Cyber Attacks and International Law on the Use of Force

Examining the thematic intersection of law, technology, and violence, this book explores cyber attacks against states and current international law on the use of force. The theory of information ethics is used to critique the law's conception of violence and to develop an informational approach as an alternative way in which to think about cyber attacks.

Cyber attacks against states constitute a new form of violence in the information age, and international law on the use of force is limited in its capacity to regulate them. This book draws on Luciano Floridi's theory of information ethics to critique the narrow conception of violence embodied in the law and to develop an alternative way to think about cyber attacks, violence, and the state. The author uses three case studies – the 2007 cyber attacks against Estonia, the Stuxnet incident involving Iran that was discovered in 2010, and the cyber attacks used as part of the Russian interference in the 2016 US presidential election – to demonstrate that an informational approach offers a means to reimagine the state as an entity and cyber attacks as a form of violence against it.

This interdisciplinary approach will appeal to an international audience of scholars in international law, international relations, security studies, cyber security, and anyone interested in the issues surrounding emerging technologies.

Samuli Haataja is an academic at Griffith Law School, Griffith University, where he teaches across a range of courses on public international law. His research explores the intersection of law and technology in the context of international law and emerging technologies, and he has published in various journals including *Law, Innovation and Technology* and the *Cambridge International Law Journal.* Dr Haataja is also a member of the Program on the Regulation of Emerging Military Technologies (PREMT) and the Institute of Electrical and Electronics Engineers Society on Social Implications of Technology (IEEE SSIT).

Emerging Technologies, Ethics and International Affairs
Steven Barela, Jai C. Galliott, Avery Plaw, Katina Michael

This series examines the crucial ethical, legal and public policy questions arising from or exacerbated by the design, development and eventual adoption of new technologies across all related fields, from education and engineering to medicine and military affairs. The books revolve around two key themes:

- Moral issues in research, engineering and design
- Ethical, legal and political/policy issues in the use and regulation of technology

This series encourages submission of cutting-edge research monographs and edited collections with a particular focus on forward-looking ideas concerning innovative or as yet undeveloped technologies. Whilst there is an expectation that authors will be well grounded in philosophy, law or political science, consideration will be given to future-orientated works that cross these disciplinary boundaries. The interdisciplinary nature of the series editorial team offers the best possible examination of works that address the 'ethical, legal and social' implications of emerging technologies.

Technology, Ethics and the Protocols of Modern War
Edited by Artur Gruszczak and Paweł Frankowski

Emerging Technologies in Diverse Forensic Sciences
Ronn Johnson

Cyber Attacks and International Law on the Use of Force
The Turn to Information Ethics
Samuli Haataja

For more information about this series, please visit https://www.routledge.com/Emerging-Technologies-Ethics-and-International-Affairs/book-series/ASHSER1408

Cyber Attacks and International Law on the Use of Force

The Turn to Information Ethics

Samuli Haataja

Routledge
Taylor & Francis Group
LONDON AND NEW YORK

First published 2019 by Routledge

2 Park Square, Milton Park, Abingdon, Oxon, OX14 4RN
605 Third Avenue, New York, NY 10017

Routledge is an imprint of the Taylor & Francis Group, an informa business

First issued in paperback 2020

British Library Cataloguing-in-Publication Data
A catalogue record for this book is available from the British Library

Library of Congress Cataloging-in-Publication Data
Names: Haataja, Samuli, author.
Title: Cyber attacks and international law on the use of force: the turn to information ethics / Samuli Haataja.
Description: Abingdon, Oxon; New York, NY: Routledge, 2019. | Series: Emerging technologies, ethics and international affairs | Based on author's thesis (doctoral - Griffith University, Brisbane, Australia, 2017). | Includes bibliographical references and index.
Identifiers: LCCN 2018041741
Subjects: LCSH: Information warfare (International law) | Cyberspace operations (Military science)
Classification: LCC KZ6718 .H32 2019 | DDC 341.6/3—dc23
LC record available at https://lccn.loc.gov/2018041741

ISBN: 978-1-138-48270-8 (hbk)
ISBN: 978-0-367-73221-9 (pbk)

Typeset in Times New Roman
by codeMantra

This book is dedicated to you, the reader.

Contents

Acknowledgements

This book was completed around the same time that my wife gave birth to our first child, Luka. Needless to say, it has been an exciting time in our lives in more ways than one. This book developed from my PhD research, which I completed at Griffith Law School, Griffith University. Like any major project extending over numerous years, I could not have done it alone, and I owe a debt of gratitude to a number of people who have helped me along the way. In particular, I thank Kieran Tranter and Afshin Akhtar-Khavari, who supervised my PhD research and provided valuable feedback throughout this project. I am also thankful to numerous other scholars at both Griffith University and the University of Helsinki who, through discussions and mentoring, have contributed to the development of my ideas and the overall shape of my book. I also owe gratitude to Tim McCormack and Ugo Pagallo for reviewing my original PhD and providing comments and feedback helpful for the development of this book, and to Rain Liivoja and Lyria Bennett Moses for providing me with numerous opportunities to engage with others working in the field of law and technology. Finally, my gratitude goes to my friends, family, and, most importantly, my wife Karen– without her support and encouragement, I would not have been able to complete this project.

Material from parts of this book has also been published elsewhere and reappears here with permission. An article based on Chapter 5 has been published as Samuli Haataja, 'The 2007 cyber attacks against Estonia and international law on the use of force: An informational approach' (2017) 9(2) *Law, Innovation and Technology* 159. An article based on Chapter 6 has been published as Samuli Haataja and Afshin Akhtar-Khavari, 'Stuxnet and international law on the use of force: An informational approach' (2018) 7(1) *Cambridge International Law Journal* 99.

Acronyms and abbreviations

APT	Advanced Persistent Threat
ASIO	Australian Security and Intelligence Organization
CERT	Computer Emergency Response Team
CIA	Central Intelligence Agency
DDoS	Distributed Denial-of-Service
DNC	Democratic National Committee
DNS	Domain Name System
DoS	Denial-of-Service
EU	European Union
FBI	Federal Bureau of Investigation
FSB	Federal Security Service (Russia)
G7	Group of Seven
GGE	Group of Governmental Experts
GRU	Main Intelligence Directorate (Russia)
HAVA	Help America Vote Act
IAEA	International Atomic Energy Agency
ICA	Intelligence Community Assessment
ICANN	Internet Corporation for Assigned Names and Numbers
ICJ	International Court of Justice
ICMP	Internet Control Message Protocol
ICT	Information and communication technology
IDI	Information and Communication Technology Development Index
IP	Internet Protocol
ISIS	Institute for Science and International Security
ISP	Internet Service Provider
ITU	International Telecommunication Union
LAN	Local Area Network
NATO	North Atlantic Treaty Organization
NPT	Treaty on the Non-Proliferation of Nuclear Weapons
NSA	National Security Agency (US)
OECD	Organization for Economic Cooperation and Development
P2P	Peer-to-Peer

PLC	Programmable Logic Controller
SDB	System Data Block
UN	United Nations
UNESCO	United Nations Educational, Scientific and Cultural Organization
UNGA	United Nations General Assembly
UNSC	United Nations Security Council
US	United States

1 Introduction

In international law, a classic example of the intersection between law and technology comes from the law of the sea. Prior to the modern 12 nautical mile limit of a state's territorial sea, the so-called cannon shot rule put this distance at 3 nautical miles – the distance reflecting the technological capacity of cannons at the time. Despite debates about the origins of this rule and the exact technological capacity of cannons in the seventeenth and eighteenth centuries,[1] the cannon shot rule reflects the basic idea that technology can shape how something is understood in law. In this instance, it helped shape the parameters of the legal space in which states can exercise their territorial sovereignty.[2] More generally, the relationship between law and technology is often described as being much like the race between the tortoise and the hare: technology is seen as moving fast, whereas the law is slow and constantly needs to catch up or it risks becoming outdated.[3] While not all new technologies raise legal issues, those technologies that make new things practicably possible do.[4] For example, from the invention and development of bicycles and automobiles to ride-sharing applications and driverless vehicles, new technologies have required updated laws to regulate new forms of transportation on roads, and have therefore had an impact on the law.[5]

The development of digital information and communication technologies (ICTs) in particular has also made a range of new behaviors and interactions possible for both state and non-state actors in and through cyberspace. In 2000, for instance, in the Australian state of Queensland, an individual used a laptop to remotely obtain unauthorized access to the computer systems used to operate the local council's sewerage system. He altered data, causing the system to malfunction, and this resulted in sewage escaping and causing environmental harm.[6] On the other hand, in 2013 the blueprints for the new headquarters of the Australian Security and Intelligence Organization (ASIO) were stolen from the computer system of a contractor involved in the construction process. While the identity of those responsible for the breach is unknown, the source of the intrusion was traced to servers located in China.[7] More recently, in 2017 the operation of a Cadbury chocolate factory in the Australian state of Tasmania was disrupted.

This was caused by malicious software (malware), which had spread across the globe.[8] As these incidents highlight, the development of digital ICTs enabling interactions in and through cyberspace has made a range of new things possible for both state and non-state actors, and this in turn has given rise to a number of legal issues.

Law, technology, and violence: Article 2(4) and cyber attacks

This book is concerned with a particular intersection of law and technology: international law on the use of force and cyber attacks. In this context, it explores the thematic intersection of law, technology, and violence.[9] A central aim of international law has always been an effort to regulate and limit interstate conflict and violence. In the modern context, this concern is crystallized in the cornerstone provision of the United Nations (UN) Charter: the Article 2(4) prohibition on the use of force. This provision essentially prohibits states from engaging in particular forms of violence in their international relations. However, where states seek to pursue their interests in and through cyberspace, questions arise as to whether cyber attacks can constitute uses of force that are prohibited by international law. This is particularly problematic in the cyberspace context: while espionage, for example, traditionally is not prohibited by international law,[10] the current technological context in which states operate both enables them to easily engage in a range of new activities and simultaneously renders them open to new vulnerabilities.

These issues have become increasingly pertinent in recent years. For example, in May 2017 the WannaCry ransomware infected over 300,000 computers in more than 150 countries and caused disruptions to the operation of businesses and hospitals.[11] The US government later publicly blamed North Korea for the incident.[12] The following month, in June 2017, the NotPetya malware infected computers in a range of government and private organizations in Ukraine and then spread to companies and organizations around the world.[13] NotPetya was particularly unique, as it disguised itself as a form of ransomware like WannaCry; however, it was capable of simultaneously deleting user data. In 2018, the United States disclosed that Russia was responsible for the incident, which it described as 'the most destructive and costly cyber-attack in history', resulting in billions of US dollars' worth of damage and major disruptions to global shipping and trade.[14]

While incidents such as these involve some type of harm caused by states against other states, there is considerable debate about whether cyber attacks such as these would amount to a use of force in violation of Article 2(4).[15] For example, the *Tallinn Manual 2.0 on the International Law Applicable to Cyber Operations* – a manual written by a group of international legal experts on the applicability of international law in cyberspace – provides that a cyber attack constitutes a use of force where its scale and effects are comparable to a traditional 'use of force'.[16] While this may be clear where, for instance, a cyber attack results in material effects, such as injury or death of human beings, or damage to or destruction of physical objects, it is more problematic when the effect is to undermine the integrity of information or disrupt the operation of computer systems and networks.[17]

Writing in the years following the September 11, 2001 terrorist attacks, Rosalyn Higgins maintained that among the key issues in the law on the use of force are 'What sort of harm, against whom and where, constitutes an attack on a "State" within the meaning of Article 2(4)?'[18] In the cyberspace context in particular, states from anywhere in the world can potentially cause new forms of harm against other states that might not involve bloody and destructive violence resembling traditional military offensives or the Al-Qaeda attacks on the United States. Obtaining unauthorized access to the blueprints of ASIO's new headquarters from the computer of a private contractor, or launching sophisticated ransomware attacks against other states, may therefore not be expressly prohibited by international law or constitute the type of harmful behavior with which the prohibition on the use of force was originally concerned when the UN Charter was drafted in the 1940s. Yet these behaviors in and through cyberspace reinvigorate questions about what types of state activities are prohibited by the law in the twenty-first century. Questions therefore arise about the types of harmful interactions that are, or should be, prohibited, how harm manifests in a world of increasingly ICT-dependent states, and even what the state as an entity capable of being subject to harm looks like in this world. These are among the key questions that this book seeks to explore.

Within the law on the use of force – the modern manifestation of the *jus ad bellum* – this book focuses primarily on cyber attacks and the threshold distinction between what amounts to 'force' within Article 2(4) and the measures below this threshold that are considered to breach the non-intervention principle alone. It is thus concerned with the law on the use of force in a narrow sense.[19] The term 'incidents short of war' is often used to describe a related distinction in international law: the differentiation between those measures amounting to a use of force but which fall below the higher 'armed attack' threshold.[20] Yoram Dinstein, for example, writes that

> Incidents involving the use of force, without reaching the threshold of war, occur quite often in the relations between States. Border patrols of neighbouring countries may exchange fire; naval units may torpedo vessels flying another flag; interceptor planes may shoot down aircraft belonging to another State, and so forth.[21]

On the other hand, economic coercion, for example, is not considered a form of 'force' for the purposes of Article 2(4) and would instead fall into the realm of the non-intervention principle.[22] This book seeks to demonstrate how the orthodox account of what constitutes a use of force under international law embodies a particular conceptualization of violence.[23] Consider, for instance, the above incidents, which involve the use of force according to Dinstein. Whether it is the members of the armed forces of one state inflicting harm to human soldiers of another state through kinetic weapons, or the launching of missiles or torpedoes that cause physical damage to the hulls of planes or naval vessels, in each instance the incidents involve a use of force understood as a particular form of violence involving injury or death to human beings, or damage to or destruction of physical objects.

In the context of cyber attacks, technology is challenging this conceptualization of violence. As this book illustrates, where cyber attacks result in material effects, the law has the ability to recognize them as a form of violence within the ambit of Article 2(4). However, where cyber attacks do not result in material effects and only, for example, disrupt the operation of computers and networks, they largely fall outside the conception of violence that is embodied in Article 2(4). It is argued that the reason for the conceptual challenge to how interstate violence in the cyberspace context is understood is not simply a result of new things becoming possible due to technological advances. Instead, the reasons are ontological. While ontology generally refers to the study of what is said to exist, in this book ontology is examined in the context of what exists in the eyes of the law, and therefore what the law is capable of recognizing as real.[24] As will be demonstrated, the law subscribes to a particular worldview in which violence is understood in inherently anthropocentric and materialist terms as requiring harm to human beings or damage to physical objects. The law's inability to recognize cyber attacks with non-material effects, such as damage to data or the disruption of information systems as a form of violence, is therefore due to the law's ontological constraints. This is evidenced by its limited capacity to recognize cyber attacks with non-material effects as a form of 'force' within Article 2(4).

Where cyber attacks do not result in material effects and fall below the use of force threshold, they instead tend to be considered as potential breaches of the non-intervention principle. This is a principle of international law that prohibits states from using methods of coercion to intervene in each other's internal or external affairs. It was classically concerned with 'forceful intervention',[25] but in its modern form, it is understood to prohibit states from using coercive measures not involving military force.[26] In relation to cyber attacks in particular, the non-intervention principle generally is used as a mechanism to capture those cyber attacks that fall below the use of force threshold that do not result in material effects.[27] However, as this book will show, in so doing, cyber attacks below the use of force threshold are effectively depicted as a form of non-violence and cast into the periphery of the law on the use of force. This is particularly problematic given the increasing ways in which non-material cyber attacks can be used to disrupt the proper functioning of states reliant on ICTs for their prosperity and security. As such, this book argues that by taking the potential effects that such attacks can have on states seriously, the harm caused by non-material cyber attacks can also be considered within the scope of Article 2(4) and recognized as a new form of violence that the law should limit states from engaging in

Accordingly, while technology in the context of the seventeenth- and eighteenth-century cannon helped shape the law of the sea, technology in the context of cyber attacks is both shaping and challenging how the notion of violence is understood through international law on the use of force. This book argues, however, that the reasons for this challenge are not simply technological but ontological. The harm that cyber attacks cause – particularly where there is no injury to human beings or damage to physical objects, and their effects are mainly informational – is at odds with the anthropocentric and materialist conception of violence that is embodied in existing law. Given the growing variety of ways in which states are becoming more and more dependent on ICTs as 'information societies', even cyber attacks without material effects can harm states in new ways that are not adequately accounted for by existing law. As such, cyber attacks highlight the need to rethink the notion of violence.

Violence has always been central to international law. From the Thirty Years' War and the consequent treaties of Westphalia in 1648 cementing the early foundations of the modern state; to the Geneva and Hague Conventions[28] that sought to limit the violence in warfare and continue to provide the basis for modern international humanitarian law; and the institutional efforts to limit the outbreak of interstate war following World Wars I and II that are now embodied in the UN Charter,[29] rules regulating the violence in warfare and the outbreak of violent warfare have taken a central position in the development of international law.[30] The modern state has also played a crucial role in these developments. As the primary subject of international law and the dominant organizational structure in the international system,[31] the state is the sole entity with a monopoly of violence internally within its territorial borders and internationally as the entity legitimately capable of engaging in warfare.[32] International law on the use of force is also premised on these assumptions of what the state is and on certain assumptions about what constitutes a form of violence against the state. Violence in this context traditionally involves the armed forces of one state engaging in conflicts on physical territory with kinetic weapons against the armed forces of another state. In contrast, cyber attacks by states against other states can originate from across the globe; they can be launched with a degree of anonymity; they may not breach the territorial integrity of a state nor manifest in material effects within a state; and they may not inflict harm through the usual instruments of violence that are associated with uses of military force. As an example of the new ways in which states can be harmed, and in highlighting the changing nature of violence, this book proposes that the use of cyber attacks against states also invites a rethinking of the state as the entity subject to violence. As will be shown, especially because states are increasingly dependent on ICTs for their proper functioning, they can also be harmed by cyber attacks with non-material effects. This means that cyber attacks that disrupt the functioning of states, even where they only affect information or disrupt the operation of information systems or processes, can amount to what is described as a form of 'informational violence' against the state.

An overview of information ethics

Let's return now to the questions posed earlier about the types of harmful interactions that are or should be prohibited, what harm looks like in a world of increasingly ICT-dependent states, and what the state as an entity capable of being subject to harm looks like in this world. To explore these questions, this book draws on Luciano Floridi's information ethics.[33] Chapter 2 will describe information ethics in more detail, but as an overview, information ethics can be best described as a form of environmental ethics. Like environmental ethics, which Floridi describes as 'biocentric' frameworks that are concerned with biological entities and ecosystems, and the intrinsic value of life, information ethics is also concerned with the well-being of the recipient (opposed to the agent) of any action.[34] As such, it can be described as

> an ecological ethics that … replaces biocentrism with ontocentrism. It suggests that there is something even more elemental than life, namely being – that is, the existence and flourishing of all entities and their global environment – and something even more fundamental than suffering, namely entropy.[35]

Instead of a concern with the well-being of the biosphere, information ethics is concerned with the well-being of the 'infosphere', which refers to 'the environment constituted by the totality of information entities'.[36] For methodological purposes, information ethics therefore advocates the adoption of an informational ontology that provides a minimum common denominator through which all entities can be seen in similar terms.[37]

By adopting an informational ontology – that is, by adopting a perspective from which all entities can be viewed in terms of their information structures – all entities can be seen as information entities.[38] This means that 'not only all persons, their cultivation, wellbeing, and social interactions, not only animals, plants, and their proper natural life, but also anything that exists, from paintings and books to stars and stones' can be viewed as information entities that collectively constitute the infosphere.[39] Information ethics also suggests that everything should have a basic degree of moral value pursuant to the ontological equality principle.

As a result of the ontological equality principle, every information entity, 'simply for the fact of being what it is, enjoys a minimal, initial, overridable, equal right to exist and develop in a way which is appropriate to its nature'.[40] In this context, being or existence is seen as inherently good, whereas entropy is regarded as evil. Floridi adopts a very particular definition of entropy that is different from the use of the term in thermodynamics, for example. In his use of the term, it essentially refers to any degradation of being, such as the destruction or corruption of information entities.[41]

To guide the behavior of responsible and caring agents within the infosphere, information ethics provides basic rules that aim to respect and promote the well-being of the entire infosphere.[42] Information ethics therefore provides an environmental approach to thinking about what is good for the infosphere and offers an approach that advocates respect for both the material and non-material world.[43]

In this book, the turn to information ethics signifies the development of an 'informational approach' to cyber attacks and the use of force. This involves reimagining the state as an entity and cyber attacks as capable of causing harm in the form of entropy. As will be shown, adopting this approach offers an alternative account of the harm caused by cyber attacks against states, one that is not limited by a strict separation between their material and non-material effects. It allows examination of the effects of cyber attacks on a range of entities, including various non-material entities such as websites and networks, in addition to their impact on human beings and material objects. As such, it allows for a deeper account of the harm caused by cyber attacks, in terms of both the ways in which they actually disrupt or damage computer systems or their operation within states and how this can be regarded as a form of violence against the state on a more conceptual level.

Structure of the book

This book therefore draws on information ethics to both inform its critique of the law's conception of violence and to develop an informational approach as an alternative way in which to think about cyber attacks. As part of this, it will consider three case studies: the 2007 cyber attacks against Estonia, the Stuxnet incident involving Iran that was discovered in 2010, and the cyber attacks used as part of the Russian interference in the 2016 US presidential election. These case studies were chosen as these incidents demonstrate key issues and limitations in the debate about cyber attacks and what constitutes a use of force under international law.[44] Each incident involved some form of cyber attacks believed to have been supported or conducted by state actors against other states, and therefore, they give rise to international legal issues. Each incident also involved cyber attacks with different types of effects highlighting issues in relation to the threshold distinction between the non-use of force and non-intervention principles. These incidents demonstrate the boundaries of what the law is capable of recognizing as 'force' in relation to cyber attacks and what it regards as falling below this threshold. They show some of the novel ways in which states that are increasingly reliant on ICTs can be harmed through cyber attacks, through the disruption of the operation of government services, key industrial processes, or central political processes integral to the functioning of the state. Accordingly, these three incidents will be used to both illustrate the law's shortcomings and demonstrate how an informational approach can be used to reconceptualize the state as an entity and cyber attacks as a form of violence.

Overall, this book argues that the law on the use of force embodies an ontologically constrained view of violence. Violence is seen in anthropocentric and material terms as involving damage or destruction of physical property, or injury or death to human beings. As a result, the harm associated with cyber attacks without material effects – essentially only affecting information – largely falls outside the law's existing conceptualization of violence, and consequently the legal doctrines through which interstate violence is regulated. In an effort to overcome these constraints, Floridi's information ethics will be drawn upon to reconceptualize the notion of violence and the state as the entity subject to violence. It is argued that through an informational approach, the law can be updated on an ontological level, meaning it is better equipped to recognize non-material forms of 'informational violence'. Consequently, an informational approach offers a means by which cyber attacks without material effects, which currently escape the law's conceptualization of violence, can be regarded as a form of violence capable of harming the state entity. Given the law's central concern with containing violence and limiting harmful interactions between states, informational violence can thus be brought into the law's conceptual containment.

As already mentioned, Chapter 2 focuses on Floridi's theory of information ethics. It locates Floridi's work within wider theorization about technology, and describes the parameters of information ethics. In doing so, this chapter provides the conceptual foundations on which this book will draw to critique the conception of violence embodied in existing law on the use of force. Further, it provides the basis for an informational approach that is developed in Chapter 3 and through the case studies in Chapters 5–7.

Chapter 3 explores international law and the containment of violence. It considers the ways in which international law has traditionally sought to regulate various flows of information globally, including information flows that are deemed harmful under international law. It also explores international law's historical concern with limiting the outbreak of interstate conflict and violence in what is described as the law's containment of violence. Against the traditional account of the law's containment of violence, this chapter then considers the novel nature of cyber warfare. It shows that there is an ontological gap between traditional or kinetic warfare and cyber warfare. While cyber warfare can involve death and destruction like traditional warfare, more often it lacks these characteristics and involves damage or disruption to information and networks. As a result, the law embodies a limited view of violence that lacks the ability to recognize the new forms of harm more commonly associated with cyber warfare (the ways in which this manifests in the law on the use of force doctrinally will be examined in Chapter 4). Finally, this chapter draws on information ethics to offer a reconceptualization of the state entity and the notion of violence. The state entity is described as an information system that increasingly interacts with other entities, and violence is described through the notion of entropy as the degradation of the state entity.

Chapter 4 examines the threshold distinction between the non-use of force and non-intervention principles to demonstrate the limited conception of violence embodied in Article 2(4). As shown, this is particularly evident in existing international legal scholarship on the use of force in relation to cyber attacks, as cyber attacks with material effects are deemed a form of violence within the non-use of force principle, whereas cyber attacks with non-material effects are considered through the non-intervention principle and depicted as a form of non-violence. This chapter demonstrates how an informational approach offers a means by which cyber attacks can be regarded as a form of informational violence capable of undermining the integrity and functioning of the state entity as an information system.

Chapter 5 provides the first of three case studies: the 2007 cyber attacks against Estonia. In April and May 2007, Estonia was subject to large-scale Distributed Denial-of-Service (DDoS) attacks lasting over three weeks in total, which impacted the functioning of its government and civil society. Particularly because the cyber attacks did not result in material damage, the incident is widely considered not to have constituted a use of force and is at most deemed to have breached the non-intervention principle. This incident therefore highlights the law's limited conception of violence and its inability to adequately recognize forms of informational violence against the state. An informational approach to the incident is therefore used to demonstrate that this offers a means to recognize a broader spectrum of violence. By viewing Estonia as an information system dependent on ICTs for its functioning, the cyber attacks can be seen to have caused increases in entropy by undermining Estonia's ability to interact, its autonomy, and its ability to care for and protect the entities within its region of the infosphere.

The second case study comes from the Stuxnet incident, which is examined in Chapter 6. Stuxnet is the name given to a sophisticated 'cyber weapon' discovered in 2010, which was used against Iran's uranium enrichment facility in Natanz. It is believed to have been a joint US and Israeli effort to undermine Iran's uranium enrichment program. Stuxnet is understood to have caused material damage to approximately 1000 nuclear centrifuges; largely for this reason, it is considered to have amounted to a use of force. As such, the Stuxnet incident illustrates that the law has the capacity to recognize cyber attacks with material effects as a form of violence. However, it will be shown that the law only provides a one-dimensional account of violence, which is evident in existing legal analyses of the incident in which Stuxnet's material effects are emphasized, whereas its non-material effects are not adequately accounted for. Here an informational approach will demonstrate how, in addition to the material damage to centrifuges caused by Stuxnet, it is necessary to consider the various non-material ways in which it undermined and degraded the integrity of thousands of virtual entities and processes associated with the functioning of the Natanz facility within Iran's region of the infosphere.

Chapter 7 provides the final case study, which explores Russian interference in the 2016 US presidential election. It focuses on the cyber attacks used in this context, namely, spear-phishing attacks targeting US political parties and electoral boards, and the subsequent strategic and systematic release of information in a way designed to undermine the electability of Hillary Clinton. Most legal scholars consider the incident to clearly fall below the use of force threshold, and there is debate about the applicability of the non-intervention principle to the incident. Essentially, the harm caused by the attacks is not something for which Article 2(4) can currently account. Further, because it is difficult to identify the coerciveness of the incident, it is also questionable whether Russia's actions constituted a violation of the non-intervention principle. An informational approach to the incident will be shown to offer a way in which the harm caused by the attacks against a range of entities can be taken into account, and how these attacks were designed to disrupt the proper operation of the election process and undermine the autonomy of the United States as an entity.

Chapter 8 provides a summary and comparison of the informational approach developed in relation to the case studies explored in Chapters 5–7 and examines the doctrinal implications of this approach to international law on the use of force and cyber attacks. It demonstrates how, given the prevalence of the use of various cyber attacks by states in their international relations, the conception of violence embodied in Article 2(4) must be updated to account for this state of affairs. An informational approach offers a way to overcome the law's ontological constraints in this context, enabling international law to contain informational violence on a doctrinal level.

Finally, Chapter 9 examines some of the wider conceptual implications of an informational approach for international law and thinking about violence and the state. It demonstrates that, beyond cyber attacks and international law on the use of force, information ethics also provides conceptual tools that are useful for thinking about different forms of violence and the role of the state in the infosphere more generally.

Notes

1 On the origins of the rule, see Heinz SK Kent, 'The Historical Origins of the Three-Mile Limit' (1954) 48(4) *American Journal of International Law* 537; Wyndham L Walker, 'Territorial Waters: The Cannon Shot Rule' (1945) 22 *British Yearbook of International Law* 210.

2 Under the current law, states have a right to establish a territorial sea of up to 12 nautical miles, and a state's sovereignty extends to this area. See United

Nations Convention on the Law of the Sea (adopted 10 December 1982, entered into force 16 November 1994) [1994] ATS 31, Arts 2, 3.

3 Lyria Bennett Moses, 'Agents of Change: How the Law "Copes" with Technological Change' (2011) 20(4) *Griffith Law Review* 763, 763–5.

4 According to Lyria Bennett Moses, the most direct impact of technology on the law comes from the 'capacity of new technology to enable new forms of conduct, including alteration of the means by which similar ends are achieved. The current state of technology limits in practice what actions we *can* perform, what objects we *can* create, and what relationships we *can* form.' Lyria Bennett Moses, 'Recurring Dilemmas: The Law's Race to Keep Up with Technological Change' [2007] *University of Illinois Journal of Law, Technology & Policy* 239, 245 (emphasis in original).

5 For example, on the impact of bicycle technologies on the law in the United States, see Susan W Brenner, *Law in an Era of "Smart" Technology* (Oxford University Press, 2007) 34–41. On the impact of the introduction of automobile technologies in Australia, see Kieran Tranter, 'The History of the Haste-Wagons: *The Motor Car Act 1909* (Vic), Emergent Technology and the Call for Law' (2005) 29 *Melbourne University Law Review* 843. For an overview of the legal impact of 'disruptive' technologies generally, see Neal Katyal, 'Disruptive Technologies and the Law' (2013) 102 *The Georgetown Law Journal* 1685.

6 *R v Boden* [2002] QCA 164, [5]–[11]. See also 'The cyberspace invaders' *The Age* (Melbourne, 22 June 2003) <www.theage.com.au/articles/2003/06/21/1056119529509.html> accessed 12 February 2018.

7 Ben Grubb, 'Blueprints for New ASIO Headquarters "Stolen"' *Sydney Morning Herald* (27 May 2013) <www.smh.com.au/it-pro/security-it/blueprints-for-new-asio-headquarters-stolen-20130527-2n7kz.html> accessed 12 February 2018.

8 Nicole Perlroth, 'Lasting Damage and a Search for Clues in Cyberattack' *New York Times* (6 July 2017) <https://nyti.ms/2uQoJKY> accessed 12 February 2018.

9 Cyber attacks refer to deliberate computer enabled actions used 'to alter, disrupt, deceive, degrade, or destroy adversary computer systems or networks or the information and/or programs resident in or transiting these systems or networks'. William A Owens and others (eds), *Technology, Policy, Law, and Ethics Regarding US Acquisition and Use of Cyberattack Capabilities* (National Academies Press 2009) 10–11. The term 'cyber attack' is used descriptively in this book, and therefore it is not to be confused with the notion of 'attack' that is used in the context of international humanitarian law, for example. See Michael N Schmitt, '"Attack" as a Term of Art in International Law: The Cyber Operations Context' in Christian Czosseck, Rain Ottis and Katharina Ziolkowski (eds), *2012 4th International Conference on Cyber Conflict* (NATO Cooperative Cyber Defence Centre of Excellence 2012). See also Tim McCormack, 'The Sony and OPM Double Whammy: International Law and Cyber "Attacks"' (2015) 18 *SMU Science and Technology Law Review* 379.

10 Geoffrey Demarest, 'Espionage in International Law' (1996) 24(2) *Denver Journal of International Law and Policy* 321, 338–9.

11 'Cyber-attack: US and UK Game North Korea for WannaCry' *BBC News* (19 December 2017) <www.bbc.com/news/world-us-canada-42407488> accessed 12 February 2018.

12 Ellen Nakashima and Philip Rucker, 'US Declares North Korea Carried Out Massive WannaCry Cyberattack' *The Washington Post* (19 December 2017) <http://wapo.st/2yTFsPk> accessed 12 February 2018.

13 Perlroth (n 8).

14 US Department of the Treasury, 'Treasury Sanctions Russian Cyber Actors for Interference with the 2016 US Elections and Malicious Cyber-Attacks'

(Media Release, 15 March 2018) <https://home.treasury.gov/news/press-releases/sm0312> accessed 16 March 2018. See also Ellen Nakashima, 'Russian Military was Behind "NotPetya" Cyberattack in Ukraine, CIA concludes' *Washington Post* (12 January 2018) <http://wapo.st/2AV5FxW> accessed 12 February 2018.

15 Michael N Schmitt and Sean Fahey, 'WannaCry and the International Law of Cyberspace' (*Just Security*, 22 December 2017) <www.justsecurity.org/50038/wannacry-international-law-cyberspace> accessed 27 March 2018; Michael N Schmitt and Jeffrey Biller, 'The NotPetya Cyber Operation as a Case Study of International Law' (*EJIL:Talk!*, 11 July 2017) <www.ejiltalk.org/the-notpetya-cyber-operation-as-a-case-study-of-international-law> accessed 27 March 2018.

16 Michael N Schmitt (ed), *Tallinn Manual 2.0 on the International Law Applicable to Cyber Operations* (2nd edn, Cambridge University Press 2017) 330.

17 ibid 333–4. See also Michael N Schmitt, 'Grey Zones in the International Law of Cyberspace' (2017) 42(2) *Yale Journal of International Law Online* 1, 14 <www.yjil.yale.edu/grey-zones-in-the-international-law-of-cyberspace> accessed 24 January 2018.

18 Rosalyn Higgins, *Themes and Theories: Selected Essays, Speeches, and Writings in International Law* (Oxford University Press 2009) 268. Writing in the years following the September 11, 2001 terrorist attacks in the United States, Higgins connects these questions to terrorism in particular.

19 The issues of threats of force, the requirement that uses of force (and threats of such) must occur in the 'international relations' of states, and the need for any such force to be against the territorial integrity of another state or in any way that is inconsistent with the general purposes of the UN Charter are of secondary concern. Similarly, this book does not focus on cyber attacks rising to the level of an armed attack against which states are permitted to use force in self-defense pursuant to Article 51. Instead, within the general area of law on the use of force, this book is concerned primarily with the threshold distinction between what amounts to 'force' within Article 2(4) and what does not.

20 Pursuant to Article 51 of the UN Charter, states retain their inherent right to self-defense following an armed attack. As will be discussed in Chapter 4, while an armed attack always involves a use of force, not all uses of force rise to the level of an armed attack.

21 Yoram Dinstein, *War, Aggression and Self-Defence* (3rd edn, Cambridge University Press 2001) 11. For Dinstein, 'War is a hostile interaction between two or more States, either in a technical or in a material sense. War in the technical sense is a formal status produced by a declaration of war. War in the material sense is generated by actual use of armed force, which must be comprehensive on the part of at least one party to the conflict.' ibid 15.

22 *Case Concerning Military and Paramilitary Activities in and Against Nicaragua (Nicaragua v United States of America)* (Merits) [1986] ICJ Rep 14, 108. For more detail, see Chapter 4.

23 As will be shown in Chapter 4 in particular, this is evident in the way the notion of force within Article 2(4) is interpreted. Tom Farer, for instance, writes that Article 2(4) is not concerned with economic coercion, but rather 'concerned with violence, with military force'. Tom J Farer, 'Political and Economic Coercion in Contemporary International Law' (1985) 79(2) *American Journal of International Law* 405, 410. Dinstein, in turn, writes that 'the term "force" in Article 2(4) must denote violence. It does not matter what specific means – kinetic or electronic – are used to bring it about, but the end result must be that violence occurs or is threatened.' Yoram Dinstein, *War, Aggression and Self-Defence* (5th edn, Cambridge University Press 2011) 88.

24 This is different to how the notion of 'law's ontology' is used – for example, in debates in legal theory about what the essence of the law is and the conditions for its existence. For these debates, see Paul Amselek and Neil MacCormick (eds), *Controversies About Law's Ontology* (Edinburgh University Press 1991). See also Bjarne Melkevik, 'The Concept of Law and Contemporary Philosophical Reflection' [2013] (4) *Law of Ukraine: Legal Journal* 228, 230–2. This book draws on information ethics, which is a theory that is ontologically committed to an informational ontology. This means that it adopts the view that everything can be seen as information structures and that these information structures exist. See Luciano Floridi, 'Information Ethics, Its Nature and Scope' (2006) 36(3) *Computers and Society* 21, 26–31. For more detail, see Chapter 2.

25 Lassa Oppenheim, for example, defines it as 'forcible or dictatorial interference by a State in the affairs of another State, calculated to impose certain conduct or consequences on that other State'. Robert Y Jennings and Arthur Watts (eds), *Oppenheim's International Law, Volume 1, Peace* (9th edn, Longman 1992) 430, cited in David J Harris, *Cases and Materials on International Law* (7th edn, Thomson Reuters 2010) 743.

26 See Chapter 4. This distinction is made in the Declaration on Principles of International Law Concerning Friendly Relations and Co-operation Among States in Accordance with the Charter of the United Nations UNGA Res 2625 (XXV) (24 October 1970) UN Doc A/RES/2625(XXV), and by the International Court of Justice in *Case Concerning Military and Paramilitary Activities in and Against Nicaragua* (n 22).

27 See Chapter 4. Heather Harrison Dinniss, for instance, writes that even where a cyber attack does not rise to the level of a use of force, it does not mean it is permissible, as it is likely that it will be considered an unlawful intervention. Heather Harrison Dinniss, *Cyber Warfare and the Laws of War* (Cambridge University Press 2012) 74. Similarly, Marco Roscini concludes that cyber attacks that are not destructive or severely disruptive are not uses of force, but 'may be unlawful interventions in the internal affairs of other states'. Marco Roscini, *Cyber Operations and the Use of Force in International Law* (Oxford University Press 2014) 115.

28 See, for example, the Geneva Convention for the Amelioration of the Condition of the Wounded in Armies in the Field (adopted 22 August 1864, entered into force 22 June 1865) <https://ihl-databases.icrc.org/ihl/INTRO/120?OpenDocument> accessed 12 February 2018; International Convention with Respect to the Laws and Customs of War on Land (adopted 29 July 1899, entered into force 4 September 1900) [1901] ATS 131.

29 According to Antonio Cassese, 'One of the major reactions to the devastations of the Second World War and the unfettered recourse to violence marking those dark years was the keen desire to set up a world organization that would be capable of preventing "the scourge of war" and peacefully settling all major disputes between States.' Antonio Cassese, *International Law* (Oxford University Press 2005) 40.

30 On the role of technology in this context, see Rain Liivoja, 'Technological Change and the Evolution of the Law of War' (2015) 97 *International Review of the Red Cross* 1157.

31 Christoph Schreuer, for example, writes that the sovereign state is the prototypical international actor and the 'universal standard' in international law, and that the 'structure of co-equal sovereign States' is presupposed by international law and the 'international community's constitutive set-up is dominated by it'. Christoph Schreuer, 'The Waning of the Sovereign State: Towards a New Paradigm for International Law?' (1993) 4(4) *European Journal of International Law* 447, 448. Martti Koskenniemi, in turn, notes how 'statehood as the law's

creative center' is reaffirmed in the 'universally acclaimed principles of international law ... of sovereignty, self-determination, territorial integrity, non-intervention, and consent'. Martti Koskenniemi, 'The Future of Statehood' (1991) 32(2) *Harvard International Law Journal* 397, 406.

32 See, for example, Janice E Thomson, 'State Sovereignty in International Relations: Bridging the Gap between Theory and Empirical Research' (1995) 39(2) *International Studies Quarterly* 213, 219–28. For more detail, see Chapter 3.

33 Floridi's information ethics was originally developed in Luciano Floridi, 'Information Ethics: on the Philosophical Foundation of Computer Ethics' (1999) 1 *Ethics and Information Technology* 33 and most comprehensively in Luciano Floridi, *The Ethics of Information* (Oxford University Press 2013). Others who have drawn on Floridi's information ethics in relation to international law and cyber warfare include: Mariarosaria Taddeo, 'Information Warfare: A Philosophical Perspective' (2012) 25(1) *Philosophy & Technology* 105; Mariarosaria Taddeo, 'Just Information Warfare' (2016) 35(1) *Topoi* 213; Ugo Pagallo, 'Cyber Force and the Role of Sovereign States in Informational Warfare' (2015) 28(3) *Philosophy & Technology* 407; and Massimo Durante, 'Violence, Just Cyber War and Information' (2015) 28(2) *Philosophy & Technology* 369. With regard to Floridi's information ethics and law more generally, Dan Burk provides a 'test drive' in the application of information ethics to the legal landscape of data representations. See Dan L Burk, 'Information Ethics and the Law of Data Representations' (2008) 10(2–3) *Ethics and Information Technology* 135. Massimo Durante considers information ethics in relation to how the law can be used to mediate between the real and the virtual. See Massimo Durante, 'Re-designing the Role of Law in the Information Society: Mediating Between the Real and the Virtual' (2010) 2(3) *European Journal of Legal Studies* 19. He also considers how it can be used to address legal value conflicts. See Massimo Durante, 'Dealing with Legal Conflicts in the Information Society: An Informational Understanding of Balancing Competing Interests' (2013) 26(4) *Philosophy & Technology* 437. Ugo Pagallo explores the sources of law from an information ethics perspective. See Ugo Pagallo, 'The Realignment of the Sources of the Law and their Meaning in an Information Society' (2015) 28(1) *Philosophy & Technology* 57.

34 Luciano Floridi, *Information: A Very Short Introduction* (Oxford University Press 2010) 111.

35 ibid 112.

36 Floridi, 'Information Ethics' (n 33) 44.

37 Floridi (n 24) 33.

38 ibid.

39 Floridi (n 34) 113.

40 ibid.

41 Floridi, *The Ethics of Information* (n 33) 67.

42 ibid 71. These rules are: (0) entropy ought not to be caused in the infosphere (null law); (1) entropy ought to be prevented in the infosphere; (2) entropy ought to be removed from the infosphere; and (3) the flourishing of informational entities as well as of the whole infosphere ought to be promoted by preserving, cultivating and enriching their wellbeing.

43 Luciano Floridi, *Information Ethics: An Environmental Approach to the Digital Divide* (First Meeting of the Sub-Commission on the Ethics of the Information Society, United Nations Educational, Scientific and Cultural Organization 2001) 67.

44 In addition to the relevance of these particular incidents in relation to this area of law, another reason for their selection is more practical, stemming from the public availability of information about them. All these incidents have been reported widely in the media, cyber security companies have released technical information about them and each incident is widely discussed in international

legal scholarship in relation to the use of force and/or non-intervention. As such, there is sufficient information available on these incidents to develop in-depth accounts of the events that occurred, the technical details of the attacks and secondary literature examining the legal issues surrounding the incidents.

Bibliography

Amselek P and MacCormick N (eds), *Controversies About Law's Ontology* (Edinburgh University Press 1991)

Bennett Moses L, 'Recurring Dilemmas: The Law's Race to Keep Up with Technological Change' (2007) *University of Illinois Journal of Law, Technology & Policy* 239

——— 'Agents of Change: How the Law "Copes" with Technological Change' (2011) 20(4) *Griffith Law Review* 763

Brenner SW, *Law in an Era of 'Smart' Technology* (Oxford University Press 2007)

Burk DL, 'Information Ethics and the Law of Data Representations' (2008) 10(2–3) *Ethics and Information Technology* 135

Case Concerning Military and Paramilitary Activities in and against Nicaragua (Nicaragua v United States of America) (Merits) [1986] ICJ Rep 14

Cassese A, *International Law* (Oxford University Press 2005)

'Cyber-attack: US and UK Blame North Korea for WannaCry' *BBC News* (19 December 2017) <www.bbc.com/news/world-us-canada-42407488> accessed 12 February 2018

'The Cyberspace Invaders' *The Age* (Melbourne, 22 June 2003) <www.theage.com.au/articles/2003/06/21/1056119529509.html> accessed 12 February 2018

Demarest GB, 'Espionage in International Law' (1996) 24(2) *Denver Journal of International Law and Policy* 321

Dinniss HH, *Cyber Warfare and the Laws of War* (Cambridge University Press 2012)

Dinstein Y, *War, Aggression and Self-Defence* (3rd edn, Cambridge University Press 2001)

——— *War, Aggression and Self-Defence* (5th edn, Cambridge University Press 2011)

Durante M, 'Re-designing the Role of Law in the Information Society: Mediating Between the Real and the Virtual' (2010) 2(3) *European Journal of Legal Studies* 19

——— 'Dealing with Legal Conflicts in the Information Society. An Informational Understanding of Balancing Competing Interests' (2013) 26(4) *Philosophy & Technology* 437

——— 'Violence, Just Cyber War and Information' (2015) 28(3) *Philosophy & Technology* 369

Farer TJ, 'Political and Economic Coercion in Contemporary International Law' (1985) 79(2) *American Journal of International Law* 405

Floridi L, 'Information Ethics: on the Philosophical Foundation of Computer Ethics' (1999) 1(1) *Ethics and Information Technology* 33

——— *Information Ethics: An Environmental Approach to the Digital Divide* (First Meeting of the Sub-Commission on the Ethics of the Information Society, United Nations Educational, Scientific and Cultural Organization 2001)

——— 'Information Ethics, its Nature and Scope' (2006) 36(3) *Computers and Society* 21

——— *Information: A Very Short Introduction* (Oxford University Press 2010)

——— *The Ethics of Information* (Oxford University Press 2013)

Geneva Convention for the Amelioration of the Condition of the Wounded in Armies in the Field (adopted 22 August 1864, entered into force 22 June 1865) <https://ihl-databases.icrc.org/ihl/INTRO/120?OpenDocument> accessed 12 February 2018

Grubb B, 'Blueprints for New ASIO Headquarters "Stolen"' *Sydney Morning Herald* (27 May 2013) <www.smh.com.au/it-pro/security-it/blueprints-for-new-asio-headquarters-stolen-20130527-2n7kz.html> accessed 12 February 2018

Harris DJ, *Cases and Materials on International Law* (7th edn, Thomson Reuters 2010)

Higgins R, *Themes and Theories: Selected Essays, Speeches, and Writings in International Law* (Oxford University Press 2009)

International Convention with Respect to the Laws and Customs of War on Land (adopted 29 July 1899, entered into force 4 September 1900) [1901] ATS 131

Jennings RY and Watts A (eds), *Oppenheim's International Law, Volume 1, Peace* (9th edn, Longman 1992)

Katyal N, 'Disruptive Technologies and the Law' (2013) 102 *The Georgetown Law Journal* 1685

Kent HSK, 'The Historical Origins of the Three-Mile Limit' (1954) 48(4) *American Journal of International Law* 537

Koskenniemi M, 'The Future of Statehood' (1991) 32(2) *Harvard International Law Journal* 397

Liivoja R, 'Technological Change and the Evolution of the Law of War' (2015) 97 *International Review of the Red Cross* 1157

McCormack T, 'The Sony and OPM Double Whammy: International Law and Cyber "Attacks"' (2015) 18 *SMU Science and Technology Law Review* 379

Melkevik B, 'The Concept of Law and Contemporary Philosophical Reflection' [2013](4) *Law of Ukraine: Legal Journal* 228

Nakashima E, 'Russian Military was Behind "NotPetya" Cyber Attack in Ukraine, CIA Concludes' *The Washington Post* (12 January 2018) <http://wapo.st/2AV5FxW> accessed 12 February 2018

Nakashima E and Rucker P, 'US Declares North Korea Carried Out Massive WannaCry Cyberattack' *The Washington Post* (19 December 2017) <http://wapo.st/2yTFsPk> accessed 12 February 2018

Owens WA and others (eds), *Technology, Policy, Law, and Ethics Regarding U.S. Acquisition and Use of Cyberattack Capabilities* (National Academies Press 2009)

Pagallo U, 'Cyber Force and the Role of Sovereign States in Informational Warfare' (2015) 28(3) *Philosophy & Technology* 407

——— 'The Realignment of the Sources of the Law and their Meaning in an Information Society' (2015) 28(1) *Philosophy & Technology* 57

Perlroth N, 'Lasting Damage and a Search for Clues in Cyberattack' *New York Times* (6 July 2017) <https://nyti.ms/2uQoJKY> accessed 12 February 2018

R v Boden [2002] QCA 164

Roscini M, *Cyber Operations and the Use of Force in International Law* (Oxford University Press 2014)

Schmitt MN, '"Attack" as a Term of Art in International Law: The Cyber Operations Context' in Czosseck C, Ottis R and Ziolkowski K (eds), *2012 4th International Conference on Cyber Conflict* (NATO Cooperative Cyber Defence Centre of Excellence 2012)

——— 'Grey Zones in the International Law of Cyberspace' (2017) 42(2) *Yale Journal of International Law Online* 1 <www.yjil.yale.edu/grey-zones-in-the-international-law-of-cyberspace> accessed 24 January 2018

——— (ed), *Tallinn Manual 2.0 on the International Law Applicable to Cyber Operations* (2nd edn, Cambridge University Press 2017)
Schmitt MN and Biller J, 'The NotPetya Cyber Operation as a Case Study of International Law' *EJIL:Talk!* (11 July 2017) <www.ejiltalk.org/the-notpetya-cyber-operation-as-a-case-study-of-international-law> accessed 27 March 2018
Schmitt MN and Fahey S, 'WannaCry and the International Law of Cyberspace' *Just Security* (22 December 2017) <www.justsecurity.org/50038/wannacry-international-law-cyberspace> accessed 27 March 2018
Schreuer S, 'The Waning of the Sovereign State: Towards a New Paradigm for International Law?' (1993) 4(4) *European Journal of International Law* 447
Taddeo M, 'Information Warfare: A Philosophical Perspective' (2012) 25(1) *Philosophy & Technology* 105
——— 'Just Information Warfare' (2016) 35(1) *Topoi* 213
Thomson JE, 'State Sovereignty in International Relations: Bridging the Gap Between Theory and Empirical Research' (1995) 39(2) *International Studies Quarterly* 213
Tranter K, 'The History of the Haste-Wagons: The *Motor Car Act 1909* (Vic): Emergent Technology and the Call for Law' (2005) 29 *Melbourne University Law Review* 843
UNGA Res 2625 (XXV) (24 October 1970) UN Doc A/RES/2625(XXV)
United Nations Convention on the Law of the Sea (adopted 10 December 1982, entered into force 16 November 1994) [1994] ATS 31
United States Department of the Treasury, 'Treasury Sanctions Russian Cyber Actors for Interference with the 2016 US Elections and Malicious Cyber-Attacks' (Media Release, 15 March 2018) <https://home.treasury.gov/news/press-releases/sm0312> accessed 16 March 2018
Walker WL, 'Territorial Waters: The Cannon Shot Rule' (1945) 22 *British Yearbook of International Law* 210

2 Information ethics

Introduction

This chapter describes Luciano Floridi's information ethics and provides the conceptual framework that will be used to develop an informational approach to cyber attacks and the law on the use of force. It first locates Floridi's information ethics within the philosophy of technology, outlining what Floridi describes to be the wider philosophical and technological transformations and challenges that give rise to the need for new conceptual toolkits such as information ethics. It then explores the key principles and concepts of information ethics, as well as the criticisms that have been levelled against it. These concepts – namely, the ontological equality principle, the infosphere, and entropy – will then be drawn upon to build an informational approach in subsequent chapters.

The philosophies of technology and information

Philosophy of technology

The tension between nature and technology, together with their relationship with humans, is a prominent theme in the philosophy of technology. The roots of these concerns can be traced to ancient Greek philosophy and distinctions between what is considered part of nature (the notion of *physis*) and those artifacts that are produced by humans (the notion of *techné*).[1] The Greeks saw an inherent essence in the idea of an artifact, which then comes into existence when someone produces it; humans were therefore regarded not as masters of nature, but as merely bringing the natural world to fruition.[2] In contrast, modern views of technology and the relationship between humans and technological artifacts see technology not as a part of nature, but instead in instrumental terms. Indeed, modernity is pervaded by an inherently instrumentalist philosophy of technology.[3] Technology from an instrumental view is conceptualized as tools or machines – artifacts are made by humans, but they are distinct from nature and can be used for any purpose. Accordingly, technology is regarded as value-neutral something under the control of humans through which nature can be exploited and dominated.[4] From this view, the only value that technology embodies is the value of formal efficiency – finding the most efficient way of realizing pre-existing values.[5] This view of technology also aligns with the modern belief in progress through technological advancement aimed at the fulfilment of human needs.[6] However, much of the perceived promise of technology and the benefits of its advancement were undermined by the realization that technology could not only be helpful but also extremely harmful. This was seen particularly after the deployment of nuclear weapons in World War II, and when the ecological side effects of technology became evident in the second half of the twentieth century.[7] Therefore, while technology could be used to achieve any human ends, the scientific rationality associated with modernity meant that there was a 'strange aimlessness' about what those ends were.[8]

More critical theories of technology emerged particularly in the second half of the twentieth century; they described technology and its relationship to the world very differently. Various approaches addressed the earlier view of technology as seemingly neutral, instead demonstrating the socially constructed nature of technologies[9] and the politics embodied by technologies,[10] and challenging perceived human control over technological development.[11] Critical theories of technology often regard the concept of technology more broadly as an environment or as more complex systems,[12] opposed to merely a collection of tools and machines.[13] As part of the environment in which humans live, technology shapes humans and their interactions,[14] and provides 'frameworks for ways of life'.[15] These views mark a shift from merely an instrumental view of technology as tools under human control used for whatever means they choose to considering technology as an evolving and wider environmental force that both shapes the socio-political order and is shaped by it.[16]

The philosophy of technology – that is, the conceptual framework through which technology and its relationship to humans and the natural world are understood – is particularly important in helping make sense of modern 'information societies' pervaded by technology. As part of the Europe 2020 initiatives in connection with the European Commission's 'Digital Agenda' for Europe, a group of academics from a range of disciplines from law to neuroscience reflected on the wider political, social, and policy-related impacts of information and communication technologies (ICTs).[17] The project was entitled 'The Onlife Initiative: Concept Reengineering for Rethinking Societal Concerns in the Digital Transition' (the Onlife Initiative) and resulted in the publication of *The Onlife Manifesto: Being Human in a Hyperconnected Era* (the Onlife Manifesto).[18] Its authors argue that the transformations associated with ICTs and their impact on the human condition is challenging the philosophical foundations of existing conceptual toolkits.[19] They maintain that ICTs are not simply tools, but environmental forces that are impacting on

- our self-conception (who we are)
- our mutual interactions (how we socialize)
- our conception of reality (our metaphysics)
- our interactions with reality (our agency).[20]

The authors attribute the reasons for this impact of ICTs to at least four major transformations:

- the blurring of the distinction between reality and virtuality
- the blurring of the distinction between human, machine, and nature
- the reversal from information scarcity to information abundance
- the shift from the primacy of stand-alone things, properties, and binary relations to the primacy of interactions, processes, and networks.[21]

These transformations, the authors maintain, challenge some of the basic assumptions of modernity. For example, they argue that policy-making is still largely underpinned by various 'political, social, legal, scientific and economic concepts' that remain 'deeply anchored in questionable assumptions about modernity'.[22] These include a view of the inherent distinction between technology and nature, the attribution of ethical responsibility mainly to rational humans as opposed to technological artifacts, and the pervasiveness of various mechanical metaphors – like the notion of control – within modern worldviews, structures and forms of political organization.[23] They argue that the development of ICTs is challenging these assumptions because the distinction between the artificial and natural is being blurred, ICTs can increasingly operate autonomously inviting notions of distributed responsibility, and ICTs destabilize modernity's mechanical worldviews and metaphors by enabling new forms of political organization.[24] The authors of the Onlife Initiative maintain that especially due to these transformations, existing conceptual frameworks need to be updated in order to better understand the various problems related to ICTs and to be better equipped to solving them satisfactorily.[25] Therefore, within the context of these transformations and the wider impact of ICTs, Floridi's philosophy of information and information ethics seeks to provide a conceptual framework to address the ethical challenges associated with ICTs.

Luciano Floridi's philosophy of information

Since the late 1990s, various aspects of a philosophy of technology based on information have been developed in Floridi's work.[26] Given the central role of information in the digital or 'information age',[27] Floridi has sought to develop a set of conceptual tools through a philosophy of information.[28] The basic premise of his philosophy, building on contributions by earlier figures such as Claude Shannon and Norbert Wiener,[29] is that everything in the world is made up of information.[30] Hence the entire universe and all of reality, given a particular level of abstraction, can be regarded as made up of information structures.[31] Information in this context is not understood semantically – as news or content for instance – but as 'equivalent to patterns or entities in the world'.[32] Within Floridi's philosophy of information, information is therefore regarded as 'something as fundamental and significant as knowledge, being, validity, truth, meaning, mind, or good and evil', and hence as worth philosophical investigation.[33] However, it is also a concept through which these concepts can be expressed and investigated philosophically.[34] Given the ways in which it aims to investigate information in all of its forms and at all stages in the information life cycle, Floridi seeks to provide his philosophy of information as *the* philosophy of information, and as an entirely new paradigm through which to understand the world.[35]

The fourth revolution and the 're-ontologization' of the infosphere

Accordingly, Floridi's philosophy of technology is based on his philosophy of information. His argument, much like that in the Onlife Manifesto,[36] is that ICTs have brought about radical conceptual challenges.[37] These challenges are connected to what he describes as the 'fourth revolution' in human self-understanding.[38] The origins of this revolution can be traced to the ideas of Alan Turing, and it comes after three previous revolutions that Floridi associates with Nicolaus Copernicus, Charles Darwin, and Sigmund Freud, respectively.[39] The essence of the fourth revolution is the realization that humans are intrinsically informational,[40] that we are 'above all information processors, and our capacities in this regard are not uniquely biological'.[41] As such, the fourth revolution is occurring as a result of the development of computer science and ICTs. However, its impact is not simply technological: it is affecting the human conception of the world and our place within it. According to Floridi, ICTs

> have not only provided unprecedented epistemic and engineering powers over natural and artificial realities; but by doing so they have also cast new light on who we are, how we are related to the world, and hence how we understand ourselves. Today, we are slowly accepting the idea that we are not Newtonian, standalone, and unique entities, but rather informationally embodied organisms (*inforgs*), mutually connected and embedded in an informational environment, the *infosphere*.[42]

Floridi describes the way ICTs are transforming the world as a process of 're-ontologization'. This notion refers to the radical re-engineering or re-design of something (any system – for example, a machine or artifact) to a degree that 'fundamentally transforms its intrinsic nature, that is, its ontology or essence'.[43] The term 'infosphere', in turn, is based on the notion of 'biosphere', and is used to describe not only the natural environment or digital environments like cyberspace but also the entire informational environment constituted by information entities.[44] It refers to

> the whole informational environment constituted by all informational entities, their properties, interactions, processes, and mutual relations. It is an environment comparable to, but different from, cyberspace, which is only one of its sub-regions, as it were, since the infosphere also includes offline and analogue spaces of information.[45]

In the context of Floridi's philosophy of information and the idea that everything can be viewed in informational terms, the infosphere refers to the entire environment constituted by information entities.[46]

ICTs are therefore re-ontologizing the world, transforming it into an infosphere. This is occurring mainly through the shift from analogue to digital and the growth in informational spaces.[47] Digital tools and digital resources are converging to a point where 'there is no ontological difference between *processors* and *processed*'.[48] As such, ICTs are changing the fundamental nature of even everyday objects, from fridges to cars, which are increasingly becoming capable of processing information and capable of interaction.[49] Hence they are being transformed into information entities, and they operate in a growing information space. In addition to re-ontologizing existing objects that are being seamlessly embedded into the everyday, ICTs are also creating new realities and blurring the distinctions between being online and offline: 'the digital-online is spilling over into the analogue-offline and merging with it'.[50] This is coupled with the increasing virtualization of services and resources[51] to a point where, according to Floridi, the human perspective on the ultimate nature of reality is changing from a materialist one into an informational one.[52] ICTs are therefore changing the nature of everyday objects and processes, and creating new realities within which those objects and even humans interact and exist. This results in the transformation of the world into an infosphere – a world in which, when understood informationally, everything from natural environments to artificial virtual environments, and from humans to computer software, coexists and interacts.

The impact of ICTs and the turn to information ethics

As a result of these transformations and the impact of ICTs, Floridi argues that new conceptual toolkits are required to make sense of the challenges that are brought about by technology in this context. Others have noted this too, namely, that the development of computer technologies and the new forms of behavior that they have made possible (or the substantial changes in the scope and scale of actions that are now possible) has raised new issues requiring novel theoretical approaches.[53] Accordingly, Floridi argues that there is a need to consider the conceptual nature and implications of these developments[54] in order to ensure a better understanding of technology's 'nature, its less visible implications, and its impact on human and environmental welfare'.[55] According to Floridi, there is a need to rethink the philosophical foundations on which existing concepts are based. Floridi's philosophy of information aims to contribute to this, and it provides the basis for his information ethics.

In light of the recurring concern about the relationship between the natural and the technological, Floridi's framework is based on a view of the world as an infosphere in which natural and technological environments are intertwined. One commentator has noted how, from this perspective, the relationship between humans and technology is 'intrinsically interrelated'.[56] Floridi's view stands in contrast to the modern view of technology, which sees reality as the natural environment that is capable of being mastered and controlled by humanity. He argues that, as well as the natural environment, humans need to be concerned with the non-natural environments that they have created, which increasingly are intertwined with the natural environment.[57] He maintains that

> In less than a century, we have moved from a state of submission to nature, through a state of power of potential total destruction, to the present state in which we have the means and tools to engineer entire new realities, tailor them to our needs and invent the future.[58]

Hence this involves revitalizing also the tensions between the ancient Greek notions of *physis* and *techné*. Floridi maintains that a practical reconciliation of the two is required as, 'Information societies increasingly depend upon technology to thrive, but they equally need a healthy, natural environment to flourish'.[59] Accordingly, he suggests that the best way to think about novel ethical problems is as environmental issues, and hence, a new environmental ethics is needed for the information society.[60] In this context, and as a branch of his philosophy of information, Floridi's information ethics provides a framework that is concerned with the ethical impact of ICTs on human life and society.[61]

Information ethics

The aim of information ethics is to guide the behavior of a responsible and caring agent in the infosphere – a world pervaded by information entities and organisms that in various ways store, process and interact with information. It provides what can be described as an environmental ethics of the information age – a form of *synthetic environmentalism*[62] that takes the approach of deep ecology even further.[63] Others note that it offers a 'new ontological perspective' from which to address the moral concerns particularly raised by, but not limited to, ICTs.[64] Instead of an approach tailored towards specific technologies, it focuses on the more fundamental informational nature shared by all technology (and everything else).[65] It seeks to provide a more impartial and universal approach to ethics than traditional ethical theories, and promises a form of universal applicability in a world of moral pluralism.[66] It therefore seeks to provide a normative framework that is particularly suited to addressing ethical concerns raised by the use of ICTs. Despite its promises, it has been subject to a range of criticisms. As will be demonstrated, in particular, information ethics' principle of ontological equality – whereby all entities are afforded a basic right to exist and flourish – and the notion of entropy as evil have been questioned. Before discussing these criticisms, however, we will describe the key concepts and principles of information ethics.

Information entities and the infosphere

Information ethics is concerned not simply with the well-being of the natural environment or the biosphere, but with that of the infosphere.[67] The infosphere is the totality of all entities that can logically exist, when they are understood informationally.[68] Therefore, human beings, technological artifacts and *everything else* can be understood in informational terms and considered as information entities. Accordingly, the ethical discourse of information ethics

> concerns any entity, understood informationally, that is, not only all persons, their cultivation, wellbeing, and social interactions, not only animals, plants, and their proper natural life, but also anything that exists, from paintings and books to stars and stones; anything that may or will exist, like future generations; and anything that was but is no more, like our ancestors or old civilizations.[69]

The way in which information ethics considers all entities as information entities is by perceiving the world from an informational perspective.[70] As mentioned, key to this is conceptualizing information as data structures, 'equivalent to patterns or entities in the world'.[71] This is in contrast to purely viewing information semantically, as the contents of an encyclopedia for instance, though naturally this is also included within the former conceptualization.[72] The purpose of this informational perspective – or its 'level of abstraction' in Floridi's terminology – is a grounding of information ethics to the lowest common denominator shared by everything, namely, information.[73] Viewing things informationally therefore means that everything can be abstracted to a sufficient degree and viewed as information entities. Consider, for instance, a human being and the various levels of abstraction or ways in which they can be perceived: as 'a primate, a mammal, a vertebrate, a colony of eukaryotic cells, and a congeries of subatomic particles'.[74] The highest and most inclusive level of abstraction, though, is informational.[75] All entities are therefore regarded in similar terms as information entities. By adopting this perspective, information ethics expressly commits itself to an informational ontology 'whereby human beings as well as animals, plants, artefacts and so forth are interpreted as informational entities'.[76]

Information ethics seeks to provide a universal and impartial (or at least less biased) ethics, and it aspires to be an all-inclusive ethics.[77] First, the environment with which it is concerned is not simply the biophysical environment, as 'the infosphere includes also any other environment'.[78] The natural environment, and the Internet and other digital environments that make up cyberspace, are all considered to be part of the infosphere. Second, all entities – be they books, robots or human beings – are considered as information entities, and thus as part of the infosphere. Accordingly, information ethics seeks a higher degree of impartiality and universality by expanding the concept of what counts as the center for moral claims to include 'every instance of information, no matter whether physically implemented or not.'[79] For Floridi this is the logical expansion of what counts as having moral value, to the all-inclusive position in which no line is drawn at all and everything is included within the moral circle.[80] However, while all entities are considered to have moral value, 'they do not share the same degree of dignity.'[81] Information ethics 'does not treat human beings as if they were no more important than animals or trees or indeed stones'.[82] It is important to note that the minimalism it advocates is only methodological: it simply holds 'the view that entities can be analysed by focusing on their lowest common denominator, represented by an informational ontology'.[83] It assigns worth to all entities in their capacity as information.[84] Therefore, information ethics attaches a basic degree of value to all entities that collectively form the infosphere. It advocates that, 'Not only inanimate but also ideal, intangible or intellectual objects can have a minimal degree of moral value, no matter how humble, and so be entitled to some respect'.[85] It thus seeks to provide a more inclusive, universal and impartial ethics concerned with all environments and entities.

The ontological equality principle

Consequently, from this perspective, everything in the world can be conceptualized as information entities and as part of the infosphere. Central to information ethics is the principle of ontological equality, which essentially refers to the idea that everything should have a basic right to exist. According to Floridi, every information entity 'simply for the fact of being what it is, enjoys an initial, overridable, equal right to exist and develop in a way which is appropriate to its nature'.[86] As such, every entity has some intrinsic moral value (however minimal and overridable) and is entitled to 'some equally minimal degree of moral respect'.[87] This basic right of every entity to exist is fundamental:

> every entity, as an expression of being, has a dignity, constituted by its mode of existence and essence (the collection of all the elementary proprieties that constitute it for what it is), which deserve to be respected

> and hence place moral claims on the interacting agent and ought to contribute to the constraint and guidance of his ethical decisions and behaviour.[88]

Accordingly, pursuant to the ontological equality principle, all information entities should be morally respected as part of the infosphere to which they belong.[89] Through this principle, information ethics seeks to adopt a more encompassing approach to viewing the world, one that is not even biased against the 'inanimate, lifeless, intangible, or abstract'.[90] All entities are therefore understood as enjoying some basic right to exist, and tied to this right is the right of every entity to flourish – 'to improve and enrich its existence and essence'.[91]

Goodness/being and evil/entropy

Information ethics regards the right of an entity to exist and flourish as fundamental. Being (as opposed to 'life') and every entity's contribution to the well-being of the infosphere makes up the basic notions of what is good. In contrast, evil is considered in terms of entropy (as opposed to 'suffering'). In this context, the notions of being and goodness are intertwined and intrinsic to all entities simply by virtue of their existence.[92] This means that every entity's right to exist should be considered in the context of the entire infosphere of which it forms part, and avoiding negative effects (entropy) therein. As a result, information ethics seeks to evaluate the moral duty of any

> being in terms of [its] contribution to the growth of the infosphere, and any process, action or event that negatively affects the whole infosphere – not just an information entity – as an increase in its level of entropy and hence an instance of evil.[93]

Information ethics therefore sees the world as made up of information and as fundamentally good, and views any acts that damage it as evil. Opposed to focusing its concern with the actions, characters or values of a human actor, information ethics shifts its focus towards considering the evil suffered by information entities and the infosphere.[94]

As mentioned in Chapter 1, Floridi adopts a very particular definition of the notion of entropy. In information ethics, entropy is defined as referring to 'any form of impoverishment of *Being*' – that is, 'any kind of *destruction* or *corruption* of entities understood as informational objects'.[95] Here *destruction* refers to 'the complete annihilation of the entity in question' – for instance, where it is entirely erased and completely ceases to exist.[96] *Corruption*, in turn, refers to 'a form of pollution or depletion of the entity' that is comparable to its degradation.[97] Entropy (evil) is thus understood in a metaphysical sense as the destruction or corruption of any entity that enjoys an inherent right to exist – that is, the destruction or corruption of its being (goodness).[98] The term is therefore used differently from, for example, its meaning in thermodynamics or in Shannon's information theory.[99]

In light of these concepts, information ethics provides four moral laws to guide behavior within the infosphere:

0 Entropy ought not to be caused in the infosphere (null law).
1 Entropy ought to be prevented in the infosphere.
2 Entropy ought to be removed from the infosphere.
3 The flourishing of informational entities as well as of the whole infosphere ought to be promoted by preserving, cultivating and enriching their well-being.[100]

These principles are designed to provide guidance on the actions of a responsible and caring agent within the infosphere. They are ranked in order of moral value, meaning that acting contrary to the null law is morally worse than the third principle. The general approach is to consider whether the overall state of the infosphere is better, even if some entropy is caused; hence the concern is with the global levels of entropy opposed to minor fluctuations.[101] It is important to note that the destruction or other form of impoverishment of the infosphere are not merely about the destruction of information, but about the destruction of information entities in their capacity as such.[102] From this perspective, harm or damage to an entity is considered in terms of the degradation of its being that is evident – for instance, in the corruption of its properties or in its complete destruction and the consequent increased levels of entropy in the infosphere.

With these principles, Floridi seeks to provide an ethical framework that affords 'respect for both the physical and the immaterial world'.[103] He maintains that an environmental approach that focuses on the well-being of the infosphere is best suited to this. He writes that

> Reality, both natural and immaterial, is not merely available for domination, control, and exploitation. Reality should also be an object of respect in its autonomous existence. This is what we can learn from an environmental approach.[104]

In summary, Floridi's information ethics is an environmental ethics that is concerned with the well-being of the infosphere. The infosphere is the totality of everything that exists – it is constituted by everything, from human beings to rocks to computer viruses, and the natural and virtual environments. The infosphere can be conceptualized as synonymous with reality itself once an informational level of abstraction is adopted. The level of abstraction is crucial to information ethics, and it expressly adopts an informational one. This means that all objects in the world are perceived in informational terms – that is, on a relatively high level of abstraction – and seen as information entities. It does not seek to raise animals or objects to the level of human beings, nor lower human beings to the level of objects. Instead, for methodological purposes, it simply perceives everything from an inclusive (informational) perspective so they share a common denominator. This also places emphasis on the foundational nature of information (everything can be described as such) and its importance in information societies that are increasingly dependent on ICTs that process information. As a result, given its informational ontology and concern with the overall well-being of the infosphere, information ethics provides a unique way of seeing the world pervaded by ICTs. It takes the position that all entities have a basic right to exist and flourish. Being or existence is regarded as good and taken to be more fundamental or basic than simply 'life'. In contrast, evil is understood in terms of entropy: the destruction or corruption of information entities. A responsible agent in this context seeks to avoid increasing the levels of entropy in the infosphere and strives to promote the right of all other information entities to flourish.

Criticisms of information ethics

Information ethics has been subject to a range of criticisms, which highlight and question the radical nature of some of its claims. For example, criticisms have been levelled against the ontological equality principle and the reasons why all entities should warrant moral respect. Also subject to criticism has been the perceived reduction of everything from human beings to inanimate objects into information entities, and information ethics' consequent inability to assess the differences in value that should be afforded to these entities. Finally, the viability of the notion of entropy as evil – that is, where an information entity is damaged or destroyed, violating its natural right to exist and flourish – has been criticized. These particular criticisms are the focus here, as they aid in the explanation of information ethics' conceptual foundation.[105] Below is an account of these criticisms, followed by Floridi's responses to them.

The ontological equality principle and value conflicts

Many have questioned the ontological equality principle and the reasoning behind why all information entities should have moral value. Michael Byron, for example, is critical of Floridi's all-inclusive broadening of the moral scope of information ethics. He maintains that because information is ontologically basic – as everything is constituted by information – it is odd to attribute intrinsic value to mere being in this sense. This leads to the position that since information itself is valuable, it requires people to seek maximal quantities of information to make the universe a morally better place.[106] Similarly, Philip Brey argues that information ethics does not provide a sound justification for its foundational claim that everything deserves some moral respect for its existence as an information object.[107] He argues that often there are other reasons why objects are valued.[108] Tony Doyle questions what it means for a waterfall to flourish, and why this in itself should be valued. He suggests that it would be more reasonable to attach value to natural wonders and animals, for example, where humans attach value to them or their conservation.[109] Doyle argues that Floridi only provides an 'undefended claim that all information objects have an essential moral dignity'.[110] Others have echoed these concerns, arguing that there tend to be other reasons to respect or value objects besides their inherent 'birthright' as information objects.[111] Essentially, these authors question why information entities should have moral value merely due to their existence, as the ontological equality principle asserts.

Another related criticism is that, if all entities can be considered as information entities that deserve a basic level of moral respect pursuant to the notion of ontological equality, then how can or should an assessment be made about when one entity warrants more respect than another? This has been raised by some authors, who argue that information ethics does not provide a sufficient framework to assess this. Byron, for example, argues that Floridi provides no means of assessing which information entity is more valuable – for instance, when comparing a human being and a rock.[112] Brey also makes this criticism, noting that information ethics fails to provide the means to distinguish between the value of, for instance, a human being and toxic waste.[113] Similarly, Bernd Stahl points out that Floridi does not provide a means of addressing value conflicts between entities.[114] Soraj Hongladarom also highlights this on a wider level, arguing that information ethics does not provide the means to prioritize different value systems.[115] Therefore, based on the principle of ontological equality, pursuant to which all entities are equal on a basic level, according to these authors information ethics fails to provide practical guidance on how to prioritize or assess the differences in value between information entities.

Entropy as evil

In addition to these criticisms against the ontological equality principle and the assessment of value conflicts, many also question what it means for an information entity to flourish and whether, according to the four principles provided by Floridi, all forms of entropy are morally evil. For example, Byron argues that the destruction of any object is unethical following these principles:

> Cyclones, volcanic eruptions, and tornadoes all cause moral evil when they destroy things—people, artifacts, or natural objects. When a star explodes, that's a deeply unethical event, given the extent of destruction.[116]

In addition to these natural events, Mikko Siponen questions whether human activities, such as fishing, hunting or felling trees, would be considered morally wrong using these principles because in each instance information entities are stripped of their rights to exist.[117] Further, there has even been criticism about the operation of information ethics in the context of ICT-specific issues such as computer viruses and the use of anti-virus software. For instance, Rafael Capurro maintains that these principles contradict the deletion of viruses, unsolicited emails and other forms of less useful information.[118] Siponen also considers computer viruses in this context: from an information ethics perspective, a virus would be regarded as an information entity as it is made up of a packet of information. As viruses are designed to spread and destroy information, meaning these functions are key to their nature and flourishing, then anti-virus activities in themselves would be morally wrong.[119] Accordingly, these authors are critical of what it means for an entity to flourish, and whether any instance of entropy that diminishes an entity's natural right to flourish can be regarded as morally evil.

Floridi's responses to criticisms

In defense of information ethics, Floridi has responded to these criticisms. In relation to the criticism levelled against the ontological equality principle and the reasoning behind why all information entities should be given moral respect, he maintains that information ethics is not simply about expanding the scope of ethical discourse from human and biological agents to artificial, digital or informational realities. Instead, it is about completely changing the perspective to an informational one, through which all entities are interpreted informationally; this in turn means that everything, including human, animal, social and artificial entities, is included.[120] From this informational level of abstraction, human beings are not simply reduced to information entities equal to rocks or toxic waste – Floridi emphasizes the point that the informational ontology is simply the lowest common denominator of everything. It is not meant to reduce human beings to numbers; instead, he argues that, like the Darwinian account of human beings as part of the animal kingdom that enabled them to see themselves differently, if human beings can be perceived as information organisms with reality understood as an infosphere, it makes sense to adopt an informational ontology.[121] The reason why, besides human beings, all other entities should be respected and considered as having intrinsic worth, is therefore that this should be considered the starting point. Floridi argues that:

> because we have no reasons against the intrinsic value of Being in all its manifestations, we should expand an environmental approach to all entities, including non-sentient beings. The injunction is to treat something as intrinsically valuable and hence worthy of moral respect by default, until 'proven guilty'.[122]

He therefore argues that all things should be respected *because* they have intrinsic value, and not that *if* they have intrinsic value *then* they should be respected.[123] Accordingly, the ontological equality principle is based on the idea that, in its capacity as an information entity, everything should be afforded a basic level of moral respect as a starting point. This does not mean, however, that all entities are equally valuable in their contribution to the well-being of the entire infosphere.

Following from this generally, and in relation to the assessment of the intrinsic value of different information entities specifically, Floridi maintains that information ethics is not simply about comparing the value of two information entities. He argues that it is ultimately not about comparing the intrinsic value of, for example, a work of Shakespeare with an 'airport novel'. Instead, he maintains that the issue is whether 'Goodness and Being … might be two sides of the same concept, as Evil and non-Being might be'.[124] Like many Eastern and Western philosophical traditions, he adopts this line of reasoning, arguing that there is a need to update the human conception of the universe 'in terms of an informational ontology, whereby Being is understood informationally and non-Being in terms of metaphysical entropy'.[125] In more practical terms, the assessment of whether one entity has more value than another is ultimately qualitative, involving a consideration of its contribution to the overall well-being of the infosphere: the higher it is, 'the higher its status is in the chain of morally respectable things'.[126] For instance, a biological virus must 'be destroyed for the sake of the rest of the environment and its flourishing'.[127] As such, the moral laws of information ethics are intended as basic principles that can assist in making these value assessments. Just like in environmental ethics, Floridi argues that simply having 'some universal, basic, and robust principles in place helps enormously when it comes to dealing with particular, complex, practical matters'.[128]

Collectively, the criticisms against information ethics that have been highlighted here essentially question the appropriateness of the notion of ontological equality, and whether any form of entropy should be regarded as evil. They question the idea that it is not just humans or living organisms, but all entities, that should be afforded moral respect, and whether the destruction or corruption of these entities is morally evil and should be avoided on that basis. Indeed, a degree of acceptance is needed of the wider arguments that Floridi makes about the profound impact of ICTs, the informational nature of reality and the resulting appropriateness of an environmental approach based on information. However, particularly due to its radical nature, information ethics provides a unique approach, grounded in a philosophy of information, and promises a conceptual framework through which to consider the ethical issues surrounding ICTs.

Conclusion

In a world in which societies are increasingly pervaded by and reliant on ICTs, information ethics provides a form of environmental ethics that takes this reality into account. Given its concern with the well-being of all entities that constitute the infosphere, it offers a novel way by which to consider all entities in terms of their information structures and the harm they can be subject to in terms of entropy. Drawing on this framework, the chapters that follow will demonstrate how the law's existing conceptual foundations are grounded in an inherent anthropocentrism and materialism, and how an informational approach offers a means by which to rethink these foundations in informational terms. In relation to cyber attacks in particular, this enables consideration of their impact on a broader range of entities within the infosphere – whether natural or artificial, real or virtual – and how the entropy caused by cyber attacks can be seen to constitute a form of violence against the state as an information entity.

Notes

1 Andrew Feenberg, 'What is Philosophy of Technology?' in John R Dakers (ed), *Defining Technological Literacy: Towards an Epistemological Framework* (Palgrave Macmillan 2006) 6–8.
2 ibid 8.
3 ibid 9.
4 ibid. This is in contrast to what are often described as 'substantivist' views on technology, which see technology not as value neutral but as embodying power and domination. See ibid 11–12. See also Carl Mitcham and Katinka Waelbers 'Technology and Ethics: Overview' in Jan Kyrre Berg Olsen, Stig Andur Pedersen and Vincent F Hendricks (eds), *A Companion to the Philosophy of Technology* (Wiley-Blackwell 2009) 371. For instance, Martin Heidegger's account of technology is often classed in this way. See Yoni Van Den Eede, 'Where Is the Human? Beyond the Enhancement Debate' (2015) 40(1) *Science, Technology & Human Values* 149, 151; Feenberg (n 1) 12.
5 Feenberg (n 1) 11.
6 ibid 9–11.
7 Val Dusek, 'Introduction: Philosophy and Technology' in Jan Kyrre Berg Olsen, Stig Andur Pedersen and Vincent F Hendricks (eds), *A Companion to the Philosophy of Technology* (Wiley-Blackwell 2009) 132–3.
8 Feenberg (n 1) 9.
9 On the 'social construction of technology', see, for example, Marc de Vries, *Teaching About Technology: An Introduction to the Philosophy of Technology for Non-Philosophers* (Springer 2005) 78–9; Val Dusek *Philosophy of Technology: An Introduction* (Blackwell 2006) 203–5.
10 Langdon Winner, 'Do Artifacts have Politics?' (1980) 109(1) *Daedalus* 121.
11 Mitcham and Waelbers (n 4) 373.
12 See Dusek (n 9) 32–3.
13 Andrew Feenberg, 'Critical Theory of Technology' in Jan Kyrre Berg Olsen, Stig Andur Pedersen and Vincent F Hendricks (eds), *A Companion to the Philosophy of Technology* (Wiley-Blackwell 2009) 148.
14 ibid.
15 Feenberg (n 1) 14.
16 Feenberg (n 13) 146–8.
17 Luciano Floridi (ed), *The Onlife Manifesto: Being Human in a Hyperconnected Era* (Springer 2015) xi–xiv.
18 ibid 1; The Onlife Initiative, 'The Onlife Manifesto' in Luciano Floridi (ed), *The Onlife Manifesto: Being Human in a Hyperconnected Era* (Springer 2015).

19 Floridi (n 17) 2–3.
20 ibid 2.
21 ibid.
22 The Onlife Initiative (n 18) 8.
23 ibid.
24 ibid.
25 Floridi (n 17) 3.
26 Luciano Floridi, 'The Philosophy of Information: Ten Years Later' (2010) 41(3) *Metaphilosophy* 402, 402–3. Floridi's major works currently include: Luciano Floridi, *Information: A Very Short Introduction* (Oxford University Press 2010); Luciano Floridi, *The Philosophy of Information* (Oxford University Press 2011); Luciano Floridi, *The Ethics of Information* (Oxford University Press 2013); and Luciano Floridi, *The Fourth Revolution* (Oxford University Press 2014).
27 Hilmi Demir maintains that the notion of the information age is traceable to developments in the 1940s and generally refers to the 'age when computers have become an essential part of our daily lives'. It is a time 'dominated by information and communication technologies'. Hilmi Demir, 'The Fourth Revolution: Philosophical Foundations and Technological Implications' (2010) 23(1–2) *Knowledge, Technology & Policy* 1. Terrell Ward Bynum uses the term to refer to 'technical and scientific developments in the 1940s that enabled a remarkable "explosion" of new products and innovations in the 1950s and beyond'. It was then the exponential growth of the social and ethical issues caused by these developments that warranted the use of the notion of the term 'information revolution'. Terrell Ward Bynum, 'Philosophy in the Information Age' (2010) 41(3) *Metaphilosophy* 420.
28 Floridi defines his philosophy of information as 'the philosophical field concerned with (a) the critical investigation of the conceptual nature and basic principles of information, including its dynamics, utilization, and sciences; and (b) the elaboration and application of information-theoretic and computational methodologies to philosophical problems.' Floridi, *The Philosophy of Information* (n 26) 14. As Patrick Allo notes, it is not simply 'about the concepts of information and computation, it is also concerned with applications of informational and computational methods and models to philosophical problems'. Patrick Allo, 'Putting Information First: Luciano Floridi and the Philosophy of Information' (2010) 41(3) *Metaphilosophy* 247.
29 For Norbert Wiener, physical objects and processes were made up of 'patterns of information encoded with an ever-changing flux of matter-energy', and any irreversible loss of physical information constituted thermodynamic entropy. He also viewed humans as 'fundamentally informational' – that is, as patterns of information – and the flourishing of a person – which depended on information processing – as the overall purpose of life. See Otávio Bueno, 'Structuralism and Information' 41(3) (2010) *Metaphilosophy* 365, 424–7.
30 According to Patrick Allo, while there had clearly been an 'informational turn' in philosophy, 'Floridi gave that turn a more radical twist by claiming that taking the informational turn means redefining philosophy.' Allo (n 28) 247.
31 This is Floridi's notion of 'informational structural realism' – the idea that the nature of reality is ultimately informational and can be regarded as 'mind-independent and constituted by structural objects that are neither substantial nor material (they might well be, but we have no need to suppose them to be so) but informational'. Luciano Floridi, 'A Defence of Informational Structural Realism' (2008) 161(2) *Synthese* 219, 241. See also Bynum (n 27) 432–3; Donald Gillies, 'Informational Realism and World 3' (2010) 23(1–2) *Knowledge, Technology, & Policy* 7, 20; Philip Brey, 'Do We Have Moral Duties Towards Information Objects?' (2008) 10(2–3) *Ethics and Information Technology* 109, 112.

32 Floridi, *Information: A Very Short Introduction* (n 26) 110.
33 Floridi, *The Ethics of Information* (n 26) xii.
34 ibid.
35 Bynum describes Floridi's philosophy of information as an ambitious project aimed at creating a 'new philosophical paradigm' founded on the concept of information, see Bynum (n 27) 431. According to Hilmi Demir, Floridi has in many ways defined the modern field of philosophy of information. See Demir (n 27) 3.
36 As the chair of the group of scholars, however, it is likely that he contributed to the shape of those arguments. See Floridi (n 17) 1–3.
37 Floridi, *The Philosophy of Information* (n 26) 2–3.
38 Floridi, *The Fourth Revolution* (n 26) 90–4.
39 In essence, Floridi maintains that 'today we acknowledge that we are not immobile, at the centre of the universe (Copernican revolution), we are not unnaturally separate and diverse from the rest of the animal kingdom (Darwinian revolution), and we are very far from being standalone Cartesian minds entirely transparent to ourselves (Freudian or neuroscientific revolution). Floridi, *The Ethics of Information* (n 26) 14. See also Floridi, *The Fourth Revolution* (n 26) 87–90.
40 Demir (n 27) 3.
41 Michael Byron, 'Floridi's Fourth Revolution and the Demise of Ethics' (2010) 23(1–2) *Knowledge, Technology, & Policy* 135, 136. According to Wolfgang Hofkirchner, the essence of Floridi's overarching argument is that 'the fourth revolution associated with ICTs imposes an unescapable infosphere on humans in which they are transformed into informational agents; this increases the importance of the management of the information life cycle; and this in turn requires ethical considerations that shape the infosphere'. Wolfgang Hofkirchner, 'How to Design the Infosphere: The Fourth Revolution, the Management of the Life Cycle of Information, and Information Ethics as a Macroethics' (2010) 23(1–2) *Knowledge, Technology, & Policy* 177, 178.
42 Floridi, *The Ethics of Information* (n 26) 14 (emphasis in original). See also Floridi, *The Fourth Revolution* (n 26) 90–100.
43 Floridi, *The Ethics of Information* (n 26) 6. See also Floridi, *Information: A Very Short Introduction* (n 26) 11; Luciano Floridi, 'A Look into the Future Impact of ICT on our Lives' (2007) 23(1) *The Information Society* 59, 60.
44 Floridi, *The Ethics of Information* (n 26) 6.
45 Floridi, *The Fourth Revolution* (n 26) 41. See also Floridi, *The Ethics of Information* (n 26) 6; Luciano Floridi, 'Information Ethics: on the Philosophical Foundation of Computer Ethics' (1999) 1(1) *Ethics and Information Technology* 33, 44. Floridi argues that, as an evolving concept, the infosphere 'can also be used as synonymous with reality, once we interpret the latter informationally'. See Floridi, *The Fourth Revolution* (n 26) 41.
46 According to Hongladarom, it is 'the whole environment in which information plays a key, constitutive role; that is, the sum total of all information there is in a given environment'. Soraj Hongladarom, 'Floridi and Spinoza on Global Information Ethics' (2008) 10(2–3) *Ethics and Information Technology* 175, 176. On how this concept has been used in relation to computer game environments, for example, see Miguel Sicart, *The Ethics of Computer Games* (MIT Press 2011).
47 Floridi, *The Ethics of Information* (n 26) 7.
48 ibid (emphasis in original).
49 ibid 8–9.
50 ibid 8. Floridi describes this experience as 'onlife'. See also Luciano Floridi, 'Global Information Ethics: The Importance of Being Environmentally Earnest' (2007) 3(3) *International Journal of Technology and Human Interaction* 1, 3.
51 Floridi, *The Ethics of Information* (n 26) 12.

52 Floridi writes that, 'We are changing our everyday perspective on the ultimate nature of reality from a historical and materialist one, in which physical objects and mechanical processes play a key role, to a hyperhistorical and informational one.' Floridi, *The Fourth Revolution* (n 26) 50.

53 See Bernd Stahl, 'Discourses on Information Ethics: The Claim to Universality' (2008) 10(2–3) *Ethics and Information Technology* 97. Bernd Stahl maintains that Floridi's information ethics appears 'uniquely suited for addressing the novel issues arising from the way current technology changes our use of information in private life, organizations and society'. ibid.

54 Floridi writes that, 'The development of information and communication technologies (ICTs) has not only brought enormous benefits and opportunities but also greatly outpaced our understanding of their conceptual nature and implications, while raising problems whose complexity and global dimensions are rapidly expanding, evolving, and becoming increasingly serious.' Luciano Floridi, 'The Information Society and Its Philosophy: Introduction to the Special Issue on "The Philosophy of Information, Its Nature, and Future Developments"' (2009) 25(3) *The Information Society* 153, 154.

55 ibid.

56 Van Den Eede (n 4) 151.

57 Luciano Floridi, *Information Ethics: An Environmental Approach to the Digital Divide* (First Meeting of the Sub-Commission on the Ethics of the Information Society, United Nations Educational, Scientific and Cultural Organization 2001) 63.

58 ibid 62.

59 Floridi, *The Ethics of Information* (n 26) 305.

60 Floridi (n 57) 66. Hongladarom maintains that Floridi's view is 'an adaptation of the ancient view' on ethics, in which nature, in the form of the infosphere, is given supreme importance. See Hongladarom (n 46) 182.

61 Floridi, *The Ethics of Information* (n 26) xii. For an overview of the evolution of Floridi's information ethics as a project, see Rafael Capurro, 'On Floridi's Metaphysical Foundation of Information Ecology' (2008) 10(2–3) *Ethics and Information Technology* 167, 167–8.

62 Synthetic here refers to the use of the term both in the holistic/inclusive and artificial sense. See Floridi, *The Ethics of Information* (n 26) 18.

63 Floridi, *The Ethics of Information* (n 26) 133. Deep ecology, rejecting the anthropocentric view of nature as only having instrumental value to humans, holds that it has intrinsic value in itself. See Dusek (n 9) 187. See also Arne Naess, 'The Shallow and the Deep, Long-Range Ecology Movement: A Summary' (1973) 16(1–4) *Inquiry* 95.

64 Joseph E Brenner, 'A Logic of Ethical Information' (2010) 23(1–2) *Knowledge, Technology, & Policy* 109, 111.

65 Massimo Durante, 'The Value of Information as Ontological Pluralism' (2010) 23(1–2) *Knowledge, Technology, & Policy* 149, 151.

66 Hongladarom (n 46) 175. Hongladarom also notes that instead of the value of the individual that underpins liberal theories, for Floridi instead it is 'the whole ontic substance, the whole of reality itself' undergirding the value. ibid 184.

67 Luciano Floridi, 'Information Ethics, its Nature and Scope' (2006) 36(3) *Computers and Society* 21, 23.

68 Floridi (n 45) 44.

69 Floridi, *Information: A Very Short Introduction* (n 26) 113.

70 The level of abstraction is the point of view from which to analyse things – the perspective and degree of abstraction from which things are conceptualized. Specifically, it is defined as 'a finite but non-empty set of observables, which are expected to be the building blocks in a theory characterized by their

very choice'. Floridi, *The Ethics of Information* (n 26) 32. Information ethics is 'committed to a LoA [level of abstraction] that interprets reality—that is, any system—informationally'. ibid 35.

71 Floridi, *Information: A Very Short Introduction* (n 26) 110. For a critique of Floridi's conception of information, see Pieter Adriaans, 'A Critical Analysis of Floridi's Theory of Semantic Information' (2010) 23(1–2) *Knowledge, Technology, & Policy* 41. See also Floridi's reply: Luciano Floridi, 'The Philosophy of Information as a Conceptual Framework' (2010) 23(1) *Knowledge, Technology & Policy* 253, 259–60.

72 Floridi maintains that all entities 'will be described as clusters of data, that is, as informational objects. More precisely, our agent A (like any other entity) will be a discrete, self-contained, encapsulated package containing (i) the appropriate data structures, which constitute the nature of the entity in question, that is, the state of the object, its unique identity, and its attributes; and (ii) a collection of operations, functions, or procedures, which are activated by various interactions or stimuli (that is, messages received from other objects or changes within itself), and correspondingly define how the object behaves or reacts to them. At this level of analysis, informational systems as such, rather than just living systems in general, are raised to the role of agents and patients of any action, with environmental processes, changes, and interactions equally described informationally.' Floridi, *Information: A Very Short Introduction* (n 26) 111.

73 Brenner (n 64) 111.

74 Tony Doyle, 'A Critique of Information Ethics' (2010) 23(1–2) *Knowledge, Technology & Policy* 163, 164.

75 ibid.

76 Floridi (n 67) 33. Floridi uses the terms information(al) entities and information(al) objects interchangeably.

77 Floridi, *The Ethics of Information* (n 26) 65.

78 Floridi (n 45) 50.

79 ibid 43. Elsewhere, Floridi writes that information ethics is 'impartial and universal because it brings to ultimate completion the process of enlargement of the concept of what may count as a center of a (no matter how minimal) moral claim, which now includes every instance of being understood informationally … no matter whether physically implemented or not'. Floridi (n 67) 26.

80 Doyle (n 74) 164–6. Tony Doyle, however, is critical of this. He maintains that merely highlighting 'an apparent trend in moral philosophy towards greater inclusiveness', whatever its merits, 'is not an *argument* for expanding the moral circle'. ibid 166 (emphasis in original). For Floridi's reply, see Floridi (n 71) 269–73.

81 Floridi (n 45) 50.

82 Floridi (n 67) 33.

83 ibid.

84 ibid 30.

85 ibid 31.

86 Floridi (n 45) 44. This notion, according to Doyle, is comparable to 'the utilitarian principle that everyone's happiness (or interests or preferences) be weighed equally or to [John] Rawls's assumption that the veil of ignorance ensures equality for the contractors in the original position'. Doyle (n 74) 165. See also Hongladarom (n 46) 184.

87 Floridi (n 67) 30. See also Luciano Floridi, 'Information Ethics: A Reappraisal' (2008) 10(2–3) *Ethics and Information Technology* 189, 192.

88 Floridi (n 45) 44.

89 Durante (n 65) 150.

90 Luciano Floridi and Jeff Sanders, 'The Foundationalist Debate in Computer Ethics' in Richard A Spinello and Herman T Tavani (eds), *Readings in CyberEthics* (2nd edn, Jones and Bartlett 2004) 92.
91 Floridi (n 45) 45.
92 Durante (n 65) 152. See also Floridi (n 87) 201; Floridi, *The Ethics of Information* (n 26) 322–3.
93 Floridi (n 45) 45.
94 Bynum (n 27) 433–4.
95 Floridi, *The Ethics of Information* (n 26) 67 (emphasis in original).
96 ibid.
97 ibid.
98 Floridi (n 87) 193.
99 See Floridi, *The Ethics of Information* (n 26) 65–7. Floridi writes that, 'Both in thermodynamics and in information theory, entropy is a syntactic and quantitative concept: neither information nor entropy refers to the actual meaning, content, interpretation (semantics), or to the existence and nature (ontology) of the system. In IE [information ethics], we still treat the two concepts of information and entropy as being related, but we are concerned with the semantic and ontological nature of information. For example, as the infosphere becomes increasingly meaningful and rich in content, the amount of information increases (what one may call, for the sake of clarity) *metaphysical entropy* decreases. Thus, in IE, entropy is not merely a syntactic concept, but, as the opposite of semantic and ontic information, it indicates the decrease or decay of information leading to absence of form, pattern, differentiation, or content in the infosphere. It is therefore most emphatically *not* the physicists' or engineers' concept of entropy.' ibid 66–7 (emphasis in original).
100 Floridi, *The Ethics of Information* (n 26) 71; Floridi (n 45) 47; Floridi (n 67) 32.
101 See Floridi, *The Ethics of Information* (n 26) 71–2.
102 Durante (n 65) 157.
103 Floridi (n 57) 67.
104 ibid. Hongladarom maintains that these principles form a clear basis for an environmental ethics, a motto of which could be 'let all things flourish'. Hongladarom (n 46) 176.
105 For a convenient collation of these and other criticisms that have been made against information ethics, and Floridi's reply to those criticisms, see Floridi, *The Ethics of Information* (n 26) Chapter 16.
106 Byron (n 41) 142. See also Floridi's reply, Floridi (n 71) 267–9.
107 Brey (n 31) 111.
108 ibid 112. See also Floridi's reply: Floridi (n 87) 191–5. Floridi, *The Ethics of Information* (n 26) 322–3.
109 Doyle (n 74) 166–7.
110 ibid 168. For Floridi's reply, see Floridi (n 71) 269–73.
111 Richard Volkman, 'Why Information Ethics Must Begin with Virtue Ethics' (2010) 41(3) *Metaphilosophy* 380, 395. Richard Volkman maintains that what a thing is, and whether and how it should be respected, depend on the purposes and values that are attached to it by people – something that the principle of ontological equality and information ethics' universalism and impartialism do not capture. See ibid 393–4. For Floridi's reply, see Floridi, 'The Philosophy of Information: Ten Years Later' (n 26) 414–17. Similarly, Rafael Capurro maintains that value is generally a relationship and not merely a property of an object. See Capurro (n 61) 168. See also Floridi's reply, Floridi (n 87) 199–201.
112 Byron (n 41) 142. See also Floridi's reply, Floridi (n 71) 267–9.
113 Brey (n 31) 112. See also Floridi's reply, Floridi (n 87) 191–5; Floridi, *The Ethics of Information* (n 26) 322–3.

114 Stahl (n 53) 103–104. See also Floridi's reply, Floridi (n 87) 190–1.
115 Hongladarom notes the difficulty of how to prioritize different value systems (for example, North American and European Union models of privacy) from an information ethics perspective. See Hongladarom (n 46) 186.
116 Byron (n 41) 144. See also Floridi's reply, Floridi (n 71) 267–9.
117 Mikko Siponen, 'A Pragmatic Evaluation of the Theory of Information Ethics' (2004) 6(4) *Ethics and Information Technology* 279, 287.
118 Capurro (n 61) 170. See also Floridi's reply, Floridi (n 87) 199–201.
119 Siponen (n 117) 287.
120 Floridi, *The Ethics of Information* (n 26) 307–8.
121 ibid 308–9.
122 ibid 318.
123 ibid.
124 ibid 322.
125 ibid 322–3.
126 ibid 317.
127 ibid.
128 ibid 314.

Bibliography

Adriaans P, 'A Critical Analysis of Floridi's Theory of Semantic Information' (2010) 23(1–2) *Knowledge, Technology, & Policy* 41

Allo P, 'Putting Information First: Luciano Floridi and the Philosophy of Information' (2010) 41(3) *Metaphilosophy* 247

Brenner JE, 'A Logic of Ethical Information' (2010) 23(1–2) *Knowledge, Technology, & Policy* 109

Brey P, 'Do We Have Moral Duties Towards Information Objects?' (2008) 10(2–3) *Ethics and Information Technology* 109

Bueno O, 'Structuralism and Information' 41(3) (2010) *Metaphilosophy* 365

Bynum TW, 'Philosophy in the Information Age' (2010) 41(3) *Metaphilosophy* 420

Byron M, 'Floridi's Fourth Revolution and the Demise of Ethics' (2010) 23(1–2) *Knowledge, Technology, & Policy* 135

Capurro R, 'On Floridi's Metaphysical Foundation of Information Ecology' (2008) 10(2–3) *Ethics and Information Technology* 167

de Vries M, *Teaching About Technology: An Introduction to the Philosophy of Technology for Non-Philosophers* (Springer 2005)

Demir H, 'The Fourth Revolution: Philosophical Foundations and Technological Implications' (2010) 23(1–2) *Knowledge, Technology & Policy* 1

Doyle T, 'A Critique of Information Ethics' (2010) 23(1–2) *Knowledge, Technology & Policy* 163

Durante M, 'The Value of Information as Ontological Pluralism' (2010) 23(1–2) *Knowledge, Technology, & Policy* 149

Dusek V, *Philosophy of Technology: An Introduction* (Blackwell 2006)

——— 'Introduction: Philosophy and Technology' in Olsen JKB, Pedersen SA and Hendricks VF (eds), *A Companion to the Philosophy of Technology* (Wiley-Blackwell 2009)

Feenberg A, 'What is Philosophy of Technology?' in Dakers JR (ed), *Defining Technological Literacy: Towards an Epistemological Framework* (Palgrave Macmillan 2006)

——— 'Critical Theory of Technology' in Olsen JKB, Pedersen SA and Hendricks VF (eds), *A Companion to the Philosophy of Technology* (Wiley-Blackwell 2009)

Floridi L, 'Information Ethics: On the Philosophical Foundation of Computer Ethics' (1999) 1(1) *Ethics and Information Technology* 33

——— *Information Ethics: An Environmental Approach to the Digital Divide* (First Meeting of the Sub-Commission on the Ethics of the Information Society, United Nations Educational, Scientific and Cultural Organization 2001)

——— 'Global Information Ethics: The Importance of Being Environmentally Earnest' (2007) 3(3) *International Journal of Technology and Human Interaction* 1

——— 'A Look into the Future Impact of ICT on Our Lives' (2007) 23(1) *The Information Society* 59

——— 'A Defence of Informational Structural Realism' (2008) 161(2) *Synthese* 219

——— 'Information Ethics: A Reappraisal' (2008) 10(2–3) *Ethics and Information Technology* 189

——— 'The Information Society and Its Philosophy: Introduction to the Special Issue on "The Philosophy of Information, Its Nature, and Future Developments"' (2009) 25(3) *The Information Society* 153

——— *Information: A Very Short Introduction* (Oxford University Press 2010)

——— 'The Philosophy of Information as a Conceptual Framework' (2010) 23(1) *Knowledge, Technology & Policy* 253

——— 'The Philosophy of Information: Ten Years Later' (2010) 41(3) *Metaphilosophy* 402

——— *The Philosophy of Information* (Oxford University Press 2011)

——— *The Ethics of Information* (Oxford University Press 2013)

——— *The Fourth Revolution* (Oxford University Press 2014)

——— (ed), The Onlife Manifesto: Being Human in a Hyperconnected Era (Springer 2015)

Floridi L and Sanders JW, 'The Foundationalist Debate in Computer Ethics' in Spinello RA and Tavani HT (eds), *Readings in CyberEthics* (2nd edn, Jones and Bartlett 2004)

Gillies D, 'Informational Realism and World 3' (2010) 23(1–2) *Knowledge, Technology, & Policy* 7

Hofkirchner W, 'How to Design the Infosphere: the Fourth Revolution, the Management of the Life Cycle of Information, and Information Ethics as a Macroethics' (2010) 23(1–2) *Knowledge, Technology, & Policy* 177

Hongladarom S, 'Floridi and Spinoza on Global Information Ethics' (2008) 10(2–3) *Ethics and Information Technology* 175

Mitcham C and Waelbers K, 'Technology and Ethics: Overview' in Olsen JKB, Pedersen SA and Hendricks VF (eds), *A Companion to the Philosophy of Technology* (Wiley-Blackwell 2009)

Naess A, 'The Shallow and the Deep, Long-Range Ecology Movement. A Summary' (1973) 16(1–4) *Inquiry* 95

The Onlife Initiative, 'The Onlife Manifesto' in Floridi L (ed), *The Onlife Manifesto: Being Human in a Hyperconnected Era* (Springer 2015)

Sicart M, *The Ethics of Computer Games* (MIT Press 2011)

Siponen M, 'A Pragmatic Evaluation of the Theory of Information Ethics' (2004) 6(4) *Ethics and Information Technology* 279

Stahl BC, 'Discourses on Information Ethics: The Claim to Universality' (2008) 10(2–3) *Ethics and Information Technology* 97

Van Den Eede Y, 'Where Is the Human? Beyond the Enhancement Debate' (2015) 40(1) *Science, Technology & Human Values* 149

Volkman R, 'Why Information Ethics Must begin with Virtue Ethics' (2010) 41(3) *Metaphilosophy* 380

Winner L, 'Do Artifacts have Politics?' (1980) 109(1) *Daedalus* 121

3 Technology, violence, and law

Introduction

This chapter explores the ways in which international law historically has sought to regulate various global information flows, violence and technology, and how the novel nature of cyber warfare requires a rethinking of the harm caused by cyber attacks against the state. The first section provides a historical overview of how international law has sought to regulate various information flows and deemed certain forms of information harmful. It also outlines the growing dependence of states on ICTs for their well-being and prosperity, as well as the threats they have become vulnerable to from cyberspace. The chapter then considers international law and containment of violence, exploring the ways in which international law has sought to limit interstate violence, the role of the sovereign state in this context, and how the Article 2(4) prohibition on the use of force is the modern continuation of the effort to contain interstate violence. The third section examines how cyber warfare challenges the traditional understanding of warfare, in what is identified as an ontological gap between kinetic and cyber warfare. Finally, drawing on information ethics, an informational reconceptualization of the state and the notion of violence is proposed. This chapter argues that an informational approach offers a means to broaden international law's containment of violence to also forms of informational violence, enabling a recognition of how cyber attacks can harm the state as an information entity.

International law and information

Vast amounts of information or data now flow across the globe – in 1992, the amount of Internet traffic was approximately 100 gigabytes per day, whereas in 2016 this figure was approximately 26,000 gigabytes per second.[1] Indeed, given various developments such as the increased globalization of the world economy, increases in data transfer between public and private sectors and a vast growth in the volume of existing data and its transfer and processing, information itself has become a 'crucial raw material' in the global economy.[2] Since the early development of ICTs and the ability for information to be transferred across the world – between governmental, corporate, and individual actors instantaneously, with little regard for territorial borders – there have been calls to regulate these data flows. The concerns for the regulation of such data flows date back to the 1970s and 1980s, when there was already a sense that information, in the context of 'transborder data flows', was becoming increasingly important.[3] The development and fusion of computer and telecommunication technology was seen to lead to the growth of information societies – that is, societies in which 'information is a predominant factor in economic, social, political, and other important facets of life'.[4] Already, information was regarded as the successor to industrial processes – similar to the way in which mechanical systems were succeeded by electronics.[5] Various concerns were associated with these developments, centered primarily on economic development and the protection of personal privacy. For instance, in 1980 the Organization for Economic Cooperation and Development (OECD) issued guidelines for transborder data flows that sought to protect personal data while ensuring minimal barriers to these data flows, given their economic advantages.[6] Similarly, in a United Nations Educational, Scientific and Cultural Organization (UNESCO) affiliated conference in 1984, the importance of regulating transborder data flows was highlighted. There was a call to 'create some kind of international highway code for informatics' to regulate transborder data flows and avoid chaos, especially given that the technologies enabling these flows formed 'the nervous system of nations'.[7] It was also predicted that:

> The next five to ten years will be crucial regarding the flow of data from one country to another: we can foresee that in the future it will not be territorial disputes or concerns of national supremacy but the control and possession of information that will be the source of major conflicts as this lies at the root of everything: of development, of security, of defence, of education, and of culture itself.[8]

These predictions were made prior to the development of the World Wide Web, and they demonstrate that already in the 1980s there was a sense that information was becoming more and more central, and rules were needed to regulate international data flows. This need was foreseen to expand beyond the economic realm and that of personal privacy into all aspects of society, and even into international security and conflict.[9]

In fact, even prior to these developments in the 1980s, early telegraphic communication technologies contributed greatly to an international concern to regulate new technologies that operated mostly regardless of national borders. The International Telegraph Union, for example, as the first public international union, was formed as an international response to issues raised by new technology.[10] It sought to promote the free flow of data by ensuring the telegraphic infrastructure of states was sufficient to 'ensure the rapid transmission' of information, and that this infrastructure could cater for state communications on a permanent basis, 'day and night, without interruption'.[11] In addition to promoting the free flow of data in this way, international law has also sought to limit the flows of information deemed harmful or contrary to international law. Data or information in this context refers to analogue data – that is, the transmission of telephone, telegraph, television, and radio data.[12] For example, the 1936 International Convention Concerning the Use of Broadcasting in the Cause of Peace sought to prohibit any transmission of information detrimental to or incompatible with the internal order of a state (propaganda), and false information likely to harm 'good international understanding'.[13] Additionally, the International Telegraph Union's successor, the International Telecommunication Union (ITU), has sought to allocate and register radio frequencies to 'avoid harmful interference between radio stations of different countries' and to 'coordinate efforts to eliminate harmful interference between radio stations of different countries'.[14] These provisions were also targeted at preventing offshore pirate radio stations in the 1950s and 1960s from broadcasting on unauthorized wavelengths and from broadcasting material that was being used without authorization.[15] They were aimed at controlling flows of information that, for example, harmed the various political, social, and economic interests of states. Similarly, the United Nations Convention on the Law of the Sea requires states to cooperate in the suppression of 'unauthorized broadcasting' from the high seas, thereby seeking to prevent 'the transmission of sound radio or television broadcasts' that are contrary to international law.[16] Harmful interference to the radio services or communications of those authorized to broadcast them is also addressed by a later ITU convention,[17] amounting to a general prohibition on deliberate radio interference or 'jamming'.[18] International law, therefore, historically has sought to regulate the international flow of information and deemed certain forms of information harmful.

Despite successful international efforts by states to regulate various analogue data flows, the current regulation and governance of digital data flows – for instance, the Internet – stem from a more complex landscape of public and private actors.[19] While originally regulated by a smaller technical community, the technical protocols and standards of the Internet are currently regulated by a combination of private actors such as the Internet Corporation for Assigned Names and Numbers (ICANN) and increasingly the UN-affiliated ITU, which itself is made up of state and non-state actors.[20] When it comes to particular uses of the Internet, states have sought to restrict certain activities involving the use of computer systems and data. In addition to censorship laws and restrictions on harmful communications within states' domestic jurisdictions,[21] states have, through international efforts such as the Convention on Cybercrime,[22] deemed certain criminal uses of networks and improper use of information therein unlawful. For example, the Convention on Cybercrime seeks to regulate certain harmful uses of networks and data through the harmonization of national laws. It includes provisions relating to illegal access to computer systems without right,[23] and the interception of non-public data being transferred between computer systems.[24] It also includes provisions relating to intentional interference – that is, the 'damaging, deletion, deterioration, alteration or suppression of computer data'[25] and interference with the functioning of computer systems, which refers to 'the serious hindering without right of the functioning of a computer system by inputting, transmitting, damaging, deleting, deteriorating, altering, or suppressing computer data'.[26] Information in the context of the Internet and the harm that can stem from criminal activities in cyberspace is thus increasingly regulated by international law. However, the harmful data flows between states that have the potential to undermine international peace and security have only become a more recent concern, particularly given the increased dependence of states on digital ICTs.

Within the UN General Assembly (UNGA), various resolutions on 'Developments in the Field of Information and Telecommunications in the Context of International Security' have been adopted since they originally were introduced by Russia in 1998.[27] Here the First Committee of the UN General Assembly (the Disarmament and International Security Committee) has highlighted a number of international issues surrounding the use of ICTs. These include the role of science and technology in relation to international security and the positive opportunities associated with these technologies in terms of developing civilization, international cooperation, and the circulation of information. In addition to concerns that these technologies can be used for criminal or terrorist purposes, fears have also been expressed that they 'can potentially be used for purposes that are inconsistent with the objectives of maintaining international stability and security and may adversely affect the integrity of the infrastructure of States to the detriment of their security in both civil and military fields'.[28]

The Second Committee (the Economic and Financial Committee) has in turn adopted a number of resolutions encouraging a 'global culture of cybersecurity'.[29] These resolutions highlight a range of international issues relating to ICTs. The resolution adopted in 2003, for example, notes the growing dependence of governments, businesses, and other organizations, as well as individuals, on information technologies,[30] and the threats and vulnerabilities that arise as a result of the ICT-enabled interconnectivity.[31] Additionally, it highlights the need to respect others' legitimate interests and recognize the possibility of one's actions or inactions harming others, given the pervasiveness of ICTs in societies.[32] The resolution adopted in 2004 in turn notes the role of ICTs in the promotion of socioeconomic development and in the provision of goods and services.[33] The resolution adopted in 2009 emphasizes that confidence and security in the use of ICTs are among 'the main pillars of the information society',[34] and it emphasizes the increasing contribution of ICTs 'to many of the essential functions of daily life, commerce and the provision of goods and services, research, innovation and entrepreneurship, and to the free flow of information among individuals and organizations, Governments, business and civil society'.[35] The resolution also notes how the reliable functioning of ICT infrastructure and the integrity of information affect global welfare.[36] Additionally, following the Edward Snowden revelations, the Third Committee (the Social, Cultural and Humanitarian Committee) has expressed a 'deep concern' about the negative impact of mass-scale surveillance and data interception programs on human rights to privacy.[37]

Finally, initially in 2004, the First Committee established a Group of Governmental Experts (GGE) to examine existing and potential threats from cyberspace. In the 2013 report, the GGE affirmed the application of existing international law and UN Charter principles in this context, noting that law is needed to ensure 'an open, secure, peaceful and accessible ICT environment'.[38] The report also concluded that state sovereignty applied to both the 'ICT-related activities' of states and to 'their jurisdiction over ICT infrastructure within their territory'.[39] It was also noted that the use of ICTs 'has reshaped the international security environment' and that, while such 'technologies bring immense economic and social benefits; they can also be used for purposes that are inconsistent with international peace and security'.[40] In the 2015 report, the GGE focused particularly on norms of behavior for states in relation to their ICT activities. These included that states should not conduct or support ICT activities that cause damage to the critical infrastructure of other states.[41] Therefore, as illustrated by various resolutions by the UN General Assembly, it has been recognized by the international community at the UN level that ICTs and information are becoming increasingly fundamental to the functioning and prosperity of modern societies.

Accordingly, states as industrial societies have used basic ICTs, such as telegraphic and radio technologies, to transmit data across borders since the nineteenth century. Also, through various international efforts, they have sought to regulate and secure global ICT infrastructures and information flows. Increasingly, however, ICTs are not simply a means of communication but intrinsically intertwined into the fabric of modern society. The hallmark of 'postindustrial' or 'information societies' is that these societies are increasingly not just using ICTs, such as radios or telephones in communications, but instead becoming dependent on digital ICTs and on information as a resource. As Ugo Pagallo maintains,

> whereas over the past centuries, human societies have used information and communication technology (ICT), but have been mainly dependent on technologies that revolve around energy and basic resources, today's societies are increasingly dependent on ICT and, furthermore, on information as a vital resource. Essential functions of today's societies, such

> as governmental services, transportation and communication systems, business processes or energy production and distribution networks, depend on the use of computer platforms.[42]

With technological advancement and increasing digitalization of essential societal functions, states have also become vulnerable to attacks on information through information. For example, the notion of critical infrastructure is defined within the context of the European Union (EU) as those assets or systems 'essential for the maintenance of vital societal functions, health, safety, security, economic or social well-being of people'[43] – essentially referring to physical infrastructure that is vital for the proper functioning of society. The term critical *information* infrastructure, in turn, is used to describe both the essential ICT infrastructures and those that are essential for the operation of the aforementioned physical critical infrastructures.[44] Accordingly, the proper functioning of the infrastructure of information societies is intertwined with ICTs, meaning that states have also become vulnerable to informational threats. Various cyber attacks provide novel informational means through which to disrupt information systems or undermine the integrity of the information upon which these systems rely. Distributed Denial-of-Service (DDoS) attacks, for example, can flood a computer system with information and disrupt its operation, and malicious software such as computer viruses can be designed to alter information and undermine the proper operation of information systems. Therefore, as states are becoming increasingly reliant on ICTs, they are becoming vulnerable to information flows that are capable of harming them in new ways. Information is effectively flowing into how interstate uses of force are conceptualized, and thereby challenging traditional understandings of interstate violence and the ability of law to regulate and contain interstate violence.

International law and the containment of violence

This section explores the relationship between international law and violence. It demonstrates how the containment of violence through international law is central to the UN Charter-based international legal order. It explores the tension between violence within the contemplation of positive law and violence that is outside the realm of law. In international law, this tension is evident in the law's relationship with war and violence. Through international law, states have sought to contain the violence associated with warfare by limiting the authority to wage violence to the sovereign state and by limiting the violence inherent in warfare through law. In the modern context, the prohibition on the use of force provides the doctrinal limitation on the most intense forms of violent coercion, and the modern means by which international law seeks to contain violence. Against this depiction of international law's containment of violence, the next section will then demonstrate how cyber attacks are challenging this containment.

Violence, the state and law

Walter Benjamin distinguished between two forms of violence: law-making violence and law-preserving violence.[45] He described law-making violence as the violence evident in the establishment of every legal order.[46] Law-preserving violence, on the other hand, refers to legal violence used to preserve the legal order.[47] He maintained that law has an interest in the monopoly of violence in order to preserve itself, as 'violence, when not in the hands of the law, threatens it not by the ends that it may pursue but by its mere existence outside the law'.[48] In the context of interstate relations, there is also an implicit distinction between forms of violence that are part of the legal order and those that are external to it, and hence considered outside the law. This is evident particularly in the classical realist image of war and its placement outside the confines of law. According to Michael Walzer, for classical realists:

> War is a world apart, where life itself is at stake, where human nature is reduced to its elemental forms, where self-interest and necessity prevail. Here men and women do what they must to save themselves and their communities, and morality and law have no place. *Inter arma silent leges*: in time of war the law is silent.[49]

Interstate violence was therefore classically seen as taking place in a state of nature in which the law was silent. Martti Koskenniemi describes a similar imagery:

> For the classical realists, the founding violence of law – the violence which could not be encompassed by law because it was its precondition – was an act of physical force, sending in the military to occupy a territory or to overthrow (or uphold) a government, war, aggression, sovereignty: great moments of historical significance. These were the *a priori* on which the law was based and could not, therefore, be captured within law.[50]

This tension between violence that is outside the law and the legal order, and violence that is captured by the law and within the legal order is implicit in the general relationship between law and violence. Despite the various forms of violence that may often escape the law, or in which the law is even implicit, the central focus of international law is, as Koskenniemi highlights, the physical violence surrounding the military forces of states engaging in inherently territorial conflicts.[51] International law is therefore concerned particularly with the violence associated with war and its containment through and within positive law.

In international law, the notion of violence is largely defined by specific legal vocabularies. For instance, the term 'violence' itself is often only mentioned in relation to illegitimate uses of force, and hence contrasted with seemingly legitimate forms of violence such as 'military offensives'.[52] However, even on a personal level, the meaning of the notion of violence is debated. In this context, violence generally is understood as direct intentional harm to a human being.[53] Harm here can take various forms – from physical to psychological harm or some form of deprivation.[54] Despite general agreement on the core meaning of violence as at least direct intentional harm to human beings,[55] there is a hesitance to extend the notion of violence beyond physical acts causing suffering or death to humans – to cover 'violence against things', for instance.[56] In the international context, international humanitarian law is arguably closely concerned with violence on a personal level,[57] including a concern about violence towards civilian objects,[58] and even violence towards the natural environment as it concerns the survival of individuals.[59] On the other hand, the law on the use of force is aimed at containing the outbreak of violent interstate conflict. As will be shown, it embodies a particular understanding of what constitutes a prohibited form of interstate violence, and in seeking to limit the use of violence by states in their international relations, constitutes a relatively recent phenomenon in international law.

While the modern UN Charter prohibition on the use of force marks a shift away from the traditional 'war' vocabulary,[60] from a historical perspective it nonetheless marks a continuation of the containment of violence discourse evident in international law and thinking about international order.[61] One of the central aims of the UN Charter system is the maintenance of international peace and security through the peaceful settlement of disputes, and therefore the containment of the violence associated with war.[62] Unlike previously, when war was considered a legitimate form of statecraft under international law, the UN Charter era is characterized by a general prohibition on the use of force. As such, in contrast to the classical realist depiction of war as a form of legally unfettered violence within a state of nature, the modern idea of war is more akin to an orderly duel.[63] Now war, or armed conflict between states,[64] while temporally deviating from periods of peace, occurs in a legal space.[65] Both the entry into war and the conduct of warfare itself are heavily regulated by law. The modern institution of war, according to Hedley Bull, is part of certain rules of coexistence that allow states to limit violence with the aim of maintaining international order.[66] According to Bull, these rules seek to confine legitimate violence exclusively to the state by confining

> legitimate violence to a particular kind of violence called 'war', and treating war as violence that is waged on the authority of a sovereign state. Furthermore, the rules seek to limit the causes or purposes for which a sovereign state can legitimately begin a war ... the manner in which sovereign states conduct war ... [and] restrict the geographical spread of a war.[67]

Bull's account demonstrates how one of the central aims of international law is to contain violence. He also notes how the modern concept of war came about from a process of limiting and containing violence, opposed to its historical alternative of 'more ubiquitous violence'.[68] International law has therefore sought to capture the violence inherent in war in particular and bring it under the control of law.

As Bull's account also highlights, the sovereign state is also central to international law's containment of violence. The classic Hobbesian image of the state as a Leviathan is one of an 'artificial man' whose soul comes from its sovereignty.[69] Generally the state is described as an anthropomorphic entity,[70] and its territorial 'body' is conceptualized as a container of modern society that separates its internal or domestic affairs from its external or foreign affairs.[71] It is a territorially bound unit with supreme authority within its boundaries, and this authority is also recognized externally by other states.[72] Internally, the state's sovereignty is manifested in its exclusive jurisdiction over its internal matters – its governing authority and resulting effective control of everything including legislation, taxation, immigration, citizenship, and law enforcement.[73] Externally, this authority is recognized by other states and embodied in the international legal obligation of non-intervention.[74] To maintain or defend its supreme authority in these dimensions, states hold a monopoly of legitimate violence.[75] Internally, this monopoly manifests in the legitimate authority to enforce the law and to maintain order, and externally the state holds the sole legal capacity to engage in violence in the form of war.[76] Therefore, the state classically is viewed as a legal and territorial entity effectively controlling law and violence internally, and being the sole entity capable of legitimately engaging in violence internationally.

This imagery of the state as a person or actor is also evident in international law. States are, according to Antonio Cassese, 'the *dramatis personae* (the characters of the play) on the international scene'.[77] To exist as a state, an entity must have a permanent human population, a defined natural (opposed to purely artificial or virtual) territory, a government, and the capacity to enter into relations with other states.[78] Without these features, an entity is generally not considered a state.[79] Territory is a particularly important element of statehood, and it goes to the very essence of the state – both in terms of its existence and as the dimension within which states 'perform' their activities.[80] Additionally, for the purposes of international law, the state is deemed a single and largely coherent entity. For instance, under the laws of state responsibility, regardless of the internal makeup of the state, the entire state as an entity is deemed responsible for the conduct of any of its 'organs' that is deemed internationally wrongful.[81] As such, the law conceptualizes the state as a fixed territorial entity with sovereignty.[82]

Given their sovereignty, states are entitled to be free from interference by other equally sovereign states. Here the legal principles of non-intervention and non-use of force are central to the containment of violence within the UN Charter system. The non-intervention principle embodies the idea that states should be free to make their own choices in relation to their political, social, economic, and cultural system, and foreign policy.[83] Other states should not coerce them – for instance, through economic means. The non-intervention principle thus aims to protect states from coercive interference by other states. As such, when the activities of a state rise above mere espionage or diplomatic pressure that may infringe on another state's sovereignty, and instead aim to affect the state's freedom in making the choices 'which must remain free ones',[84] then those actions are regarded as unlawful and in breach of the non-intervention principle. The non-use of force principle on the other hand is considered as 'the very cornerstone of the human effort to promote peace in a world torn by strife'.[85] It seeks to prohibit those forms of coercion that, while technically also breaching the non-intervention principle, rise to a higher threshold. It essentially prohibits states from using more intense forms of coercion, such as the use of armed force, in their international relations.

The forms of coercion and violence captured by these legal principles are often conceptualized on a spectrum of intensity. Rosalyn Higgins, for example, argues that military force or intervention is at one end of the spectrum, whereas 'any interference at all' is at the other end.[86] Similarly, Myres McDougal and Florentino Feliciano distinguish between low-level coercion that 'includes all coercion not accelerated to the levels of intensity and magnitude that signal impermissible coercion' and forms of 'coercion of relatively great scope and intensity, including the most intense and extensive violence'.[87] Accordingly, the most intense forms of violent coercion are generally conceptualized as uses of force, whereas the less intense measures or forms of interference below the threshold only constitute breaches of the non-intervention principle or the sovereignty of a state. As will be shown in Chapter 4, in the debates about the threshold distinction between these principles, the more intense forms of coercion involving harm to human beings or damage to physical objects are seen to be captured by the non-use of force principle as they affect the conceptual 'body' of the state. On the other hand, those forms of coercion below this threshold are effectively depicted as forms of non-violence that only affect the 'personality of the state'.[88] As such, the notion of 'force' in this context reflects an extension of the general core understanding of violence as 'direct intentional acts of harm', to 'direct (or indirect)[89] intentional acts of harm to a state'. Harm in this context generally requires some form of injury to humans or damage to physical objects for the law to be capable of recognizing it as a form of prohibited interstate violence. Therefore, the non-use of force and non-intervention principles are central to modern international law's containment of violence, and consequently form part of the effort by states to contain violence through and within the law.

Technology

In addition to the conceptual containment of violence within the confines of law, states have also sought to contain or control weapons technologies as the instruments of violence. Generally, and as a hallmark of modernity, technology is regarded in instrumental terms as a means through which deadly conflict can be waged and through which human beings can dominate nature. Simultaneously, given the potentially excessive violence that can be inflicted on human beings with technological means (from the crossbow to explosive bullets and nuclear weapons), technology itself is something that must be contained, and law is seen as the mechanism by which this can be done. For example, through various arms-control treaties such as the Treaty on the Non-Proliferation of Nuclear Weapons,[90] the law seeks to contain and control the development, spread and deployment of various weapons technologies. Again the sovereign state is central to this effort, particularly given the resource-intensive nature of these weapons development projects, and because international agreements to prohibit or limit these technologies are dependent on state consent.[91] The law thus reflects the idea that to maintain international order, states should retain a monopoly over the technological means of violence – only state actors should be in possession of such weapons, and efforts by non-state actors (from criminals to terrorist organizations) to obtain these weapons should be restricted to ensure international peace and security.

In addition to the role of states in limiting military weapons technologies, they have often also been the main drivers behind the development of military and related technologies. A key technological development that started as a military and research project was the development of what is now the Internet. This can be traced to the Cold War superpower rivalry and the potential for annihilation linked to the concern of the use of nuclear weapons technologies during the time. Communication during, or in the advent of, a nuclear war was a problem with which both the military and the scientific community were concerned. This, as well as the funding for research and development obtained in the context of the superpower rivalry and space race, pushed the efforts to develop technologies enabling digital communication through networks.[92] Now cyberspace has become recognized in the military context as the fifth, virtual domain of warfare, alongside the physical land, sea, air, and outer-space domains.[93] In many ways, this is recognition of the increasing reliance of modern states and also militaries on ICTs, and the consequent vulnerabilities and opportunities this presents. The development and even deployment of various cyber weapons and other cyber-enabled activities – from widespread information-collection programs to sophisticated cyber attacks causing material damage to computer hardware – demonstrates that cyberspace has expanded the means and spaces in which states can engage in politics by other means. Hence what began partially as a need to develop communication methods in the context of the Cold War now provides new possibilities and vulnerabilities, and hence new avenues for interstate conflict such as through the use of cyber attacks.

To summarize, the containment of violence is central to international law: the authority to wage violence is limited to the sovereign state, and warfare between sovereign states is limited by legal principles that flow from state sovereignty. Within the UN Charter international legal order, the violence associated with warfare, while previously conceptually outside the realm of law, is sought to be contained by law. In this context, the prohibition on the use of force serves as a doctrinal limitation on the most intense forms of violent coercion. Additionally, the technological dimension to international law's containment of violence sees technology as a means through which violence can be inflicted. As such, the law regards technology as something that must be controlled in order to contain violence. However, as the following section will demonstrate, cyber attacks are challenging the traditional understanding of violence embodied in the law, and therefore challenging international law's containment of violence.

Cyber attacks and the containment of violence

Cyber attacks commonly are defined as deliberate computer-enabled actions used 'to alter, disrupt, deceive, degrade, or destroy adversary computer systems or networks or the information and/or programs resident in or transiting these systems or networks'.[94] As hostile information flows, cyber attacks seek to compromise computer security in one or more ways by undermining the integrity of information, undermining the operation of computer systems and/or disrupting the flow of information within a network.[95] Cyber attacks can be understood on a spectrum of intensity. At the lower end of this spectrum are those generally termed information collection operations, cyber exploitations or cyber espionage – low-intensity cyber attacks that involve unauthorized access to information and undermine its confidentiality. At the higher end of this spectrum are cyber attacks that are capable of causing material effects, such as the destruction of computer hardware. In the context of states using cyber attacks against other states in their international relations, the lower-intensity forms of cyber attacks, while questionable, are often not specifically prohibited by international law.[96] In contrast, the more intense forms of cyber attacks that cause physical destruction are more likely to constitute a form of 'force' that states are expressly prohibited from using in their international relations.[97]

The novel nature of cyber warfare

The use of cyber attacks, and therefore engaging in cyber warfare, is only possible within the technological context of ICT-driven societies.[98] Cyber warfare is, however, not simply a new means of engaging in traditional warfare that existing law is concerned with containing.[99] Instead, cyber warfare is ontologically different – particularly in relation to the entities through which it is waged, the environment in which it is waged and the harm or forms of violence that characterize it. Instead of human agents engaging in conflicts with kinetic weapons in physical environments that result in injury or death to humans, or damage or destruction of physical property, cyber warfare can involve artificial agents engaging in conflicts in virtual environments that may or may not result in similar forms of harm. Due to these characteristics, what arises is an ontological gap between the laws regulating existing warfare and cyber warfare.[100] In other words, there is a disparity between cyber warfare and the conceptual basis of international law's existing containment of violence. Summarizing the novelties of cyber warfare as a form of 'information warfare',[101] Mariarosaria Taddeo defines the latter as

> the use of ICTs within an offensive or defensive military strategy endorsed by a state and aiming at the immediate disruption or control of the enemy's resources, and which is waged within the informational environment, with agents and targets ranging both on the physical and non-physical domains and whose level of violence may vary upon circumstances.[102]

While information warfare in this definition incorporates various forms of modern conflict engaged through drones, robots, and technologically enhanced soldiers, for example, cyber warfare is a particular form of information warfare involving the use of cyber attacks. The novelties of this form of warfare, as highlighted by Taddeo's account, involve (1) the entities waging cyber warfare, (2) the environment in which it takes place, and (3) the forms of harm or violence inflicted through cyber warfare.

Entities

Unlike traditional warfare waged through human agents, cyber warfare involves a wider ontological range of agents. Taddeo highlights how the ontological status of the agents involved in waging information warfare include both 'artificial agents, such as viruses, drones and robots for example, and human agents'.[103] Therefore, in contrast to traditional warfare waged by human agents with technological artifacts against other human beings or physical objects, cyber warfare in particular involves both human and artificial entities. For example, malicious computer software such as viruses and worms can be designed to attack computer systems and networks. Once created and propagated, these artificial entities self-replicate and operate with a degree of autonomy as they are able to scan for potential targets, select them based on their potential success, self-replicate and spread into those targets, and deliver whatever payload they are designed for.[104]

Environment

Land, sea, air, and outer space constitute the four physical domains of warfare. The 'fifth domain' of cyberspace, however, is an entirely artificial, human-made virtual space. Even though the notion of space is used metaphorically in this context, cyber warfare is waged in and through the virtual environment of cyberspace. For instance, the US Department of Defense defines cyberspace as a 'global domain within the information environment' that is made up of the various networks and the data residing therein, and includes computer systems and processors.[105] The ITU instead uses the broader term 'cyber environment' to refer to the various users, networks, devices, programs, processes, and information that are directly or indirectly connected to networks.[106] In both cases, cyberspace is conceptualized as an artificial environment that is created by human technologies that enable the operation of virtual networks such as the Internet. However, with the increasing reliance of states on ICTs for their proper functioning, the effects of cyber warfare are not limited to a purely virtual environment. Cyber warfare can be waged in both physical and virtual domains, as digital 'cyber weapons' can be used to affect both informational and physical objects, or individuals in the physical domain.[107] Given its artificial nature, even cyberspace itself as an environment can be the target of cyber warfare.[108] As demonstrated earlier in this chapter, various UN General Assembly resolutions also highlight the dependence of states on ICT infrastructure, and the way the well-being and prosperity of societies are increasingly vulnerable to threats from cyberspace. As such, while cyberspace constitutes a virtual environment, it increasingly intersects and converges with the physical environment given the integration of ICTs into everything from critical infrastructure and traffic control to military equipment and communications.[109] Accordingly, unlike traditional warfare waged in the physical land, sea, air, and outer-space domains, cyber warfare is waged in and through virtual environments that increasingly are embedded into objects in the physical environment.

Harm and violence

In addition to the difference between cyber warfare and traditional warfare in relation to the agents waging warfare and where warfare is waged, perhaps the most important difference is the harm associated with cyber warfare – the forms of violence associated with the use of cyber attacks. Generally, cyber attacks are not viewed as a form of violence. For instance, those adopting a conventional view of violence, essentially as direct intentional acts of harm towards human beings, argue that cyber attacks 'cannot be sensibly understood as a form of violent action' as any potentially violent force is indirect.[110] As such, cyber attacks by themselves cannot harm a human being like energy (such as heat or a laser), or a chemical or biological agent directed towards (or being exposed to) a human can.[111] This view of violence is echoed in commentary on cyber attacks in relation to international humanitarian law, where cyber attacks are considered in terms of their violent consequences and not simply their potentially violent nature.[112] In terms of traditional accounts of the law regulating interstate violence, the notion of violence is closely connected to the physical destruction and death associated with warfare. According to Massimo Durante, this view of violence also pervades political theory: 'Violence is anthropologically founded: human beings are intrinsically violent, and violence is understood in kinetic terms as physical violence'.[113] Cyber warfare challenges this conceptualization of violence, however, as it less often involves physical violence; instead it includes forms of exploitation and disruption, or forms of 'informational violence'.[114]

Therefore, while traditional warfare is characterized by kinetic attacks, death of human beings, and destruction of physical property, cyber warfare does not necessarily have these characteristics.[115] Cyber warfare primarily affects information, meaning the effects of cyber attacks and the harm that they cause are not necessarily to human beings or physical objects. Randall Dipert, for instance, notes the novelty of cyber warfare and that, unlike traditional (or even nuclear) weapons, 'many cyberattacks will not be lethal and will not even result in permanent damage to physical objects'.[116] A cyber attack instead

> involves the disruption of an information processing system rather than the killing of human beings or the permanent destruction of physical objects. It crucially involves harm to the functioning of systems but not necessarily with permanent (hardware) destruction.[117]

While it is possible to inflict physical harm or destruction through cyber warfare, more often cyber attacks are only disruptive, and any harm they cause is to non-physical entities such as the software allowing the system to function.[118] This means that in contrast to the death and destruction associated with traditional warfare, the harm and consequent violence inherent in cyber warfare are not necessarily physical, and possibly only impact virtual entities in a virtual environment. In essence, the inherently anthropocentric and materialist understanding of violence associated with warfare is not characteristic of cyber warfare.

As such, cyber warfare challenges the traditional understandings of violence inherent in kinetic warfare, and consequently the ontology underpinning of the law regulating interstate violence.[119] This gives rise to a new tension between law and forms of 'informational violence' that the law is incapable of recognizing adequately. As a result of this ontological gap between traditional warfare and cyber warfare, as demonstrated in Chapter 4, the law embodies a limited view of violence that is particularly evident in existing legal analyses of cyber attacks and the use of force threshold.

Consequently, especially non-material cyber attacks – that is, cyber attacks with disruptive or purely informational effects – largely escape the law's conceptual containment of violence. The remainder of this chapter will develop an informational approach as a means by which the law's ontological constraints can be overcome. This enables recognition of new forms of violence that are capable of harming the state, such as informational violence, which currently escape the law's containment of violence.

An informational approach

As demonstrated in Chapter 2, information ethics provides a conceptual framework based on an informational ontology that is concerned with the well-being of the infosphere. Particularly given its promise of offering an innovative way to consider ethical issues surrounding ICTs, others have also drawn on information ethics to explore some of the ethical issues surrounding cyber warfare. For example, both Taddeo and Pagallo have considered the traditional just war principles in the context of the four moral laws of information ethics to develop their respective perspectives on the morality of cyber warfare.[120] The focus in this book, however, is not on whether cyber attacks are morally permitted or reprehensible pursuant to the moral laws of information ethics. Instead, an informational approach is used to reconceptualize the notion of violence in relation to cyber attacks. This involves rethinking the harm caused by cyber attacks in terms of the increases in entropy they produce and a reconceptualization of the state as the entity subject to violence.

Accordingly, this section first describes the state as an information entity. The state is depicted as a dynamic entity that continuously receives, processes, and communicates information from and in the physical and virtual environments (the infosphere) in which it is situated. It is an entity that is constituted by its internal components (various sub-entities and subsystems), and configured by the protocols that give it coherence as an entity. The state is therefore conceptualized as an information system, and the purpose of this entity is to care for and protect the well-being of its region of the infosphere. Subsequently, this section will consider cyber attacks as causing harm in the form of entropy and constituting a form of violence against the state. Finally, this section describes international law as providing the protocols according to which these entities operate within the international system.

The state as an information entity

Viewed informationally, the state is a non-static and continuously changing entity. Given the nature of global information infrastructures and information flows, the state entity continuously receives information from other entities. From the data flows stemming from individuals' use of the Internet, financial data flow into banks and other corporations within a state, and government communications with foreign governments and regional and international organizations – various information flows continuously move in and out of this entity. The amount of global information flows also increases over time – as captured, for instance, by the idea of 'Big Data'.[121] Similarly, more users and more devices embedded with ICTs are also constantly being connected.[122] The information storage, processing, and communication capabilities of the state also need to increase to ensure it continues to flourish. The informational substance of the state as a dynamic or non-static entity thus changes continuously over time. However, its form or pattern as an information entity persists.

The pattern or form of the state entity is evident in its systematic features. Like a 'multi-agent system' constituted by its components, the state entity is an information system capable of interaction: it has a degree of autonomy, it is adaptable, and it has an inherent purpose, towards which it gears its functions.[123] As an information system, it is situated not only in the physical world (within its territory), but also in the virtual world of cyberspace, in which it increasingly interacts with other entities. As such, the state entity has physical and virtual properties – a presence within its territorial boundaries and a virtual presence that transcends territory. This is illustrated, for example, in the idea that state sovereignty is considered not only to extend to the jurisdiction over the physical ICT infrastructure within its territory, but also to its conduct of 'ICT-related activities'.[124] Sovereignty (and the rights and obligations that flow from it) is considered to extend beyond the physical realm of international relations, to the 'ICT-related activities' that enable state entities to interact and engage both in and through cyberspace. As an information system, the state entity is capable of interaction, and of cooperating and coordinating its activities with other entities. It is capable of interacting internally with the components (the sub-entities and sub-systems) that constitute its information system, as well as externally with other entities (such as other states, international organizations, and multinational corporations), and in some cases it constitutes a component or sub-system within these larger systems (for example, in regional or international organizations). As an information system, it is autonomous in the sense that it can act independently of the other entities without being dependent on external authorization for its actions; therefore it is not dependent on other entities for its behavior. It is adaptable, as it is capable of changing or adapting its policies and strategies depending on the information it gathers from its environment, and it can change its behavior depending on the actions of other entities.[125]

While these features reflect the state entity's systematic nature, its form or pattern is also evident in the informational structures through which it is constituted and the protocols by which it operates. The state's informational structures – the organizational structures of its institutions, typically seen in the structural separation of powers between legislative, executive, and judicial institutions – configure its structure as an entity. These structures that make up the information system are 'bound together by a system of communication',[126] both internally within and between these structures, and externally between its institutions and those of other state entities.[127] The exact configuration of these structures may change among state entities (that is, the core configuration of power within the state, such as the degree or extent to which legislative, executive and judicial powers are separated). The structural configuration may also change over time (transforming states from constitutional monarchies to independent republics, for example) and can be embedded with different value systems (from secular liberal democracies to religious autocracies). However, the basic structure of these entities – their form or pattern – persists, despite continuous changes to the informational substance of these entities.[128] The system of communication binding together these structures comes from the protocols under which the communication and exchange of information occurs within this information system.

In addition to these information structures constituting the state entity as an information system, this entity also operates according to protocols that configure it and enable it to operate as a coherent and autonomous system.[129] Its internal protocols govern the interactions and information exchanges among the various sub-entities and sub-systems of which it is constituted. The overarching protocol under which each information system operates generally comes from its constitution. It configures the key sub-systems within this information system (state institutions), their functions and tasks within this system, and the protocols for interaction and information exchange between these components. Various other protocols govern the interactions of these entities and humans (administrative law), the interactions between humans and corporations and the natural environment (environmental law), and the proper behaviors, interactions, and information exchanges of humans and other entities within the physical and virtual environments of this information system (criminal law, civil law). Various protocols also govern the interactions of the information system as a whole with other information systems (public international law). Therefore, the information structures by which the state entity as an information system is constituted are bound together by various protocols, which give the system a degree of coherence over time and delineate it as an entity separate from other information systems.

As such, the state entity is an information system – a dynamic entity constituted by various sub-systems and configured by the protocols under which it operates. With increasing amounts of information flowing in and out of it, and more and more entities becoming connected to the infosphere, the state entity becomes increasingly complex over time. The primary purpose of this entity is to care for and protect the well-being of its region of the infosphere.[130] This includes the natural environment and virtual environments such as cyberspace, in which all entities increasingly coexist and interact. The state entity has an inherent responsibility to care for and protect the entities that constitute its system – a responsibility to care for their well-being and protect them from entropy. By doing so and ensuring the functioning of its components and the interactions between them, it can continue to function as a system and flourish according to its nature. Caring and protecting its region of the infosphere (as well as ensuring its well-being and flourishing) includes protecting the physical territory in which it is situated, caring for the natural environment and caring for and protecting the virtual environment.[131] The entities within these environments forming its region of the infosphere include everything from animals, humans, and corporations to virtual entities such as websites and databases. Therefore, the purpose of the state entity as an information system is to protect these entities and their interactions from entropy, and to care for the environments in which they exist.

Violence

Against this account of the state entity as an information system, the harm inflicted by cyber attacks can be rethought in terms of entropy. This means that cyber attacks can be seen as a form of violence against the state as an information entity. The starting point here is the principle of ontological equality, which provides that all entities have a basic right to exist and flourish. Harm to any entity is understood in terms of entropy – that is, as some form of damage, destruction, degradation, corruption, or pollution of an entity, impacting its very being and right to exist.[132] While Floridi maintains that the notion of harm is problematic, as it implies that the object of harm is a 'sentient being with a nervous system',[133] others connect harm to situations in which the interests or stakes of humans are harmed, even if those interests lie in physical objects such as buildings or plants.[134] However, here it is proposed that because all things should have value in themselves pursuant to the ontological equality principle, then any entity is capable of being 'harmed', even if it has no direct connection to human interests.[135] Harm in this context is to the entity's existence and right to flourish, and thus to its inherent interest to exist as an information entity. The notion of harm therefore does not need to be connected to purely human interests in objects or information entities. Instead, an entity is harmed when it is subject to entropy. This means that any form of damage or degradation of an entity constitutes harm because it undermines the entity's right to exist and flourish pursuant to the ontological equality principle.[136]

Viewing the harm inherent in any act of violence in terms of entropy, however, means that on one level, with everything viewed in informational terms, all forms of violence can be seen as 'informational violence'. For example, intentional acts of physical harm to an entity resulting in damage, destruction, injury or death – that is, physical violence – can also be seen as causing entropy and amounting to informational violence. However, in order to distinguish between physical violence and forms of violence that do not result in damage or injury to, or destruction or death of, an entity, the notion of informational violence will be used in a narrower sense. This allows a distinction between cyber attacks with material effects that can be likened to a form of physical violence, and those cyber attacks with non-material effects. The notion of informational violence is therefore used here to refer to intentional acts of non-material harm to an entity.

Other authors have also sought to reconsider the harm in cyber attacks. For example, Dipert suggests an ontological rethinking of the harm caused by cyber attacks. He maintains that this should involve a shift in 'focus away from strictly injury to human beings and physical objects toward a notion of the (mal-)*functioning* of information systems, and the other systems (economic, communication, industrial production) that depend on them'.[137] He proposes the notion of cyber harm as harm inflicted through cyberspace, in which 'the functioning of a system (a person, a machine, software or an economy) is in some way impaired or degraded'.[138] Durante also considers the notion of violence specifically from an information ethics perspective, distinguishing between informational and physical violence. He argues that physical violence arises 'when a disruptive activity damages, deteriorates, deletes or suppresses an informational object'[139] – essentially, where the entropy that is caused physically (and not only informationally) affects the information entity so that its right to exist and not to be destroyed is infringed. He considers the separate form of 'informational moral violence' to be violence that deprives an information entity of the capacity of being *that* source of information that it is.[140] He argues that moral violence in informational terms occurs when an entity is deprived of its capacity to flourish and become a specific source of information, and hence become an agent.[141] It is a form of 'radical regardlessness' towards an entity.[142]

The informational reconceptualization of violence offered here is similar to both of these accounts. Like Dipert's cyber harm, the concern is with harm to the functioning of an entity – that is, its impairment or degradation, which is captured by the notion of entropy. Also like Durante's account of physical and informational violence, a distinction is made between the two in order to highlight the material and non-material dimensions of cyber attacks. Cyber attacks without material effects can thus be seen a form of informational violence, whereas those causing material harm constitute a form of physical violence. On a more conceptual level however, in addition to the ways in which cyber attacks actually disrupt or damage computer systems or their operation within states, they can also be seen as harming the state as an entity.

Accordingly, the harm caused by cyber attacks to the state can be viewed in terms of entropy. Unlike the usual information flows into the state entity, cyber attacks are hostile information flows seeking to undermine or degrade its integrity, or disrupt or damage its ability to function. They do so particularly when they undermine its ability to interact, its autonomy, the protocols according to which it operates, and its ability to care for and protect the entities within its region of the infosphere. Both material and non-material cyber attacks have the ability to cause various degrees of increases in entropy, and as such, cyber attacks can be seen as forms of both physical and/or informational violence capable of causing increased entropy within state entities. In addition to the harm that they cause to computer systems or data, cyber attacks also constitute a form of violence against the state as an information entity.

Law

As discussed at the beginning of this section, the internal protocols according to which state entities operate (that is, domestic law) allow these entities to operate with a degree of coherence and autonomy. On the other hand, the external protocols of the international system govern the interactions of state entities. As demonstrated earlier in the chapter, various external protocols govern the information exchanges between state entities and restrict certain harmful information flows between them. In addition, from international human rights law to international environmental law and international economic law, a range of external protocols govern the interactions between and among state entities, corporations and human beings, and their interactions within the global infosphere. As such, law is among the protocols according to which state entities (and various other entities) operate within the international system, and it governs the interactions of these entities and the environments in which they interact.

Due to the law on the use of force, state entities within the UN Charter system are generally restricted from interactions involving material harm to other state entities. These external protocols seek to contain violence in the interactions of particular entities within the international system, and violence is conceptualized in an inherently anthropocentric and materialist way as requiring either harm to human beings or damage to material objects. As will be illustrated in Chapter 4, while the law is capable of recognizing cyber attacks with material effects as a form of violence that is prohibited, it does not adequately recognize and restrict cyber attacks with non-material effects, and therefore the use of forms of informational violence. This is despite the increasing ways in which informational violence can undermine or degrade the integrity and functioning of state entities. As such, due to the ontologically constrained view of violence that is embodied in the law on the use of force, it is unable to adequately recognize the ways in which informational violence can harm state entities, and this means informational violence is largely left outside the law's conceptual containment of violence.

Accordingly, an informational approach offers a means by which a broader spectrum of violence can be recognized by the law. By updating the external protocols under which the international system of state entities operates, both informational and physical violence can be seen as threats to state entities, and to international peace and security within the global infosphere. Cyber attacks are capable of producing increases in entropy by undermining the proper functioning of the state entity – particularly its autonomy and ability to interact, and its ability to care for and protect the entities within its region of the infosphere.

Conclusion

This chapter has offered an informational reconceptualization of the state and the notion of violence as a way in which to rethink the harm that cyber attacks cause and the state as the entity subject to violence. Cyber attacks can be seen as capable of harming the state as an information entity by causing increased entropy. This reconceptualization also enables the law to conceptually contain the informational violence that can be inflicted through cyber attacks. The chapter first considered various global information flows that international law has historically sought to regulate, as well as how the international community has recognized the importance of ICTs to the functioning of modern societies. It then explored international law's containment of violence and demonstrated how the law traditionally regards the state as an entity and violence that is deemed to threaten the state. Following this, the novel nature of cyber warfare was examined, and the ontological gap between kinetic and cyber warfare highlighted. Finally, an informational reconceptualization of the state entity and the notion of violence was presented, along with the argument that an informational approach offers a means to broaden the law's conceptual containment of violence.

Notes

1 CISCO, 'The Zettabyte Era: Trends and Analysis' (CISCO, 2017) <www.cisco.com/c/en/us/solutions/collateral/service-provider/visual-networking-index-vni/vni-hyperconnectivity-wp.html> accessed 5 February 2018.
2 Christopher B Kuner, *Transborder Data Flows and Data Privacy Law* (Oxford University Press 2013) 1–6.
3 See Peter Robinson, 'From TDF to International Data Services' (1987) 11(4) *Telecommunications Policy* 369.
4 William L Fishman, 'Introduction to Transborder Data Flows' (1980) 16 *Stanford Journal of International Law* 1, 2.
5 ibid.
6 See Organization of Economic Cooperation and Development, *Guidelines on the Protection of Privacy and Transborder Flows of Personal Data* (OECD, 1980) <www.oecd.org/sti/ieconomy/oecdguidelinesontheprotectionofprivacyandtransborderflowsofpersonaldata.htm> accessed 12 February 2018. See also Michael Kirby, 'The History, Achievement and Future of the 1980 OECD Guidelines on Privacy' (2010) 20(2) *Journal of Law, Information and Science* 1.
7 UNESCO Artvideo and Intergovernmental Bureau of Informatics, 'IBI Second World Conference on Transborder Data Flow Policies' (Documentary, 1984) <www.unesco.org/archives/multimedia/?pg=33&s=films_details&id=1800> accessed 25 August 2015.

8 ibid 00:00:20.

9 Fishman (n 4) 1. It was also predicted that 'political conflict about the direction, access, use, and control of transborder data flows can be expected'. Eric J Novotny, 'Transborder Data Flows and International Law: A Framework for Policy-Oriented Inquiry' (1980) 16 *Stanford Journal of International Law* 141, 142.

10 According to Bob Reinalda, the nineteenth-century international telegraph and postal unions 'responded to the expansion of modern capitalism and technology, which did not take much notice of national borders'. Bob Reinalda, *Routledge History of International Organizations: From 1815 to the present day* (Routledge 2009) 83.

11 International Telegraph Convention and Regulations (Rome, 14 January 1872) 143 CTS 411 Arts 1, 2.

12 Analogue communications, according to Henry Perritt, involve 'representing real world intelligence, such as a sound wave, by an electric signal, with essentially the same characteristics of frequency and amplitude as the real world phenomenon'. Henry Perritt, *Law and the Information Superhighway* (Wiley 1996) 7. Digital communications, in contrast, 'take millions of samples of real world soundwave or video representation per minute and represent the sample features of the real world signal by arithmetic quantities, ultimately reduced to binary digits or "bits"'. ibid.

13 International Convention Concerning the Use of Broadcasting in the Cause of Peace (adopted 23 September 1936, entered into force 2 April 1938) [1938] ATS 8 Arts 1, 3.

14 International Telecommunication Convention (adopted 21 December 1959, entered into force 1 January 1961) [1962] ATS 2 Art 4.

15 Neville Hunnings, 'Pirate Broadcasting in European Waters' (1965) 14(2) *International and Comparative Law Quarterly* 410, 413–14.

16 United Nations Convention on the Law of the Sea (adopted 10 December 1982, entered into force 16 November 1994) [1994] ATS 31 Art 109.

17 Instrument amending the Constitution of the International Telecommunication Union of 22 December 1992 (as amended 14 October 1994, entered into force 1 January 2000) [2000] ATS 8 Art 45.

18 Eric De Brabandere, 'Propaganda' in Rudiger Wolfrum (ed), *Max Planck Encyclopedia of Public International Law* (Oxford University Press 2012).

19 Lee Bygrave and Terje Michaelsen, for instance, write that the governance of the Internet 'is rather wrought by a mélange of various bodies – private and public, old and new. Viewed from afar, the governance structure resulting from these bodies' interaction appears relatively flat, open, sprawling, ad hoc and amorphous. Lines of responsibility are blurred, as are lines of competence and funding. Many of the lines straddle, if not eviscerate, traditional organizational boundaries.' Lee A Bygrave and Terje Michaelsen, 'Governors of Internet' in Lee A Bygrave and Jon Bing (eds), *Internet Governance: Infrastructure and Institutions* (Oxford University Press 2009) 92.

20 Despite its attempts, the ITU has not been able to position itself as the primary regulator of the Internet as it has in telecommunications since the late nineteenth century. See Ingo Take, 'Regulating the Internet Infrastructure: A Comparative Appraisal of the Legitimacy of ICANN, ITU, and the WSIS' (2012) 6(4) *Regulation & Governance* 499, 506.

21 For instance, Chinese efforts to block, filter and monitor Internet traffic are often described as China's 'Great Firewall': see Richard A Clarke and Robert K Knake, *Cyber War* (HarperCollins 2010) 57. In 2015, New Zealand passed a law protecting against harmful uses of digital communications, see Harmful Digital Communications Act 2015 (NZ).

22 Convention on Cybercrime (adopted 23 November 2001, entered into force 1 July 2004) [2013] ATS 9.
23 ibid Art 2.
24 ibid Art 3.
25 ibid Art 4.
26 ibid Art 5.
27 The first resolution was adopted in 1999, see UNGA Res 53/70 (4 January 1999).
28 UNGA Res 69/28 (11 December 2014).
29 UNGA Res 57/239 (31 January 2003); UNGA Res 58/199 (30 January 2004); UNGA Res 64/211 (21 December 2009).
30 UNGA Res 57/239 (n 29) 1.
31 ibid 2.
32 ibid 3.
33 UNGA Res 58/199 (n 29) 1.
34 UNGA Res 64/211 (n 29) 1.
35 ibid.
36 ibid 2.
37 UNGA Res 68/167 (18 December 2013), 2.
38 UN Group of Governmental Experts on Developments in the Field of Information and Telecommunications in the Context of International Security, 'Report of the Group of Governmental Experts on Developments in the Field of Information and Telecommunications in the Context of International Security' (24 June 2013) UN Doc A/68/98, 2.
39 ibid.
40 ibid 6.
41 UN Group of Governmental Experts on Developments in the Field of Information and Telecommunications in the Context of International Security, *Report of the Group of Governmental Experts on Developments in the Field of Information and Telecommunications in the Context of International Security* (22 July 2015) UN Doc A/70/174, 8.
42 Ugo Pagallo, 'Cyber Force and the Role of Sovereign States in Informational Warfare' (2015) 28(3) *Philosophy & Technology* 407, 409. Floridi describes these as 'hyperhistorical' societies – societies in which 'ICTs and their data *processing* capabilities are the necessary condition for the maintenance and any further development of societal welfare, personal well-being, as well as overall flourishing'. Luciano Floridi, 'Hyperhistory and the Philosophy of Information Policies' in Luciano Floridi (ed), *The Onlife Manifesto: Being Human in a Hyperconnected Era* (Springer 2015) 52 (emphasis in original).
43 Council Directive 2008/114/EC of 8 December 2008 on the identification and designation of European critical infrastructures and the assessment of the need to improve their protection [2008] OJ L 345/75 Art 2.
44 Commission of the European Communities, 'Green Paper on a European Programme for Critical Infrastructure Protection' (COM/2005/576 final, 17 November 2005) 19 (emphasis added).
45 Walter Benjamin, 'Critique of Violence' in Marcus Bullock and Michael W Jennings (eds), *Walter Benjamin: Selected Writings* (Belknap Press of Harvard University Press 2002) 241–4.
46 ibid 243, 248. According to Ari Hirvonen, Benjamin's law-making (or law-positing or law-imposing) violence is violence that is not legal or illegal, and that provides the foundation or constitution of a legal order. It 'points beyond itself in order to maintain itself'. Ari Hirvonen, 'The Politics of Revolt: On Benjamin and Critique of Law' (2011) 22 *Law and Critique* 101, 102.
47 Benjamin (n 45) 242–3. Hirvonen writes that it is a form of violence that 'preserves, maintains, conserves and confirms posited law'. Hirvonen (n 46) 102.

48 Benjamin (n 45) 239.
49 Michael Walzer, *Just and Unjust Wars: A Moral Argument with Historical Illustrations* (4th edn, Basic Books 2006) 3 (emphasis in original).
50 Martti Koskenniemi, '"The Lady Doth Protest Too Much": Kosovo, and the Turn to Ethics in International Law' (2002) 65(2) *The Modern Law Review* 159, 172 (emphasis in original).
51 For instance, in relation to the armed conflict in Kosovo, Koskenniemi notes how the, 'Obsessive talk about Kosovo makes invisible the extreme injustice of the system of global distribution of wealth, reducing it to the sphere of the private, the unpolitical, the natural, the historically determined – just like war used to be – a "social", "cultural" or "economic" *condition* of law which cannot be touched by law.' ibid (emphasis in original). Myers McDougal and Florentino Feliciano in turn describe the minimization of change by major coercion and violence as 'the most fundamental policy projected by international law', and the 'law of war' as the result of the global process to minimize coercion and violence. Myers S McDougal and Florentino P Feliciano, *The International Law of War: Transnational Coercion and World Public Order* (Martinus Nijhoff 1994) xix, xxiv–xxv. Gina Heathcote also maintains that international law on the use of force is 'the manifestation of the law/violence relationship within the international sphere' (which she argues is a gendered discourse). Gina Heathcote, *The Law on the Use of Force: a Feminist Analysis* (Routledge 2012) 11.
52 Claire Thomas, 'Why Don't we Talk About "Violence" in International Relations?' (2011) 37(4) *Review of International Studies* 1815, 1819–21. Thomas argues that the distinction between legitimate force and (illegitimate) violence is problematic as it 'constructs a discourse of legitimacy around all state violence, and it hides the violence of state action'. ibid 1821.
53 According to a dictionary definition, violence is 'behaviour involving physical force intended to hurt, damage, or kill someone or something'. Angus Stevenson (ed), *Oxford Dictionary of English* (3rd edn, Oxford University Press 2010) 1983. In contrast, 'non-violence' is defined as 'the use of peaceful means, not force, to bring about political or social change'. ibid 1209.
54 The World Health Organization, for instance, defines violence as, 'The intentional use of physical force or power, threatened or actual, against oneself, another person, or against a group or community, that either results in or has a high likelihood of resulting in injury, death, psychological harm, maldevelopment or deprivation.' Etienne G Krug and others, *World Report on Violence and Health* (World Health Organization 2002) 5.
55 Cecil AJ Coady, 'The Idea of Violence' (1986) 3(1) *Journal of Applied Philosophy* 3, 4. In the debates on the meaning of violence, some argue for a broad scope considering structural injustices as a form of violence. Newton Garver, for instance, connects the idea of violence to the notion of 'violation', arguing that violence should be understood in terms of a person being violated, opposed to merely subject to force. Newton Garver, 'What Violence Is' in Arthur K Bierman and James A Gould (eds), *Philosophy for a New Generation* (Macmillan 1970) 257. Johan Galtung also defines violence broadly, arguing that 'violence is present when human beings are being influenced so that their actual somatic and mental realizations are below their potential realizations.' John Galtung, 'Violence, Peace, and Peace Research' (1969) 6(3) *Journal of Peace Research* 167, 168. However, his definition has been criticized for its excessive breadth: see Joseph Betz, 'Violence: Garver's Definition and a Deweyan Correction' (1977) 87(4) *Ethics* 339, 343. John Keane also criticizes Galtung's account, arguing that it makes violence 'virtually synonymous with all human failures to live happily, like angels, unburdened by the curse of politics, within a universe of "symbiotic, equitable relations among diverse partners" held together by

"cooperation, friendliness and love"'. See John Keane, *Violence and Democracy* (Cambridge University Press 2004) 35. Some authors even raise the possibility that the destruction of things could constitute violence. Galtung, for instance, argues that this could be the case, at least where it involves the 'destruction of something very dear to persons referred to as consumers or *owners*'. Galtung (n 55) 170 (emphasis in original).

56 Keane (n 55) 33–4. Keane defines violence as 'the more or less intended, direct but unwanted physical interference by groups and/or individuals with the bodies of others, who are consequently made to suffer a series of effects ranging from shock, speechlessness, mental torment, nightmares, bruises, scratches, swellings, or headaches through to broken bones, heart attacks, loss of body parts, or death'. ibid. He maintains that it must have an embodied quality as it must ultimately affect the bodies of individuals. ibid 36–8.

57 Common Article 3 for instance prohibits 'violence to life and person, in particular murder of all kinds, mutilation, cruel treatment and torture' to various classes of people in and affected by armed conflict: see Geneva Convention for the Amelioration of the Condition of the Wounded and Sick in Armed Forces in the Field (adopted 12 August 1949, entered into force 21 October 1950) [1958] ATS 21 Art 3. Antonio Cassese describes international humanitarian law as designed to constrain the violence unleashed by war from spilling over its legal limits. Antonio Cassese, *Violence and Law in the Modern Age* (Polity Press 1988) 108.

58 Protocol Additional to the Geneva Conventions of 12 August 1949, and relating to the Protection of Victims of International Armed Conflicts (Protocol I) (adopted 8 June 1978, entered into force 7 December 1978) [1991] ATS 29 Art 48. On whether data can qualify as 'objects' for the purposes of the international humanitarian law principle of distinction, see Michael N Schmitt, 'Cyber Operations and the Jus in Bello: Key Issues' (2011) 87 *International Law Studies Series US Naval War College* 89, 96.

59 Protocol Additional to the Geneva Conventions of 12 August 1949, and relating to the Protection of Victims of International Armed Conflicts (Protocol I) (n 58) Arts 52, 53 and 55.

60 During the nineteenth and early twentieth centuries, war was regarded as the sovereign prerogative and an essential element of sovereignty. See Yoram Dinstein, *War, Aggression and Self-Defence* (3rd edn, Cambridge University Press 2001) 71. The early twentieth century saw a shift towards a more restricted right to war, however, as reflected in the attempts to restrict the right to war in the Covenant of the League of Nations (adopted 28 June 1919, entered into force 10 January 1920) [1920] ATS 1 Art 12. While the Covenant did not seek to abolish the right to war completely, this was the aim of the League in implementing the General Treaty for the Renunciation of War as an Instrument of National Policy (adopted 27 August 1928, entered into force 24 July 1929) 94 LNTS 57 Art 1. See also Dinstein (n 60) 77. Apart from a limited number of exceptions in this treaty, the aim was to prohibit all uses of armed force and therefore place the right to engage in war "outside the legal competence of states". Ian Brownlie, *International Law and the Use of Force by States* (Oxford University Press 1963) 91. With the UN Charter instead restraining the use of 'force', even the word 'war' was eliminated from the discourse – consequently, as Kennedy notes, the 'law of war' became the 'law of force'. David Kennedy, *Of War and Law* (Princeton University Press 2006) 78.

61 Originating from early Greek and Roman scholars and statesmen, through the medieval theologians and early modern scholastics to modern international law scholars, these debates and the frameworks of thinking about the just causes of war and the permitted forms of violence within war have varied. For an

overview of the historical development of just war theory in relation to the legality of war, see Brownlie (n 60) 3–17; Dinstein (n 60) 59–68. Anthony Anghie notes that the questions of who can wage war, when it can be waged, the limits of warfare and when a war is just are among the 'traditional questions' with which international lawyers are still occupied today, just as Francisco de Vitoria was in the early sixteenth century. Anthony Anghie, 'Francisco De Vitoria and the Colonial Origins of International Law' (1996) 5 *Social & Legal Studies* 321, 328.

62 Charter of the United Nations (adopted 26 June 1945, entered into force 24 October 1945) [1945] ATS 1 Preamble and Art 2(3). See also Antonio Cassese, *International Law* (Oxford University Press 2005) 40.

63 Carl von Clausewitz, *On War* (Penguin 1968) 101–2.

64 According to Lassa Oppenheim's widely used definition, 'War is a contention between two or more States through their armed forces, for the purpose of overpowering each other and imposing such conditions of peace as the victor pleases.' Lassa Oppenheim, *International Law, Volume 2: Disputes, War and Neutrality* (7th edn, Longmans 1952) 202 cited in Dinstein (n 60) 4.

65 See Kennedy (n 60) 5–6.

66 Hedley Bull, *The Anarchical Society: A Study of Order in World Politics* (3rd edn, Columbia University Press 2002) 40.

67 ibid 66.

68 ibid 179.

69 Thomas Hobbes, *Leviathan* (Pearson Longman 2008) 1.

70 This image pervades literature on the state, as the state is depicted as an individual 'actor' or 'person' with an identity and interests that holds rights and obligations. For instance, according to Erik Ringmar, the state 'is almost invariably talked about in anthropomorphic terms. It is seen as an "actor" or a "person"; it is a "someone" or a "subject" to whom intentions, memories, rights and obligations are attached.' Erik Ringmar, 'On the Ontological Status of the State' (1996) 2(4) *European Journal of International Relations* 439, 443. Similarly, Alexander Wendt argues that 'state personhood' pervades social science and international relations literature – states are 'actors' or 'persons' to whom properties associated with human beings, such as 'rationality, identities, interests, [and] beliefs', are attributed. Alexander Wendt, 'The State as Person in International Theory' (2004) 30(2) *Review of International Studies* 289, 289.

71 Anthony Giddens, for instance, describes the state as 'the pre-eminent form of power container, as a territorially bounded (although internally highly regionalized) administrative unity'. Anthony Giddens, *The Nation-State and Violence* (Polity Press 1985) 13. See also Peter J Taylor, 'The State as Container: Territoriality in the Modern World-System' (1994) 18(2) *Progress in Human Geography* 151. According to John Agnew, the traditional state-centered account of the spatiality of power rests on three assumptions: that 'modern state sovereignty requires clearly bounded territorial spaces'; that there is a clear distinction between domestic and foreign affairs due to the view 'that states are akin to individual persons struggling for wealth and power in a hostile world'; and that 'the territorial state acts as the geographical "container" of modern society'. John Agnew, *Geopolitics: Re-Visioning World Politics* (Routledge 1998) 51.

72 Richard Little, 'Sovereignty' in Martin Griffiths (ed), *Encyclopedia of International Relations and Global Politics* (Routledge 2005) 768–9.

73 James Crawford, 'Sovereignty as a Legal Value' in James Crawford and Martti Koskenniemi (eds), *The Cambridge Companion to International Law* (Cambridge University Press 2012) 120–1.

74 Little (n 72) 769.

75 According to Max Weber, 'a state is a human community that (successfully) claims the *monopoly of the legitimate use of physical force* within a given territory ...

The state is considered the sole source of the "right" to use violence.' Hans H Gerth and Charles W Mills (eds), *From Max Weber: Essays in Sociology* (Routledge 2009) 78 (emphasis in original). See also Stephen Kalberg, *Max Weber: Readings and Commentary on Modernity* (Blackwell 2005) 222; Bryan S Turner, *Max Weber: From History to Modernity* (Routledge 2002) 198.

76 According to Richard Little, this is how the state is understood in the classical nineteenth- and twentieth-century context, in contrast to earlier times when non-state actors such as mercenaries and pirates were mainly responsible for the violence that took place internationally. Little (n 72) 773. See also Janice E Thomson, *Mercenaries, Pirates, and Sovereigns: State-Building and Extraterritorial Violence in Early Modern Europe* (Princeton University Press 1996).

77 Cassese (n 62) 71. He also describes how insurgents 'are born from a wound in the body of a particular State'. ibid.

78 See Montevideo Convention on Rights and Duties of States (adopted 26 December 1933, entered into force 26 December 1934) 136 LNTS 19 Art 1.

79 For example, entities located solely on artificial islands and therefore without natural territory have not been considered as states, because, 'Territory must consist in a natural segment of the earth's surface.' See *Re Duchy of Sealand* (1978) 80 ILR 683, 685.

80 See Cassese (n 62) 81. He writes that: 'Most activities performed by the primary subjects of the world community, States, take place within a geographic area. Territory is crucial not only to the very existence of States (a State without territorial basis, however tiny it may be, is inconceivable). Territory also constitutes the dimension within which States employ their major activities.'

81 International Law Commission, Responsibility of States for Internationally Wrongful Acts, UNGA Res 56/83 (12 December 2001) Art 4.

82 For example, Eve Darian-Smith notes how, in traditional scholarship on the state, 'Nation-states are interpreted as continuing to function as relatively fixed political and territorial entities against which non-state actors (and things) and their relationships to places, properties, homelands, and sovereignties (however defined) are posited.' Eve Darian-Smith, *Laws and Societies in Global Contexts: Contemporary Approaches* (Cambridge University Press 2013) 179.

83 *Case Concerning Military and Paramilitary Activities in and Against Nicaragua (Nicaragua v United States of America)* (Merits) [1986] ICJ Rep 14, 108.

84 ibid.

85 ibid 153 (separate opinion of President Nagendra Singh).

86 Rosalyn Higgins maintains that intervention concerns a spectrum of activities, ranging 'from the notion of any interference at all in the state's affairs at the one end, to the concept of military intervention at the other'. Rosalyn Higgins, *Themes and Theories: Selected Essays, Speeches, and Writings in International Law* (Oxford University Press 2009) 273.

87 McDougal and Feliciano (n 51) 207.

88 See UNGA Res 2625 (XXV) (24 October 1970).

89 As discussed in Chapter 4, a use of force may also be 'indirect' according to the ICJ in *Case Concerning Military and Paramilitary Activities in and Against Nicaragua* (n 83).

90 Treaty on the Non-Proliferation of Nuclear Weapons (adopted 1 July 1968, entered into force 5 March 1970) [1973] ATS 3.

91 For example, as the ICJ in *Nicaragua v USA* noted in relation to the spread of armaments and the militarization of Nicaragua, 'in international law there are no rules, other than such rules as may be accepted by the State concerned, by treaty or otherwise, whereby the level of armaments of a sovereign State can be limited, and this principle is valid for all States without exception'. *Case Concerning Military and Paramilitary Activities in and Against Nicaragua* (n 83) 135.

92 See Jon Bing, 'Building Cyberspace: A Brief History of Internet' in Lee A Bygrave and Jon Bing (eds), *Internet Governance: Infrastructure and Institutions* (Oxford University Press 2009) 8–12, 20.
93 Clarke and Knake (n 21) 44–7.
94 William A Owens and others (eds), *Technology, Policy, Law, and Ethics Regarding US Acquisition and Use of Cyberattack Capabilities* (National Academies Press 2009) 10–11.
95 Herman Tavani, for example, describes the three dimensions of computer security as data security, system security and network security. See Herman T Tavani, 'The Conceptual and Moral Landscape of Computer Security' in Kenneth E Himma (ed), *Internet Security: Hacking, Counterhacking, and Society* (Jones and Bartlett 2007) 30–1.
96 See, for example, Geoffrey Demarest, 'Espionage in International Law' (1996) 24(2) *Denver Journal of International Law and Policy* 321, 338–9. Similarly, Michael Schmitt writes that the revelations by Edward Snowden about the US National Security Agency's information collection program 'illustrate the international community's unease with cyber operations that target other states or their citizens, even when … perhaps lawful under current understandings of international law'. Michael N Schmitt, 'The Law of Cyber Warfare: Quo Vadis?' (2014) 25 *Stanford Law and Policy Review* 269, 276. Scott Shackelford also notes how 'both outer space and cyberspace are domains in which intelligence gathering has been widely tolerated, even though the outcry has been greater in the case of cyber espionage than orbital reconnaissance'. Scott J Shackelford, *Managing Cyber Attacks in International Law, Business, and Relations: In Search of Cyber Peace* (Cambridge University Press 2014) 274 (citations omitted).
97 These issues are examined in more detail in Chapter 4.
98 A useful descriptive (opposed to legal) definition of cyber war comes from Richard Clarke and Robert Knake, who define it as referring to 'actions by a nation-state to penetrate another nation's computers or networks for the purposes of causing damage or disruption'. Clarke and Knake (n 21) 6.
99 See, for example, Michael N Schmitt, 'Classification of Cyber Conflict' (2012) 17(2) *Journal of Conflict & Security Law* 245, 246.
100 Taddeo argues that there is an 'ontological hiatus' between traditional warfare and information warfare – the former involves 'human beings and physical objects' while the latter 'involves artificial and non-physical entities alongside human beings and physical objects'. Mariarosaria Taddeo, 'Just Information Warfare' (2016) 35(1) *Topoi* 213, 216. This ontological hiatus or gap affects just war theory that underpins the law on the use of force, as it 'rests on an anthropocentric ontology, i.e. moral discourse is solely concerned with respect for human rights and disregards all non-human entities'. ibid. Dipert also notes similar ontological problems: see Randall R Dipert, 'The Ethics of Cyberwarfare' (2010) 9(4) *Journal of Military Ethics* 384, 399, 400.
101 This is in contrast to the usual military definition of information warfare, which focuses mainly on a range of methods that are used to manipulate or deceive adversaries through information, or deny them access to information during conflict. Martin C Libicki, *What is Information Warfare?* (National Defense University 1995) x–xi. See also Jason Barkham, 'Information Warfare and International Law on the Use of Force' (2001) 34 *New York University Journal of International Law and Politics* 57, 60–2. Taddeo uses this term to highlight the essentially informational nature of cyber warfare – hence locating it within the other means of ICT-enabled warfare. See Mariarosaria Taddeo, 'Information Warfare: A Philosophical Perspective' (2012) 25 *Philosophy & Technology* 105, 114.
102 Taddeo (n 101) 114.
103 ibid 113.

104 Thomas M Chen and others, 'Electronic Attacks' in Hossein Bidgoli (ed), *Handbook of Information Security: Information Warfare, Social, Legal, and International Issues and Security Foundations* (John Wiley & Sons 2006) 54–5. The term 'payload' refers broadly to 'the things that can be done once a vulnerability has been exploited'. Owens and others (n 94) 88. The payload of a computer worm, for example, can be 'virtually anything' and does not need to be destructive. See Chen and others (n 104) 55.

105 Joint Chiefs of Staff, Joint Publication 1-02, *Department of Defense Dictionary of Military and Associated Terms* (US Department of Defense, 8 November 2010, as amended through 15 June 2015) 58 <www.hsdl.org/?view&did=750658> accessed 12 February 2018.

106 International Telecommunication Union, 'Series X: Data Networks, Open System Communications and Security. Telecommunication Security: Overview of Cybersecurity' (ITU, 2008) 2 <www.itu.int/rec/T-REC-X.1205-200804-I/en> accessed 12 February 2018.

107 Taddeo (n 101) 113.

108 Sean P Kanuck, 'Information Warfare: New Challenges for Public International Law' (1996) 37 *Harvard International Law Journal* 272, 288. See also Chen and others (n 104) 48.

109 See Charles Jaeger, 'Cyberterrorism and Information Security' in Hossein Bidgoli (ed), *Handbook of Information Security: Information Warfare, Social, Legal, and International Issues and Security Foundations* (John Wiley & Sons 2006) 22–3.

110 Thomas Rid, *Cyber War Will Not Take Place* (Oxford University Press 2013) 12.

111 ibid 12–13. Thomas Rid maintains that any such violence is indirect, requiring the code to unleash the pre-existing violent potential of the target system – for instance, causing a nuclear reactor to explode or emit radiation, a dam to unleash large amounts of water or a pacemaker to be disrupted. ibid 13.

112 The *Tallinn Manual*'s Group of Experts examine the notion of 'cyber attack' in the context of the law of armed conflict (international humanitarian law). Rule 92 provides that a cyber attack is a cyber operation 'that is reasonably expected to cause injury or death to persons or damage or destruction to objects'. Michael N Schmitt (ed), *Tallinn Manual 2.0 on the International Law Applicable to Cyber Operations* (2nd edn, Cambridge University Press 2017) 415. The commentary then distinguishes between the use of violence against targets and non-violent operations such as cyber espionage, with the former rather than the latter constituting violence. The Group of Experts goes on to define 'acts of violence' generally as those releasing kinetic force, with the exception of non-kinetic 'chemical, biological, or radiological' means also constituting attacks. They note that the crux lies in the effects caused. Hence an attack is defined by its consequences and not its nature: '"violence" must be considered in the sense of violent consequences and is not limited to violent acts.' ibid 415–16.

113 Massimo Durante, 'Violence, Just Cyber War and Information' (2015) 28 *Philosophy & Technology* 369, 376. Durante also investigates the notion of violence in order to consider how cyber war is different from traditional war and how force is conventionally understood: ibid 372–9.

114 Although cyber warfare can sometimes be used as a precursor to or an enabler of physical attacks, such as in the case of the suspected Israeli airstrike on a Syrian nuclear facility, where it is believed that Israel first used cyber attacks to disable Syrian air defense radars. See Clarke and Knake (n 21) 6–8. The notion of informational violence will be discussed later in the chapter.

115 According to Durante, 'War is no longer based only or even mostly on kinetic armed attacks but also on political, economic, ideological and informational

strategies intended to exploit someone else's informational resources.' Durante (n 113) 369–70. Taddeo similarly writes that existing laws on warfare focus 'on violent warfare, bloodshed and physical damage' – and while essential characteristics of kinetic warfare, they are not peculiar of information or cyber warfare. Taddeo (n 100) 217.

116 Dipert (n 100) 385.

117 Randall R Dipert, 'The Essential Features of an Ontology for Cyberwarfare' in Panayotis A Yannakogeorgos and Adam B Lowther (eds), *Conflict and Cooperation in Cyberspace: The Challenge to National Security* (CRC Press 2013) 36.

118 However, as Taddeo notes, cyber warfare is not simply a 'non-sanguinary, cheap and less military-based version of classic warfare', as it too can be 'as bloody and violent as traditional warfare'. Taddeo (n 101) 112.

119 Dipert, for example, also notes how 'cyberwarfare involves aspects of damage or harm that are typically not addressed by law, such as harm to the functioning of information and other systems that might not harm physical objects or persons'. Dipert (n 100) 395.

120 These authors mainly adopt the four principles of information ethics and merge them with just war principles to consider the legitimacy of the circumstances in which cyber attacks, for instance, can be used. Taddeo, drawing on the four moral laws of information ethics and the notion of ontological equality, maintains that the moral evaluation of cyber warfare needs to consider the consequences of a cyber attack for both humans and the information infrastructure that is being disrupted. Therefore, she argues that non-physical harm to the infosphere can be considered in conjunction with the harm to physical entities. See Taddeo (n 100) 221–2. Pagallo similarly argues that, pursuant to the ontological equality principle, the lawfulness of not merely physical but also virtual force can be determined pursuant to the laws of information ethics. See Pagallo (n 42) 416–19.

121 See James Manyika and others, *Big Data: The Next Frontier for Innovation, Competition, and Productivity* (McKinsey Global Institute 2011) iv.

122 The projected number of mobile devices by 2021 is 11.6 billion, which equates to 1.5 mobile devices per capita. See CISCO, 'Cisco Visual Networking Index: Global Mobile Data Traffic Forecast Update, 2016–2021' (CISCO, 2017) 3 <www.cisco.com/c/en/us/solutions/collateral/service-provider/visual-networking-index-vni/mobile-white-paper-c11-520862.pdf> accessed 5 February 2018. Similarly, with the Internet of Things, more objects are becoming embedded with ICTs and are capable of communicating and interacting. See Luigi Atzori and others, 'The Internet of Things: A Survey' (2010) 54(15) *Computer Networks* 2787.

123 These features are based on Floridi's description of the state as a multi-agent system or 'MAS'. He maintains that it is teleological, interactive, autonomous and adaptable. Luciano Floridi, *The Fourth Revolution* (Oxford University Press 2014) 180–1. Alexander Wendt, in considering states as persons, discusses their similarity to organisms. Many of these features are similar to those attributed to states as 'multi-agent systems' by Floridi. Wendt maintains that, much like organisms, (1) states are individual as they each have a 'distinct system with its own history'; (2) states are organized; (3) states are homeostatic, as they actively resist their own degradation (which is achieved through a spatial and political closure of the boundary between the domestic and international realms, and the internal structure of the state 'that channels the behaviour of their members toward the goal of state survival'); (4) states are autonomous, as 'their behaviour is determined partly independent of their environment'; however, (5) unlike organisms, they are incapable of reproduction. Alexander Wendt, 'The State as Person in International Theory' (2004) 30(2) *Review of International Studies* 289, 307–9.

124 UN Group of Governmental Experts on Developments in the Field of Information and Telecommunications in the Context of International Security (n 38) 8.

125 On the features of a multi-agent system in computer science, see Michael Wooldridge, *An Introduction to Multiagent Systems* (John Wiley & Sons 2002) 3.

126 Norbert Wiener, *Cybernetics: or Control and Communication in the Animal and the Machine* (Technology Press 1948) 33, cited in Terrell Ward Bynum 'Norbert Wiener and the Rise of Information Ethics' in Jeroen Van Den Hoven and John Weckert (eds), *Information Technology and Moral Philosophy* (Cambridge University Press 2008) 12.

127 Similarly, Anne-Marie Slaughter argues that states have become 'disaggregated' into networks of actors, making up what she describes as a 'world of governments, with all the different institutions that perform the basic functions of governments – legislation, adjudication, implementation – interacting both with each other domestically and also with their foreign and supranational counterparts'. Anne-Marie Slaughter, *A New World Order* (Princeton University Press 2005) 5.

128 Bynum, writing about Norbert Wiener's 'cybernetic account of human nature', maintains that for Wiener 'a person consists of a complex pattern of information embodied in matter and energy. Although the *substance* changes, the *form* must persist if the person is to flourish or even exist. Thus a human being is an "information object", a dynamic form, or pattern persisting in an ever-changing flow of matter and energy'. Bynum (n 126) 12 (emphasis in original).

129 In cyberspace, the informational constraints of computer code – that is, the various protocols, algorithms and data structures – provide the logical (opposed to physical or legal) constraints to which all entities are subject. See Timothy Colburn and Gary Shute, 'Abstraction, Law, and Freedom in Computer Science' (2010) 41(3) *Metaphilosophy* 345, 346. Lawrence Lessig famously argued that 'code is law' – that is, that computer code is central to regulating behaviour in cyberspace. Lawrence Lessig, *Code Version 2.0* (Basic Books 2006) 5.

130 The notion of an entity's 'region of the infosphere' is drawn from Floridi's informational analysis of business. See Luciano Floridi, *The Ethics of Information* (Oxford University Press 2013) 289–90.

131 Similarly, Nazli Choucri, after noting how the conventional way of thinking about national security is in terms of defending a country's borders from military intrusions, argues that twenty-first century imperatives call for a reconsideration of this. She argues that 'national security must be seen as a function of four distinct but interconnected dimensions, each with its characteristic features, variables, and complexities: external security, internal security, environmental security, and cyber security'. Nazli Choucri, *Cyberpolitics in International Relations* (MIT Press 2012) 38.

132 As Floridi writes, it is an 'impoverishment of *Being*'. Floridi (n 130) 67 (emphasis in original).

133 Floridi suggests avoiding 'using the term "harm" – a zoocentric, not even biocentric, word, which implicitly leads to the interpretation of *P* [the patient] as a sentient being with a nervous system – in favor of "damage", an ontocentric, more neutral term, with "annihilation" as the level of most severe damage or highest degree of metaphysical entropy.' ibid 182.

134 Joel Feinberg considers the various ways in which an extended notion of harm can be used. For example, 'By smashing windows, vandals are said to harm people's property; neglect can harm one's garden; frost does harm to crops.' Joel Feinberg, *Harm to Others* (Oxford University Press 1984) 32. Similarly,

according to Feinberg, machines can be harmed where their functioning is impaired and someone has an interest in its proper functioning. However, where no one has such an interest, the machine can only be described as 'broken' and not harmed. ibid 33.

135 This is in contrast to the way Feinberg describes harm. In relation to rocks, for example, he writes that 'For a rock to be coherently described as broken or damaged, it must either have some special value to a human being (say, as an art object) or have some function in a larger complex that has now been impaired.' ibid.

136 This is not to say that any degree of entropy is always wrong and therefore, for example, that a computer virus cannot be destroyed because of its inherent right to flourish. Instead, even if any entropy in itself is considered evil, it must be considered within the wider contribution of the entity to the well-being of the infosphere. To this end, a normative assessment based on the four moral laws is required, and consideration given to the increases in global entropy. As discussed in Chapter 2, the general approach is to consider whether the overall state of the infosphere is better, even if some entropy is caused, and hence the concern is with the global levels of entropy opposed to minor fluctuations. See Floridi (n 130) 71–2.

137 Dipert (n 100) 386 (emphasis in original).

138 ibid 397.

139 Durante (n 113) 383 (emphasis in original).

140 ibid 382–3.

141 ibid 383.

142 ibid. This 'radical regardlessness' is 'the conceptual core or the essence of violence' for Durante: see ibid 378. He likens this to the deprivation of the human right to be free from torture, and argues that both physical and moral violence from an informational standpoint can be considered as 'violence', justifying recourse to force: see ibid 383–4.

Bibliography

Agnew J, *Geopolitics: Re-Visioning World Politics* (Routledge 1998)

Anghie A, 'Francisco De Vitoria and the Colonial Origins of International Law' (1996) 5 *Social & Legal Studies* 321

Artvideo and Intergovernmental Bureau of Informatics, 'IBI Second World Conference on Transborder Data Flow Policies' (Documentary, 1984) <www.unesco.org/archives/multimedia/?s=films_details&pg=33&id=1800> accessed 25 August 2015

Atzori L and others, 'The Internet of Things: A Survey' (2010) 54(15) *Computer Networks* 2787

Barkham J, 'Information Warfare and International Law on the Use of Force' (2001) 34 *New York University Journal of International Law and Politics* 57

Benjamin W, 'Critique of Violence' in Bullock M and Jennings MW (eds), *Walter Benjamin: Selected Writings* (Belknap Press of Harvard University Press 2002)

Betz J, 'Violence: Garver's Definition and a Deweyan Correction' (1977) 87(4) *Ethics* 339

Bing J, 'Building Cyberspace: A Brief History of Internet' in Bygrave LA and Bing J (eds), *Internet Governance: Infrastructure and Institutions* (Oxford University Press 2009)

Brownlie I, *International Law and the Use of Force by States* (Oxford University Press 1963)

Bull H, *The Anarchical Society: A Study of Order in World Politics* (3rd edn, Columbia University Press 2002)
Bygrave LA and Michaelsen T, 'Governors of Internet' in Bygrave LA and Bing J (eds), *Internet Governance: Infrastructure and Institutions* (Oxford University Press 2009)
Bynum TW, 'Norbert Wiener and the Rise of Information Ethics' in Van Den Hoven J and Weckert J (eds), *Information Technology and Moral Philosophy* (Cambridge University Press 2008)
Case Concerning Military and Paramilitary Activities in and Against Nicaragua (Nicaragua v United States of America) (Merits) [1986] ICJ Rep 14
Cassese A, *Violence and Law in the Modern Age* (Polity Press 1988)
——— *International Law* (Oxford University Press 2005)
Charter of the United Nations (adopted 26 June 1945, entered into force 24 October 1945) [1945] ATS 1
Chen TM and others, 'Electronic Attacks' in Bidgoli H (ed), *Handbook of Information Security: Information Warfare, Social, Legal, and International Issues and Security Foundations* (John Wiley & Sons 2006)
Choucri N, *Cyberpolitics in International Relations* (MIT Press 2012)
CISCO, 'Cisco Visual Networking Index: Global Mobile Data Traffic Forecast Update, 2016–2021' (CISCO, 2017) <www.cisco.com/c/en/us/solutions/collateral/service-provider/visual-networking-index-vni/mobile-white-paper-c11-520862.pdf> accessed 5 February 2018
——— 'The Zettabyte Era: Trends and Analysis' (CISCO, 2017) <www.cisco.com/c/en/us/solutions/collateral/service-provider/visual-networking-index-vni/vni-hyperconnectivity-wp.html> accessed 5 February 2018
Clarke RA and Knake RK, *Cyber War* (HarperCollins 2010)
Clausewitz C, *On War* (Penguin 1968)
Coady CAJ, 'The Idea of Violence' (1986) 3(1) *Journal of Applied Philosophy* 3
Colburn T and Shute G, 'Abstraction, Law, and Freedom in Computer Science' (2010) 41(3) *Metaphilosophy* 345
Commission of the European Communities, 'Green Paper on a European Programme for Critical Infrastructure Protection' (COM/2005/576 final, 17 November 2005)
Convention on Cybercrime (adopted 23 November 2001, entered into force 1 July 2004) [2013] ATS 9
Council Directive 2008/114/EC of 8 December 2008 on the Identification and Designation of European Critical Infrastructures and the Assessment of the Need to Improve Their Protection [2008] OJ L 345/75
Covenant of the League of Nations (adopted 28 June 1919, entered into force 10 January 1920) [1920] ATS 1
Crawford J, 'Sovereignty as a Legal Value', in Crawford J and Koskenniemi M (eds), *The Cambridge Companion to International Law* (Cambridge University Press 2012)
Darian-Smith E, *Laws and Societies in Global Contexts: Contemporary Approaches* (Cambridge University Press 2013)
De Brabandere E, 'Propaganda' in Wolfrum R (ed), *Max Planck Encyclopedia of Public International Law* (Oxford University Press 2012)
Demarest G, 'Espionage in International Law' (1996) 24(2) *Denver Journal of International Law and Policy* 321

Dinstein Y, War, *Aggression and Self-Defence* (3rd edn, Cambridge University Press 2001)
Dipert RR, 'The Ethics of Cyberwarfare' (2010) 9(4) *Journal of Military Ethics* 384
——— 'The Essential Features of an Ontology for Cyberwarfare' in Yannakogeorgos PA and Lowther AB (eds), *Conflict and Cooperation in Cyberspace: The Challenge to National Security* (CRC Press 2013)
Durante M, 'Violence, Just Cyber War and Information' (2015) 28 *Philosophy & Technology* 369
Feinberg J, *Harm to Others* (Oxford University Press 1984)
Fishman WL, 'Introduction to Transborder Data Flows' (1980) 16 *Stanford Journal of International Law* 1
Floridi L, *The Ethics of Information* (Oxford University Press 2013)
——— *The Fourth Revolution* (Oxford University Press 2014)
——— 'Hyperhistory and the Philosophy of Information Policies' in Floridi L (ed), *The Onlife Manifesto: Being Human in a Hyperconnected Era* (Springer 2015)
Galtung J, 'Violence, Peace, and Peace Research' (1969) 6(3) *Journal of Peace Research* 167
Garver N, 'What Violence Is' in Bierman AK and Gould JA (eds), *Philosophy for a New Generation* (Macmillan 1970)
General Treaty for the Renunciation of War as an Instrument of National Policy (adopted 27 August 1928, entered into force 24 July 1929) 94 LNTS 57
Geneva Convention for the Amelioration of the Condition of the Wounded and Sick in Armed Forces in the Field (adopted 12 August 1949, entered into force 21 October 1950) [1958] ATS 21
Gerth H and Mills CW (eds), *From Max Weber: Essays in Sociology* (Routledge 2009)
Giddens A, *The Nation-State and Violence* (Polity Press 1985)
Harmful Digital Communications Act 2015 (NZ)
Heathcote G, *The Law on the Use of Force: A Feminist Analysis* (Routledge 2012)
Higgins R, *Themes and Theories: Selected Essays, Speeches, and Writings in International Law* (Oxford University Press 2009)
Hirvonen A, 'The Politics of Revolt: On Benjamin and Critique of Law' (2011) 22 *Law and Critique* 101
Hobbes T, *Leviathan* (Pearson Longman 2008)
Hunnings N, 'Pirate Broadcasting in European Waters' (1965) 14(2) *International and Comparative Law Quarterly* 410
Instrument Amending the Constitution of the International Telecommunication Union of 22 December 1992 (as amended 14 October 1994, entered into force 1 January 2000) [2000] ATS 8
International Convention Concerning the Use of Broadcasting in the Cause of Peace (adopted 23 September 1936, entered into force 2 April 1938) [1938] ATS 8
International Law Commission, Responsibility of States for Internationally Wrongful Acts, UNGA Res 56/83 (12 December 2001) UN Doc A/RES/56/83
International Telecommunication Convention (adopted 21 December 1959, entered into force 1 January 1961) [1962] ATS 2
International Telecommunication Union, 'Series X: Data Networks, Open System Communications and Security. Telecommunication Security: Overview of Cybersecurity' (ITU, 2008) <www.itu.int/rec/T-REC-X.1205-200804-I/en> accessed 12 February 2018

International Telegraph Convention and Regulations (Rome, 14 January 1872) 143 CTS 411
Jaeger C, 'Cyberterrorism and Information Security' in Bidgoli H (ed), *Handbook of Information Security: Information Warfare, Social, Legal, and International Issues and Security Foundations* (John Wiley & Sons 2006)
Joint Chiefs of Staff, Joint Publication 1–02, Department of Defense Dictionary of Military and Associated Terms (US Department of Defense, 8 November 2010, as amended through 15 June 2015) <www.hsdl.org/?view&did=750658> accessed 25 August 2015
Kalberg S, *Max Weber: Readings and Commentary on Modernity* (Blackwell 2005)
Kanuck SP, 'Information Warfare: New Challenges for Public International Law' (1996) 37 *Harvard International Law Journal* 272
Keane J, *Violence and Democracy* (Cambridge University Press 2004)
Kennedy D, *Of War and Law* (Princeton University Press 2006)
Kirby M, 'The History, Achievement and Future of the 1980 OECD Guidelines on Privacy' (2010) 20(2) *Journal of Law, Information and Science* 1
Koskenniemi M, '"The Lady Doth Protest Too Much": Kosovo, and the Turn to Ethics in International Law' (2002) 65(2) *The Modern Law Review* 159
Krug EG and others (eds), *World Report on Violence and Health* (World Health Organization 2002)
Kuner CB, *Transborder Data Flows and Data Privacy Law* (Oxford University Press 2013)
Lessig L, *Code Version 2.0* (Basic Books 2006)
Libicki MC, *What is Information Warfare?* (National Defense University 1995)
Little R, 'Sovereignty' in Griffiths M (ed), *Encyclopedia of International Relations and Global Politics* (Routledge 2005)
Manyika J and others, *Big Data: The Next Frontier for Innovation, Competition, and Productivity* (McKinsey Global Institute 2011)
McDougal MS and Feliciano FP, *The International Law of War: Transnational Coercion and World Public Order* (Martinus Nijhoff 1994)
Montevideo Convention on Rights and Duties of States (adopted 26 December 1933, entered into force 26 December 1934) 136 LNTS 19
Novotny EJ, 'Transborder Data Flows and International Law: A Framework for Policy-Oriented Inquiry' (1980) 16 *Stanford Journal of International Law* 141
Oppenheim L, *International Law, Volume 2: Disputes, War and Neutrality* (7th edn, Longman 1952)
Organization of Economic Cooperation and Development, *Guidelines on the Protection of Privacy and Transborder Flows of Personal Data* (OECD, 1980) <www.oecd.org/sti/ieconomy/oecdguidelinesontheprotectionofprivacyandtransborderflowsofpersonaldata.htm> accessed 12 February 2018
Owens WA and others (eds), *Technology, Policy, Law, and Ethics Regarding U.S. Acquisition and Use of Cyberattack Capabilities* (National Academies Press 2009)
Pagallo U, 'Cyber Force and the Role of Sovereign States in Informational Warfare' (2015) 28(3) *Philosophy & Technology* 407
Perritt H, *Law and the Information Superhighway* (Wiley 1996)
Protocol Additional to the Geneva Conventions of 12 August 1949, and Relating to the Protection of Victims of International Armed Conflicts (Protocol I) (adopted 8 June 1978, entered into force 7 December 1978) [1991] ATS 29
Re Duchy of Sealand (1978) 80 ILR 683

Reinalda B, *Routledge History of International Organizations: From 1815 to the Present Day* (Routledge 2009)
Rid T, *Cyber War will Not Take Place* (Oxford University Press 2013)
Ringmar E, 'On the Ontological Status of the State' (1996) 2(4) *European Journal of International Relations* 439
Robinson P, 'From TDF to International Data Services' (1987) 11(4) *Telecommunications Policy* 369
Schmitt MN, 'Cyber Operations and the Jus in Bello: Key Issues' (2011) 87 *International Law Studies Series US Naval War College* 89
——— 'Classification of Cyber Conflict' (2012) 17(2) *Journal of Conflict & Security Law* 245
——— 'The Law of Cyber Warfare: Quo Vadis?' (2014) 25 *Stanford Law and Policy Review* 269
——— (ed), *Tallinn Manual 2.0 on the International Law Applicable to Cyber Operations* (2nd edn, Cambridge University Press 2017)
Shackelford SJ, *Managing Cyber Attacks in International Law, Business, and Relations: In Search of Cyber Peace* (Cambridge University Press 2014)
Slaughter AM, *A New World Order* (Princeton University Press 2005)
Stevenson A (ed), *Oxford Dictionary of English* (3rd edn, Oxford University Press 2010)
Taddeo M, 'Information Warfare: A Philosophical Perspective' (2012) 25 *Philosophy & Technology* 105
——— 'Just Information Warfare' (2016) 35(1) *Topoi* 213
Take I, 'Regulating the Internet Infrastructure: A Comparative Appraisal of the Legitimacy of ICANN, ITU, and the WSIS' (2012) 6(4) *Regulation & Governance* 499
Tavani HT, 'The Conceptual and Moral Landscape of Computer Security' in Himma KE (ed), *Internet Security: Hacking, Counterhacking, and Society* (Jones and Bartlett 2007)
Taylor PJ, 'The State as Container: Territoriality in the Modern World-System' (1994) 18(2) *Progress in Human Geography* 151
Thomas C, 'Why Don't We Talk About "Violence" in International Relations?' (2011) 37(4) *Review of International Studies* 1815
Thomson JE, *Mercenaries, Pirates, and Sovereigns: State-Building and Extraterritorial Violence in Early Modern Europe* (Princeton University Press 1996)
Treaty on the Non-Proliferation of Nuclear Weapons (adopted 1 July 1968, entered into force 5 March 1970) [1973] ATS 3
Turner BS, *Max Weber: From History to Modernity* (Routledge 2002)
UN Group of Governmental Experts on Developments in the Field of Information and Telecommunications in the Context of International Security, *Report of the Group of Governmental Experts on Developments in the Field of Information and Telecommunications in the Context of International Security* (24 June 2013) UN Doc A/68/98
——— Report of the Group of Governmental Experts on Developments in the Field of Information and Telecommunications in the Context of International Security (22 July 2015) UN Doc A/70/174
UNGA Res 2625 (XXV) (24 October 1970) UN Doc A/RES/2625(XXV)
UNGA Res 53/70 (4 January 1999) UN Doc A/RES/53/70
UNGA Res 57/239 (31 January 2003) UN Doc A/RES/57/239

UNGA Res 58/199 (30 January 2004) UN Doc A/RES/58/199

UNGA Res 64/211 (21 December 2009) UN Doc A/RES/64/211

UNGA Res 68/167 (18 December 2013) UN Doc A/RES/68/167

UNGA Res 69/28 (11 December 2014) UN Doc A/RES/69/28

United Nations Convention on the Law of the Sea (adopted 10 December 1982, entered into force 16 November 1994) [1994] ATS 31

Walzer M, *Just and Unjust Wars: A Moral Argument with Historical Illustrations* (4th edn, Basic Books 2006)

Wendt A, 'The State as Person in International Theory' (2004) 30(2) *Review of International Studies* 289

Wiener N, *Cybernetics: Or Control and Communication in the Animal and the Machine* (Technology Press 1948)

Wooldridge M, *An Introduction to Multiagent Systems* (John Wiley & Sons 2002)

4 Cyber attacks and international law on the use of force and non-intervention

Introduction

This chapter examines cyber attacks and international law on the use of force and non-intervention. It argues that, in the context of cyber attacks, the threshold distinction between the non-use of force and non-intervention principles highlights the law's ontologically constrained view of violence. As a result, while the law is capable of regulating cyber attacks with material effects, its capacity is limited – particularly in relation to cyber attacks without material effects.

The chapter is divided into two parts, and each part contains two sections examining the non-use of force and non-intervention principles, respectively. The first part considers these principles of international law in the non-cyber context. It demonstrates that the law conceptualizes what amounts to interstate violence through the use of force doctrine. Violence in this context requires physical damage or harm (as associated with uses of armed force), whereas those measures below this threshold are considered through the non-intervention principle and effectively depicted as a form of non-violence. The second part of the chapter then considers the law on the use of force and non-intervention in relation to cyber attacks. It argues that, while the law has the capacity to regulate cyber attacks resulting in material damage to physical objects or harm to human beings, as a result of its ontological constraints, the law lacks the capacity to adequately deal with cyber attacks without material effects. Instead, these cyber attacks are viewed as possible breaches of the non-intervention principle and effectively depicted as forms of non-violence outside the conception of violence embodied in the law on the use of force. This is particularly problematic given the degree to which states increasingly rely on ICTs for their proper functioning.

The use of force and non-intervention

The prohibition on the use of force

International law on the use of force and non-intervention subscribes to a particular view of the state and violence. The state is a legally constituted entity that is geographically located in physical space – an entity with a permanent population, a defined territory, a government and the capacity to enter into relations with other states.[1] The state is therefore conceptualized as a territorial entity,[2] with an aggregate of human individuals, possessing a government in control of the territory, and with a separate existence from other entities.[3] The law represents these entities as states, as sovereign equals within the UN Charter system[4] that are prohibited from intervening in each other's domestic affairs[5] and from using force against each other's territorial integrity or political independence.[6] The law on the use of force and non-intervention is premised on this view of the state as a static and inherently territorial entity, and only violence of a specific type are deemed to threaten the state and international peace and security.

As highlighted in Chapter 3, international law's modern discourse on the containment of interstate violence revolves around the use of force doctrine.[7] The formal state of war has been rendered legally obsolete, and states are prohibited from using force in their international relations.[8] Article 2(4) of the UN Charter provides that all member states of the United Nations:

> shall refrain in their international relations from the threat or use of force against the territorial integrity or political independence of any state, or in any other manner inconsistent with the Purposes of the United Nations.[9]

This 'cardinal principle'[10] of international law has been described as 'the very cornerstone of the human effort to promote peace in a world torn by strife'.[11] Its legal force derives not only from treaty law, but also from customary international law,[12] and it is considered to have the status of a *jus cogens* norm.[13]

The Article 2(4) prohibition on the use of force – particularly the meaning of the notion of 'force' that it embodies – represents the central doctrine through which interstate violence is understood. As the debates about the provision's scope – from the history of its drafting to the issues raised by destructive non-kinetic weapons technologies – reveal, the generally accepted meaning is premised on a particular worldview. The law subscribes to an ontology in which the state's territorial sovereignty is central and physical violence in particular is considered to pose a threat to states and the international order. As such, Article 2(4) is deemed to prohibit uses of armed force depicted as akin to physical violence harming the conceptual body of the state, whereas measures falling below this threshold are considered through the non-intervention principle as only affecting the personality of the state. What follows is an examination of the notion of 'force' that is contained within Article 2(4), and the non-intervention principle as it is relevant in this context to those measures below the use of force threshold to illustrate how international law draws the conceptual boundaries between violence and non-violence.

The ambiguity of the notion of 'force' contained in Article 2(4) has given rise to various debates about its meaning.[14] This central notion is not defined in the UN Charter and has been disputed.[15] While acts of military aggression by states are clearly considered to constitute uses of force,[16] controversy has surrounded what other types of force may fall within its ambit. Some argue that force is understood to refer only to armed force and consequently that political and economic coercion fall outside its ambit.[17] This view aligns with the intention of the drafters and the UN Charter as a whole, and seeks to avoid the difficulties associated with distinguishing between permissible and impermissible forms of coercion.[18] The opposite view holds that the notion of force should include political and economic coercion too, as the UN Charter does not specify the prohibition to be on the use of *armed* force and because the use of such methods can be as threatening to the political independence of a state as military force.[19] Both positions therefore view the use of traditional armed force or military force as clearly included within the scope of the notion of force, but the debate is about how far beyond this it extends.

As the UN Charter does not define 'force', international law specifies that the ordinary meaning of the term within the context of the object and purpose of the UN Charter should be considered.[20] A dictionary definition of force defines it as 'coercion or compulsion, especially with the use or threat of violence'.[21] Coercion, however, can be understood in violent and non-violent terms, resulting in a definition that is perhaps excessively broad.[22] When considering the broader context and the object and purpose of the UN Charter, there is a clear desire to prevent the outbreak of war and the violence experienced in the context of the world wars. For example, among the provisions in the Preamble to the UN Charter is the expression of a determination 'to save succeeding generations from the scourge of war, which twice in our lifetime has brought untold sorrow to mankind'.[23] One of the ways in which this is sought to be achieved is by ensuring, through 'the acceptance of principles and the institution of methods, that armed force shall not be used, save in the common interest'.[24] Given the overarching purpose of the UN Charter and the desire to protect future generations from the horrors of war, the notion of force should be understood within this context.[25]

However, while Article 2(4) refers to a use of 'force', the Preamble refers to a qualified form of *armed* force. Looking at the UN Charter as a whole, in addition to the 'miscellaneous' and other related provisions about the entry into force of the UN Charter,[26] the term 'force' appears five times. In addition to the Preamble and Article 2(4) contexts already mentioned, it appears in Articles 41, 44 and 46. All of these are contained in Chapter 7 of the UN Charter, which deals with the authority of the UN Security Council. Essentially, Chapter 7 provides the UN Security Council with the power to 'determine the existence of any threat to the peace, breach of the peace, or act of aggression' and to decide on the measures that will be taken to 'maintain or restore international peace and security' should such circumstances arise.[27] Measures in this context include economic and diplomatic measures 'not involving the use of armed force';[28] should they prove or be deemed inadequate, the UN Security Council can take action through, for instance, 'operations by air, sea, or land forces'.[29] Further, Article 44 provides other procedural considerations for when the UN Security Council has made its decision 'to use force' in this context,[30] and Article 46 mentions the relevant committee with which the UN Security Council shall make any plans 'for the application of armed force'.[31]

Therefore, in addition to Article 2(4), in each other instance where the notion of 'force' appears, it clearly appears in connection with the qualified form of *armed* force or directly related to its use. Generally, according to this logic, it is understood that because everywhere else in the UN Charter the notion of force refers to armed force, the Article 2(4) prohibition must also refer to that.[32] However, others interpret it in the opposite way. Distinguishing the instances in which *armed* force is referred to, from the general prohibition on the use of force in the unqualified sense, they maintain that 'force' in the context of Article 2(4) is not limited to armed force.[33] Further ambiguity and confusion on what constitutes 'force' comes from Article 51. Here, it is stated that the UN Charter as a whole does not impair the inherent right of self-defense available to states subject to an 'armed attack'.[34] While an 'armed attack' invariably presumes a 'use of force', it is not so vice versa – a use of force does not necessarily always rise to the level of an 'armed attack' against which the use of force in self-defense is permitted.[35] As such, there is ambiguity in interpreting the notion of 'force' within the context of the object and purpose of the UN Charter.

In such instances of ambiguity, or where there is need for additional support for a particular meaning that results from the application of the rules of treaty interpretation, recourse may be had to the preparatory work of the treaty (the *travaux préparatoires*).[36] According to the intention of the drafters of the UN Charter, as evident in the preparatory work, the notion of 'force' referred to military force and suggestions by the Brazilian delegation to include economic coercion were rejected.[37] This was largely because of the experiences in the world wars; it was deemed at the time of drafting that armed force specifically was 'simply too destructive to be considered an acceptable means of pursuing changes or advancing other policy'.[38] Therefore, according to the intention of the drafters, Article 2(4) is a prohibition on the use of armed force, and not economic or political coercion.

This view is also supported by later UN General Assembly resolutions. For example, the 1970 Declaration on Friendly Relations aligns with this interpretation, referring to the prohibition on the use of force in the context of military force.[39] It only refers to economic and political matters in relation to the duty not to intervene in the internal matters of a state.[40] Here, too, there was opposition to this view as Eastern European states and most developing countries argued that force should include 'all forms of pressure, including those of a political and economic character, which have the effect of threatening the territorial integrity or political independence of any state'.[41] They argued that the notion of force should be 'interpreted broadly so as to cover forms of coercion other than armed force'.[42] This was in contrast to Western states that maintained that force only referred to armed force.[43] The opposing view advocated by Eastern European states and many developing countries was rejected, however, meaning that political and economic coercion was to be treated under the non-intervention principle instead. Therefore, despite these debates, the 1970 Declaration on Friendly Relations was unanimously adopted and it characterizes political and economic coercion as potential breaches of the non-intervention principle. As such, these forms of coercion were distinguished from uses of armed force and not considered to fall under Article 2(4).[44] Accordingly, the orthodox interpretation, supported by later UN General Assembly resolutions, is that Article 2(4) is intended to prohibit uses of armed force – specifically the violence associated with militaries using kinetic weapons in conflicts with other states.

As the UN Charter was drafted even prior to the 'age of jets, rockets and nuclear weapons',[45] questions have also emerged about whether the use of non-kinetic weapons, such as chemical and biological weapons, constitutes use of armed force. Ian Brownlie famously maintained that such weapons should constitute uses of force due to the common reference to them as 'weapons' and, more importantly, due to their employment 'for the destruction of life and property'.[46] He placed importance not only on the weapon-like nature of the instruments used, but also on their destructive effects, in determining whether their use would breach Article 2(4). Similarly, the International Court of Justice (ICJ) in its Advisory Opinion on the Legality of the Threat or Use of Nuclear Weapons[47] maintained that Article 2(4) does not refer to specific weapons meaning the provision applies 'to any use of force, regardless of the weapons employed'.[48] Accordingly, even with the development of chemical, biological and nuclear weapons technologies, the uses of force contemplated to be prohibited by Article 2(4) clearly requires the use of weapon-like instruments capable of causing injury or death to humans, or damage or destruction of physical property.

In addition to these forms of military force, some have also discussed whether physical non-military force can constitute force for the purposes of Article 2(4). Again, Brownlie remarks that:

> More difficult to regard as a use of force are deliberate and forcible expulsion of population over a frontier, release of large quantities of water down a valley, and the spreading of fire through a built up area or woodland across a frontier.[49]

Nonetheless, he argues that, for instance in circumstances where one state controlling the upper reaches of a river releases water downstream, the 'deliberate employment of natural forces by a state in such circumstances can probably be regarded as a use of force'.[50] Albrecht Randelzhofer also maintains that generally non-military force would not constitute a breach of Article 2(4), and that only the non-intervention principle would apply in such circumstances.[51] The exception to this is in extreme circumstances where 'the use of physical non-military force may produce the effects of an armed attack prompting the right of self-defence'.[52] In such cases, the use of force would not only breach Article 2(4) but also rise to the level of an armed attack warranting self-defense under Article 51.[53] Consequently, physical non-military force can in exceptional circumstances be analogous to armed military force and hence fall within the ambit of Article 2(4).[54]

In contrast to armed force, economic coercion or force is not prohibited by Article 2(4). Whether it is termed 'economic coercion',[55] 'economic diplomacy',[56] 'economic force'[57] or an economic 'weapon',[58] the use of such measures is rejected as falling under the prohibition on the use of force generally due to their effects. This is despite arguments by some that the effects of economic coercion can be as severe as the use of armed force. Cassandra La-Rae Perez, for instance, maintains that 'Economic and trade sanctions have the potential to devastate a civilian population and to rock the economic and political stability of a developing state.'[59] Similarly, Jordan Paust and Albert Blaustein, referring to the 1973 Arab oil embargo, maintain that it constituted 'coercion … of such mounting intensity and efficacy that it can be authoritatively proscribed as a violation of basic Charter goals and of Article 2(4)'.[60] Echoing the concerns of many developing countries in the context of the 1970 Declaration on Friendly Relations, these authors argue that in some circumstances the effects of economic coercion can be contrary to the UN Charter ideals and even a violation of Article 2(4). However, as has been shown, the orthodox view remains that Article 2(4) only applies to armed force.[61] Economic coercion is therefore generally not considered a recognized form of 'force' under the Article 2(4) prohibition.

While direct uses of armed force clearly fall within the scope of Article 2(4), the question of whether indirect uses of armed force – for instance, situations in which states actively support the use of force by other actors – has also emerged. The ICJ was faced with this issue in the case of *Nicaragua v USA*.[62] There the United States was found to have breached Article 2(4) through its involvement in, and by supporting in various ways, the armed activities of the contras in Nicaragua.[63] Specifically, these included US involvement in the laying of mines in Nicaraguan ports and the destruction of various oil pipelines, oil terminals and oil-storage tanks through air and sea attacks.[64] As well as a level of involvement in these attacks, the United States had also provided the contras with various forms of support. The ICJ was satisfied that over the years this support had included 'logistic support, the supply of information on the location and movement of the Sandinista troops, the use of sophisticated methods of communication, the deployment of field broadcasting networks, [and] radar coverage'.[65] These forms of support, however, were not considered uses of force. Instead, the ICJ found that the 'financial support, training, supply of weapons, intelligence and logistic support' provided to the contras breached the non-intervention principle.[66] The ICJ specifically noted that the 'arming and training' of the contras also constituted a use of force against Nicaragua, in contrast to 'the mere supply of funds', which only constituted an intervention.[67] An indirect use of armed force can therefore also constitute a breach of Article 2(4).

Overall, the prevailing interpretation of Article 2(4) is that force is limited to armed force.[68] Tom Farer maintains that the preparatory work clearly illustrates a desire to 'outlaw war as an instrument of state policy', and hence that the provision is 'concerned with violence, with military force, not with economic coercion'.[69] Similarly, Oscar Schachter argues that the UN Charter was designed to 'outlaw war in its classic sense, that is, the use of military force to acquire territory or other benefits from another state'.[70] Accordingly, the notion of 'force' generally is understood as 'armed force', as opposed to economic and political coercion, which falls below this threshold. As alluded to earlier, these forms of coercion may, however, constitute breaches of the non-intervention principle.

Therefore, Article 2(4) prohibits the use of armed force – it is concerned with a particular type of interstate violence that involves material damage or harm. It subscribes to particular ontological assumptions about the state and the forms of violence that are deemed to threaten the state and international order. As the following section will demonstrate, international law also protects states from non-violent coercion, particularly those measures below the use of force that are embodied in the modern form of the non-intervention principle protecting the 'personality of the state'.[71] However, these distinctions demonstrate the law's ontologically constrained view of violence, as only physical violence associated with uses of armed force is seen as a threat to the state, whereas those instances of 'non-violence' below this threshold are deemed outside the scope of the prohibition on the use of force.

The non-intervention principle

The meaning of the notion of 'force' is relatively settled as armed force, despite the aforementioned debates about how to interpret its scope. This is in contrast to the less clear notion of intervention.[72] The classic definition of intervention provided by Lassa Oppenheim is 'forcible or dictatorial interference by a State in the affairs of another State, calculated to impose certain conduct or consequences on that other State'.[73] Indeed, until the twentieth century, the principle of non-intervention was only associated with the use of forceful means.[74] For instance, in the International Law Commission's first session in 1949, a draft provision entailing a duty on states to refrain from intervention was discussed.[75] In this context, Hans Kelsen argued that if such a duty were interpreted in accordance with existing international law at the time, it would have meant 'intervention by the threat or use of force'.[76] It was only after the world wars that the non-use of force principle took over and developed to deal specifically with military or armed force. As a result, other non-forceful but nonetheless coercive means instead began to be recognized as breaches of the non-intervention principle.[77] Therefore, classically the non-intervention principle only applied to forceful interventions. While technically the principle continues to encompass both armed and non-armed forms of coercion, in the context of use of force analysis, it is now generally referred to only in relation forms of coercion falling below the Article 2(4) threshold.

Unlike the non-use of force principle, which exists in both treaty and customary form, the non-intervention principle generally is regarded as a principle of customary international law, and therefore it cannot be found in a specific treaty provision alone. Nonetheless, it can be read within various treaty provisions. For instance, Article 2(1) of the UN Charter states that the United Nations is based on the notion of sovereign equality.[78] Sovereign equality in turn entails various elements, including the notion 'that the personality of the state is respected, as well as its territorial integrity and political independence'.[79] The principle is also alluded to in Article 2(7) of the UN Charter, which provides that the United Nations cannot 'intervene in matters which are essentially within the domestic jurisdiction of any state'.[80] Similarly, the principle can be seen in various regional treaties.[81]

For the content of the non-intervention principle, two key declarations by the UN General Assembly stand out. The 1965 Declaration on the Inadmissibility of Intervention[82] condemns all forms of interference with the personality of a state[83] and the similarly worded 1970 Declaration on Friendly Relations[84] states that such actions are in violation of international law:

> No State or group of States has the right to intervene, directly or indirectly, for any reason whatever, in the internal or external affairs of any other State. Consequently, armed intervention and all other forms of interference or attempted threats against the *personality of the State* or against its political, economic and cultural elements, are in violation of international law.[85]

While the 1970 Declaration on Friendly Relations is not a treaty, and does not have binding force as such, it is regarded as an authoritative statement of the principle. This is because it was adopted unanimously by the UN General Assembly, and also because it was heavily relied upon by the ICJ in *Nicaragua v USA* as support for the existence and content of the principle in customary international law.[86]

The ICJ in *Nicaragua v USA* discussed the principle of non-intervention, stating that

> A prohibited intervention must accordingly be one bearing on matters in which each State is permitted, by the principle of State sovereignty, to decide freely. One of these is the choice of a political, economic,

> social and cultural system, and the formulation of foreign policy. Intervention is wrongful when it uses methods of coercion in regard to such choices, which must remain free ones. The element of coercion, which defines, and indeed forms the very essence of, prohibited intervention, is particularly obvious in the case of an intervention which uses force.[87]

This principle is thus regarded as containing two elements: first, there must be an intervention; and second, it must coercively impact on those choices that should be made freely by states.[88] Unlike uses of force, which require a degree of physicality, the non-intervention principle applies to those forms of coercion that only affect the 'personality of the state' by impacting on the matters that states should be able to decide freely.[89] For example, in *Nicaragua v USA*, as noted above, the US actions amounted to a use of force because it was involved in various attacks and in the 'arming and training' of the contras. In contrast, the other forms of support provided by the United States, which included logistical, informational and communicational support, only amounted to an intervention.[90] The support itself constituted the intervention, whereas the coerciveness was satisfied as the ICJ found that the United States did this with the intention 'to coerce the Government of Nicaragua in respect of matters in which each State is permitted, by the principle of State sovereignty, to decide freely'.[91]

The ICJ in *Nicaragua v USA* also discussed the relationship of the non-intervention principle to the non-use of force. Essentially, the non-intervention principle is broader than the non-use of force principle; however, generally it is only referred to when coercive activities do not reach the level of a prohibited use of force. For instance, when discussing actions that would amount to a prohibited intervention, the ICJ noted that actions amounting to a 'use of force' would be 'wrongful in the light of both the principle of non-use of force, and that of non-intervention.'[92] With respect to the 'use of force', the ICJ distinguished between forms of force depending on their gravity. It distinguished 'the most grave forms of use of force (those constituting an armed attack) from other less grave forms'.[93] Here it also noted that certain conduct may amount to a breach of 'the principle of the non-use of force and an intervention in the internal affairs of a State, that is, a form of conduct which is certainly wrongful, but is of lesser gravity than an armed attack'.[94] Therefore, according to the ICJ, there are three different types of coercion that can be distinguished by their gravity. These are (1) forms of coercion affecting matters that states are free to decide (prohibited interventions),[95] (2) coercive armed force (prohibited uses of force), and (3) coercive armed force rising to the level of an armed attack (against which the use of force is permitted in self-defense).[96] Coercion, however, remains the operative element – 'the very essence' of prohibited interventions and 'obvious' in uses of force.[97]

Coercion is therefore a key element separating those acts by states that may be considered to be in breach of the non-intervention principle from legitimate pressure. Maziar Jamnejad and Michael Wood, for example, stress that it is 'a crucial limit' for the non-intervention principle:

> Without it, any act which had an effect on another state could fall within the prohibition. The requirement of coerciveness not only removes minor international friction from the scope of the principle, but means that it only applies to those acts that to some degree 'subordinate the sovereign will' of another state.[98]

Others have also described the non-intervention principle as 'the doctrinal mechanism to express the outer limits of permissible influence that one state may properly exert upon another'[99] and 'the frontier between diplomatic pressure which is tolerable to the pressured and various degrees of coercion which are not'.[100]

In exploring the meaning of force within Article 2(4), and the non-intervention principle as it is relevant to the threshold distinction between these principles, this part of the chapter has examined the way in which the law conceptualizes interstate violence. Violence is regarded as something inherently physical – as associated with uses of armed force – as opposed to those non-forceful measures that fall within the ambit of the non-intervention principle and are seen to affect only the personality of the state. Particularly where there is neither harm to human beings nor damage to physical property, the law lacks the adequate ability to recognize this as a form of violence. Instead, it is depicted as being below the use of force threshold and within the scope of the non-intervention principle alone, and effectively equates to a form of non-violence. As a result, as will be demonstrated below, while the law is capable of regulating cyber attacks that result in material damage or harm, it lacks the capacity to sufficiently deal with cyber attacks with non-material effects.

Cyber attacks, the use of force, and non-intervention

This part of the chapter considers existing literature on cyber attacks and the use of force and non-intervention. It demonstrates that the law's ontologically constrained view of violence is evident in the dominant approaches to the application of these doctrines to cyber attacks. As the law is centrally concerned with protecting the state entity from the physical violence associated with uses of armed force, it has the capacity to regulate cyber attacks with material effects. This is evident in the fact that cyber attacks with material effects, such as damage or destruction of property, or injury or death to human beings, are considered the easy cases for the use of force analysis. The more complex instances of cyber attacks, however, affecting the functionality of ICTs or otherwise disruptive attacks without material effects, are generally not considered as uses of force because they do not fit into existing conceptualizations of violence. These cyber attacks below the use of force threshold are considered potential breaches of the non-intervention principle instead, and effectively depicted as forms of non-violence. Given the degree to which even non-material cyber attacks can threaten the security of states increasingly reliant on ICTs, treating these attacks as a form of non-violence outside the scope of Article 2(4) does not adequately account for the new ways in which states can be harmed, and it effectively undermines international order by enabling states to pursue their political ends through seemingly 'non-violent' means.

Cyber attacks and the prohibition on the use of force

Given the increased dependence of states on ICTs and cyberspace that was demonstrated in Chapter 3, states have become vulnerable to cyber attacks and also acquired the capability to engage in cyber warfare. Technology has therefore made it possible for states to engage in new ways both in and through cyberspace, raising questions about the application of international law in this context. While some early views held that cyberspace should be a zone entirely outside the control of states,[101] today it is mostly accepted that international law applies in cyberspace, and that it is not a law-free zone.[102] As a zone within the realm of law, international lawyers and scholars have also considered the question of how the law should be applied in the cyber context, and the most common techniques for doing so have been through analogy or the extension of existing law. A range of areas of law have been considered, including the law regulating the use and proliferation of nuclear weapons,[103] international telecommunications law,[104] aviation law,[105] outer space law,[106] the law governing Antarctica[107] and the law of the sea.[108] Through analogy or extension, these laws are used or offered as ways of conceptualizing how the law already applies, or how it could apply, to state activities in cyberspace, including to cyber attacks.[109] Given the general prohibition on the use of force in international law, the question of whether and when a cyber attack constitutes a use of force has been a central focus. With no hard law on the use of cyber attacks specifically, an important soft law instrument comes from the *Tallinn Manual 2.0 on the International Law Applicable to Cyber Operations* (*Tallinn Manual*).[110] The *Tallinn Manual* is a study authored by a Group of Experts led by Michael Schmitt. The first version was published in 2013 and an updated version was published in 2017.[111] The *Tallinn Manual* considers both the *jus ad bellum* and *jus in bello* in relation to cyber warfare. On the central questions relating to the law on the use of force – whether the use of cyber attacks is prohibited, and if so, when the use of cyber attacks is prohibited – the *Tallinn Manual* provides the following two rules:

> Rule 68 – Prohibition of threat or use of force
>
> A cyber operation that constitutes a threat or use of force against the territorial integrity or political independence of any State, or that is in

> any other manner inconsistent with the purposes of the United Nations, is unlawful.[112]
>
> Rule 69 – Definition of use of force
>
> A cyber operation constitutes a use of force when its scale and effects are comparable to non-cyber operations rising to the level of a use of force.[113]

As such, the *Tallinn Manual* seeks to answer what are among the key questions for international law in relation to cyber attacks, namely whether the law on the use of force extends to cyber attacks, and if so, what sort of harm amounts to 'force' that is prohibited by the law.[114] Essentially, the answer it provides is that the law on the use of force applies to cyber attacks, and a cyber attack constitutes a use of force when it is comparable 'in scale and effects' to a non-cyber use of force. While this is clear, according to the *Tallinn Manual*, in instances where people are killed or physical objects are destroyed, it is less clear where no injury to human beings or damage to physical objects occurs.[115]

In the broader international legal scholarship on whether or not cyber attacks amount to a use of force, three different approaches are evident. The 'instrument approach' is essentially concerned with the nature of the instrument used – where a 'weapon' or similar instrument is used to inflict the force, then it may amount to a use of armed force. The 'target approach', in turn, focuses on the target of the cyber attack – where this is important infrastructure, for instance, it should be considered a use of force. Finally, the 'effects approach' is concerned with the effects of cyber attacks and whether they are comparable with those of conventional military attacks.[116] Few adopt one of these approaches on its own, and they are more often used to distinguish between various considerations in assessing whether a cyber attack amounts to a use of force. Marco Roscini combines the 'instrument approach' and 'effects approach', suggesting that whether or not a cyber attack amounts to a use of force must be determined by the weapons (instruments) used; however, 'weapons' are defined by the harmful effects of the instrument in question.[117] Accordingly, for Roscini it is the 'instrument used that defines armed force, but the instrument is identified by its (violent) consequences'.[118] Similarly, William Boothby adopts the position that a cyber weapon is defined by its violent consequences – where a means of cyber attack is 'designed, intended or used, in order to have violent consequences, that is, to cause death or injury to persons or damage or destruction of objects'.[119] As these combined approaches already highlight, the effects of a cyber attack are particularly important in the analysis of cyber attacks and the use of force.

The 'instrument approach' considers the nature of the instrument being used and whether it constitutes a weapon, and therefore a use of 'armed' force. This was also the approach traditionally used in distinguishing armed force from economic and political coercion.[120] As Schmitt notes, this determination generally

> depends on the type of the coercive instrument – diplomatic, economic, or military – selected to attain the national objectives in question. The first two types of instruments might rise to the level of intervention, but they do not engage the normatively more flagrant act of using force.[121]

The problem with adopting a purely 'instrument approach' in relation to cyber attacks comes from their non-physical nature and non-weapon-like qualities.[122] The essential question, according to Heather Harrison Dinniss, is 'whether a bitstream of malicious code is sufficiently militaristic or weapon-like to meet the required definition of "armed" force'.[123] Unlike conventional weapons, cyber attacks are, at their core, 'simply written instructions that are translated into the 0s and 1s of binary code, the language of machines'.[124] Cyber weapons are therefore at odds with the conventional understanding of what constitutes a weapon, particularly as they lack the physicality associated with weapons. Further, weapons generally generate destructive effects through kinetic force, and while chemical and biological weapons, for instance, do so through non-kinetic force, they are nonetheless widely recognized and regarded as weapons.[125] Cyber weapons, in contrast, can reside on small USB drives and be released by the mere stroke of a key.[126] However, focusing purely on the instrument used is problematic in the cyber context, given the non-weapon-like nature of digital code and that, from this perspective, even potentially destructive cyber attacks may be excluded from constituting a use of 'armed force'.[127] Similarly, as discussed earlier in the chapter, the approach taken in relation to chemical and biological weapons was concerned with both their weapon-like nature and their destructive effects. Indeed, the nature of the weapon technology is generally not an issue, as it depends on how it is used. A laser beam, for instance, can be used for beneficent medical purposes or for destructive and lethal purposes.[128] As Daniel Silver argues, 'when we assign one of those technologies to the "armed force" category, it is not because of its inherent lethality but because of the potential destructiveness of the way it is being used or the purpose for which it is deployed'.[129] Cyber weapons therefore lack the physicality and weapon-like nature of what are traditionally understood as weapons, despite their potential to cause destruction.

The 'target approach' is concerned primarily with the target of the cyber attack in determining whether or not it would amount to a use of force. The key factor here is the value of the computer system or network to a state's critical national interests.[130] Roscini uses the example of a cyber attack against critical infrastructure:

> A week-long cyber attack that shuts down the national grid, and thus leaves millions of people without electricity, cripples the financial

> market and the transport system, and prevents government communications is likely to be treated as a use of force, whether or not physical damage ensues.[131]

In contrast, he maintains that a similar attack on a (non-critical) network such as that of a university would not amount to a use of force.[132] Similarly, Eric Talbot Jensen suggests that attacks on critical infrastructure from *any source* (including cyber attacks) would amount to a use of force.[133] As Duncan Hollis notes, however, cyber attacks can range from merely disruptive to highly destructive, and if the focus is simply on the 'critical' nature of the target, then very minor attacks can potentially be considered uses of force.[134] Consequently, while the target of a cyber attack is an important consideration, reliance on the target approach alone is problematic.

From the 'effects approach', a cyber attack is assessed based on its effects. This approach has attracted the most support, and its focus is on the evaluation of whether the effects of a cyber attack are akin to a use of armed force. For instance, the *Tallinn Manual*'s Group of Experts, while considering several criteria, highlighted the severity of an attack as the 'most significant' criterion to be considered.[135] While an early example of this view considered that cyber attacks causing *any* destructive effect against information, for instance, would amount to an unlawful use of force, more recent views only consider those attacks with tangible effects as qualifying.[136] As such, according to the prevailing view, cyber attacks that have material effects such as damage to physical objects or injury to human beings constitute the 'easy cases' that most clearly amount to a use of force. Reliant on Brownlie's effects-based approach focusing particularly on whether there was any 'destruction of life or property',[137] Jason Barkham argues that cyber attacks that cause instantaneous destruction akin to that caused by conventional weapons are 'relatively easy' to regard as constituting uses of force.[138] Schmitt also notes that the narrow category of cyber attacks 'specifically intended to directly cause physical damage to tangible property or injury or death to human beings' are 'easily dealt with'.[139] For Dinniss, 'it appears to be clear' that a cyber attack will constitute a use of force where it 'results in a physical consequence, namely destruction of physical property, injury or loss of lives'.[140] According to Herbert Lin, 'the ambiguities are fewest when cyber attacks cause physical damage to property and loss of life in ways that are comparable to kinetic attacks and traditional war'.[141] Roscini, in turn, maintains that if a cyber attack caused physical damage to property or injury to persons then the position that it would amount to a use of force is 'virtually uncontested'.[142] Similarly, Katharina Ziolkowski notes the 'nearly uniform opinion among scholars'; she adopts the position that a cyber attack amounts to a use of force 'if it results in death, physical injury or the destruction of property'.[143] Silver also argues that a cyber attack will most likely constitute a use of force where 'its direct and foreseeable effects are physical injury or property damage'.[144] Christopher

Joyner and Catherine Lotrionte find it 'persuasive' that cyber attacks that 'directly and intentionally result in non-combatant deaths and destruction' constitute uses of force.[145] Yoram Dinstein also maintains that the crux of whether a cyber attack amounts to a use of force is not the means used, but its 'violent consequences'.[146] Finally, the *Tallinn Manual's* Group of Experts maintained that, generally, 'Acts that injure or kill persons or damage or physically destroy or damage objects are uses of force',[147] and that where cyber attacks involve similar consequences they will qualify as uses of force.[148] Therefore, despite their non-physical nature as weapons, cyber attacks can also constitute a use of force under Article 2(4) – especially if it has material effects.

In the *Tallinn Manual*'s commentary to Rules 68 and 69, the Group of Experts also considered eight criteria to aid in the determination of when a cyber attack constitutes a use of force. These criteria were based on criteria that Schmitt first suggested in the late 1990s,[149] and they have been widely cited since.[150] Therefore, the following eight criteria were regarded by the Group of Experts as a non-exhaustive list of factors to consider in distinguishing armed force from other forms of coercion, and specifically in determining the circumstances in which a cyber attack would amount to a use of force in breach of Article 2(4).[151]

1 *Severity.* Compared with economic and political coercion, coercion through the use of armed force 'threaten[s] physical injury or destruction of property to a much greater degree'.[152] Cyber attacks causing physical harm to people or destruction of property will thus generally amount to a use of force, whereas those causing purely inconvenience or irritation will never qualify.
2 *Immediacy.* The negative effects of armed force are more immediately visible than those of other forms of coercion. Where the effects are immediate, there are fewer opportunities to resolve the situation peacefully or mitigate its harmful effects.
3 *Directness.* In terms of the chain of causation, the consequences of armed force are more directly linked to the act itself, whereas the effects of other forms of coercion are indirect and dependent on other contributing factors. Hence cyber attacks in which the cause and effect are clearly linked are most likely to constitute uses of force.
4 *Invasiveness.* Armed force usually intrudes through the borders of a target state, whereas acts of economic coercion usually occur outside those borders. Cyber attacks will be most invasive when they penetrate the most secure systems, as opposed to mere exploitation of vulnerabilities in more openly accessible systems. Cyber attacks concentrated into a particular state will also increase their perceived invasiveness.
5 *Measurability of effects.* The negative consequences of armed force are usually easier to measure and quantify, compared with other forms of coercion. While the consequences of cyber attacks are generally less

apparent, those attacks that result in more specifically measurable effects are more likely to constitute a use of force.

6 *Military character.* Generally, cyber attacks that occur in close connection to uses of military force will increase the likelihood of them constituting uses of force.

7 *State involvement.* Where there is a high degree of clear state involvement in a cyber attack, it is more likely that other states will regard it as a use of force.

8 *Presumptive legitimacy.* Under both domestic and international law, it is generally presumed that the application of violence is illegitimate (unless authorized – for instance, in self-defense). In contrast, economic and political coercion generally are regarded as permissible. Similarly, propaganda and espionage are not expressly prohibited under international law and are generally permitted. Accordingly, cyber attacks that only amount to economic coercion or espionage, for instance, are less likely to constitute uses of force.[153]

As Schmitt noted when he originally coined these criteria, given the new forms of coercion made possible by cyber attack technologies, these criteria are useful in rethinking the boundaries of the use of force 'box' so that it can be expanded to fill in gaps in the law that have been revealed by cyber attacks.[154] Accordingly, under the approach taken by the *Tallinn Manual*, cyber attacks will constitute a use of force when they are invasive attacks that directly cause immediately visible, severe and quantifiable effects such as death or destruction. This aligns with the dominant position in the scholarly literature on cyber attacks and the use of force: essentially that where cyber attacks have destructive physical effects causing injury to humans or damage to property, they will constitute a use of force as prohibited by Article 2(4). These are considered the easy cases.

The more complex cases come from those cyber attacks that do not directly cause visible physical harm or damage. Non-material cyber attacks, such as those that disrupt the operation of computer systems or networks without destruction of hardware, or that only undermine the integrity of information, are more difficult to characterize as uses of force. For example, according to Dinniss, those instances 'where the effect of the attack is not to destroy the information, but to degrade the information target to the extent that it cannot be relied upon' are particularly problematic.[155] Barkham also highlights the problems with cyber attacks that only undermine the integrity of data, as opposed to actually destroying it. He uses the examples of Distributed Denial-of-Service (DDoS) attacks and industrial espionage, which can 'rob the property of its value without causing any actual physical damage'.[156] However, he maintains that such attacks would not be considered uses of force as there is no weapon involved nor any property destroyed.[157] Scott Shackelford also maintains that difficulties arise in relation to 'pure information' attacks involving electronic means to access or alter information without 'damag[ing] any physical components in the traditional sense'.[158] Boothby questions whether 'damage to data within a computer system that does not affect the facility or service that the targeted computer system provides constitutes damage'.[159] He adopts the position taken by the Group of Experts and maintains that the data resident on a computer system can only properly be regarded as an object of an attack under limited circumstances. The attack must impact on the functioning of a computer systems or network to the degree where repairs are needed for it to be able to operate again.[160] Roscini also notes a similar problem in relation to intangible property, questioning:

> Whether data as such can be equated to physical property for the purposes of Article 2(4), so that their deletion, alteration or corruption qualifies as a use of force even without physical damage or incapacitation of infrastructure, is a question that it is very difficult to answer.[161]

Roscini cites Schmitt's position that this generally will not be the case, except perhaps where the data are 'designed to be immediately convertible into tangible objects, like banking data'.[162] Similarly, Georg Kerschischnig also highlights the problems associated with the need for physical damage or destruction under the use of force doctrine. He argues that '[t]he strict limitation to physical damage clearly does not reflect the realities of cyberspace'[163] and suggests redefining the notion of destruction to include non-physical damage to intangible properly such as data.[164]

Accordingly, most authors within the scholarship on cyber attacks and the use of force highlight particularly how the harm caused by cyber attacks is problematic. This is especially where cyber attacks only have non-material effects that do not fit easily within the law on the use of force. Nonetheless, the general position remains under existing law that unless a cyber attack causes material effects, such as injury or death to human beings or damage or destruction of physical property, it cannot be seen as a use of force.

Cyber attacks and the non-intervention principle

In the literature on cyber attacks and the use of force and non-intervention, as within the general literature on these principles discussed earlier, those measures not constituting a use of force are instead considered unlawful interventions, provided the element of coercion is present. While the non-intervention principle has not received as much scholarly attention as cyber attacks and the use of force, most nonetheless maintain that the principle is applicable.[165] For example, according to Russell Buchan, this principle creates

> a legal framework that can protect States from cyber attacks which, although not producing physical damage and thus not qualifying as an

> unlawful use of force, nevertheless have the effect of coercing a State into adopting a course of conduct that it is freely entitled to determine itself.[166]

Similarly, while the original *Tallinn Manual* only provided limited commentary on the non-intervention principle,[167] the 2017 version considers the principle in more depth. The *Tallinn Manual* provides:

> Rule 66 – Intervention by States
> A State may not intervene, including by cyber means, in the internal or external affairs of another State.[168]

The Group of Experts took the position adopted by the ICJ in *Nicaragua v USA* that in order to amount to a prohibited intervention, any act must be coercive in nature and it must affect the internal or external affairs of the target state.[169] They maintained that the 'internal or external affairs' generally refer to matters that states have the sovereign prerogative to decide.[170] The Group of Experts defined the notion of 'coercion' (which is not defined under international law), as 'an affirmative act designed to deprive another state of its freedom of choice, that is, to force that State to act in an involuntary manner or involuntarily refrain from acting in a particular way'.[171] The Group of Experts expressly noted that, in this context, cyber attacks do not need to be physical in nature, and therefore DDoS attacks attempting to compel another state to change its foreign policy can amount to a breach of the non-intervention principle.[172]

Within the legal scholarship on cyber attacks and the use of force, the general tendency is to consider the non-intervention principle as a secondary category into which to push the problematic cyber attacks that do not easily fit existing understandings of what amounts to a use of force. Roscini argues that cyber attacks that do not produce destructive consequences or severely disrupt critical infrastructure 'may be unlawful interventions in the internal affairs of other states, but are not a use of force'.[173] He maintains there is no difficulty in qualifying cyber attacks as breaching the non-intervention principle when used 'to coerce another State in order to obtain from it the subordination of the exercise of its sovereign rights and to secure from it advantages of any kind'.[174] Similarly, Dinniss argues that cyber attacks with minimal effects or not manifesting in the physical sphere will likely be considered as unlawful interferences instead.[175] Joyner and Lotrionte also argue that cyber attacks that do not amount to force in the 'literal sense … may be viewed as a form of intervention that can produce certain harmful or coercive effects in other states'.[176] Mary O'Connell emphasizes that even though a cyber attack does not amount to a use of force, international law nonetheless prohibits cyber attacks under the principle of non-intervention.[177]

Therefore, according to the prevailing view, those cyber attacks without material effects similar to those traditionally associated with uses of armed force cannot be considered uses of force. In contrast to these 'easy cases', the more difficult ones arise where cyber attacks do not have clear material effects akin to what is normally understood as 'force' within Article 2(4). Those cyber attacks below this threshold, provided the element of coercion is present, are instead considered as potential breaches of the non-intervention principle.

This distinction between cyber attacks with material and non-material effects arises as a result of the law's ontologically constrained view of violence. Destructive cyber attacks with material effects resembling physical violence fit easily within the law's conceptualization of violence. The harm caused by such attacks – in the form of injury to human beings or damage to material objects – is something the law is capable of recognizing. This is regardless of whether the harm or damage is inflicted through kinetic force, non-kinetic weapons, destructively used non-military force or indeed cyber attacks. In each case, the harm caused subscribes to the conception of violence embodied in Article 2(4). However, those cyber attacks without material effects largely fall outside this conceptualization of violence. The harm or damage caused is mainly virtual entities and processes – non-material cyber attacks mainly impact the functioning of computer systems and networks or the integrity of data. Given the tendency to cast these cyber attacks outside the scope of Article 2(4) and as potential breaches of the non-intervention principle alone, they are seen to affect a state's legal personality and not constitute a form of harm that can be viewed as a use of force.

The tendency to view non-material cyber attacks as forms of non-violence through the lens of the non-intervention principle is problematic. Given the degree to which states increasingly rely on ICTs for their functioning, regarding non-material cyber attacks as mainly affecting the personality of the state does not adequately capture the harm that these attacks can cause, and how their use by states to pursue political aims can undermine international peace and security. Further, by not taking this new form of violence seriously, the law fosters a grey area of uncertainty that effectively enables states to use seemingly non-violent actions in and through cyberspace.[178] Therefore, viewing cyber attacks with non-material effects as forms of non-violence outside the scope of Article 2(4), and as potential violations of the non-intervention principle alone, does not adequately recognize the harm such attacks can cause.

Conclusion

This chapter has examined the way in which international law, through the non-use of force and non-intervention principles, draws the boundaries of what constitutes violence and non-violence in interstate relations. It argued that the distinction between these legal principles in relation to cyber attacks reveals the ontologically limited conception of violence embodied in Article 2(4). This is particularly evident in how cyber attacks with material effects can easily be regarded as uses of force, whereas non-material cyber attacks tend to be considered as breaches of the non-intervention principle alone, only affecting the legal personality of the state.

The following chapters will consider the threshold distinction between the non-use of force and non-intervention principles in relation to three prominent cyber attack incidents against states: the 2007 cyber attacks against Estonia, the Stuxnet incident and the Russian interference in the 2016 US presidential elections. Each chapter will demonstrate the problems arising from Article 2(4)'s limited conception of violence in regulating cyber attacks, and how an informational approach to each incident offers a means of overcoming these limitations and recognizing the new ways in which cyber attacks can harm states.

Notes

1 Montevideo Convention on Rights and Duties of States (adopted 26 December 1933, entered into force 26 December 1934) 136 LNTS 19 Art 1. See also James R Crawford, *The Creation of States in International Law* (Oxford University Press 2006) 45–6.
2 A state's territory, over which it has sovereignty under international law, includes its land, the airspace above it and, for coastal states, parts of the sea: *Case Concerning Military and Paramilitary Activities in and Against Nicaragua (Nicaragua v United States of America)* (Merits) [1986] ICJ Rep 14, 111.
3 See Crawford (n 1) 45–66.
4 Charter of the United Nations (adopted 26 June 1945, entered into force 24 October 1945) [1945] ATS 1 Art 2(1).
5 The notion of sovereign equality includes various elements, including 'that the personality of the state is respected, as well as its territorial integrity and political independence'. Leland M Goodrich and others, *Charter of the United Nations: Commentary and Documents* (3rd and rev edn, Columbia University Press 1969) 37.
6 Charter of the United Nations (n 4) Art 2(4).
7 Christine Gray describes Article 2(4) (and Article 51 which provides the self-defence exception to this rule) as providing 'a new terminology and the first expression of the basic rules in their modern form'. Christine Gray, *International Law and the Use of Force* (Oxford University Press 2000) 2–3.
8 In contrast to the Covenant of the League of Nations (adopted 28 June 1919, entered into force 10 January 1920) [1920] ATS 1, which sought to encourage states to respect and preserve the territorial integrity and political independence of states against aggression (Article 10), and the General Treaty for the Renunciation of War as an Instrument of National Policy (adopted 27 August 1928, entered into force 24 July 1929) 94 LNTS 57, which condemned war as a means of solving disputes and renounced it as a form of national policy (Article 1), the UN Charter instead prohibits the use of force. See Charter of the United Nations (n 4) Art 2(4).
9 Charter of the United Nations (n 4) Art 2(4). Article 2(4) not only prohibits uses of force, it also prohibits any threats of force. The ICJ has noted that threats involve a 'declared readiness' or otherwise 'signalled intention' to use force and, for example, 'it would be illegal for a State to threaten to secure territory from another State, or to cause it to follow or not follow certain political or economic paths'. *Legality of the Threat or Use of Nuclear Weapons*

(Advisory Opinion) [1996] ICJ Rep 226, 246. Further, it is generally accepted that Article 2(4) only applies to uses of force between states – that is, the use of force must take place in the 'international' relations of states – and therefore the provision does not apply to internal (non-international) conflicts. See Goodrich and others (n 5) 50. The requirement that the use of force (or threat thereof) must be 'against the territorial integrity or political independence of any state' has been interpreted by some to restrict the scope of Article 2(4) only to situations in which the territorial integrity or political independence is somehow diminished. See, for example, Anthony D'Amato, 'The Invasion of Panama was a Lawful Response to Tyranny' (1990) 84(2) *American Journal of International Law* 516, 520. However, the generally accepted position is that this phrase was not meant to restrict the application of Article 2(4) and that even short armed incursions that are not intended to deprive another state of its territory are covered by the prohibition. See Albrecht Randelzhofer, 'Article 2(4)' in Bruno Simma and others (eds), *The Charter of the United Nations: A Commentary* (Oxford University Press 2002) 123. The final phrase, also prohibiting uses of force that are 'in any other manner inconsistent with the Purposes of the United Nations', is generally taken to act as a 'catch-all' provision and to prohibit all other forms of uses of force that may not otherwise be covered. See Yoram Dinstein, *War, Aggression and Self-Defence* (3rd edn, Cambridge University Press 2001) 82. However, here too there has been a debate: see Ian Brownlie, *International Law and the Use of Force by States* (Oxford University Press 1963) 267–8; Bert VA Röling, 'The Ban on the Use of Force and the UN Charter' in Antonio Cassese (ed), *The Current Legal Regulation of the Use of Force* (Martinus Nijhoff 1986) 4. Therefore, under the UN Charter, the use of force is generally prohibited, unless in self-defence or where authorized by the UN Security Council (Article 51 of the UN Charter permits states to use force in self-defence against an armed attack, and Article 42 of the UN Charter permits the Security Council to authorize the use of force to maintain or restore international peace and security).

10 *Case Concerning Military and Paramilitary Activities in and Against Nicaragua* (n 2) 151 (separate opinion of President Nagendra Singh).

11 ibid 153.

12 *Case Concerning Military and Paramilitary Activities in and Against Nicaragua* (n 2) 92–7.

13 Gray (n 7) 24; Crawford (n 1) 131. See also *Case Concerning Military and Paramilitary Activities in and Against Nicaragua* (n 2) 100.

14 Although, as Christine Gray points out in the context of the drafting history of the UN Charter provisions, 'consensus was attained only at the price of ambiguity'. Gray (n 7) 46.

15 Randelzhofer (n 9) 117; Michael N Schmitt, 'Computer Network Attack and the Use of Force in International Law: Thoughts on a Normative Framework' (1999) 37 *Columbia Journal of Transnational Law* 885, 904.

16 See UNGA Res 3314 (XXIX) (14 December 1974) UN Doc A/RES/29/3314.

17 For instance, Sadurska notes that, 'Although Article 2(4) of the Charter does not specify the type of coercion it forbids, most writers assume that it refers to the physical use of armed force alone.' Sadurska (n 9) 242 (citations omitted).

18 Goodrich and others (n 5) 48.

19 ibid 48–9. For instance, Oscar Schacter notes the ambiguity in the term 'force': 'It can be used in a wide sense to embrace all types of coercion: economic, political, and psychological as well as physical.' Oscar Schachter, 'The Right of States to Use Armed Force' (1984) 82 *Michigan Law Review* 1620, 1624.

20 See Vienna Convention on the Law of Treaties (adopted 23 May 1969, entered into force 27 January 1980) [1974] ATS 2 Art 31.

21 Angus Stevenson (ed), *Oxford Dictionary of English* (3rd edn, Oxford University Press 2010) 683.
22 See Tom J Farer, 'Political and Economic Coercion in Contemporary International Law' (1985) 79(2) *American Journal of International Law* 405, 406.
23 Charter of the United Nations (n 4) Preamble.
24 ibid.
25 This is also the only reference to the notion of 'war' contained in the UN Charter, as the term was eliminated from legal discourse and replaced by the 'law of force'. See David Kennedy, *Of War and Law* (Princeton University Press 2006) 78.
26 Charter of the United Nations (n 4) Chs 16–19.
27 ibid Art 39.
28 ibid Art 41.
29 ibid Art 42.
30 ibid Art 44.
31 ibid Art 46.
32 For instance, Albrecht Randelzhofer takes this approach, see Randelzhofer (n 9) 118. Dinniss adopts a similar reasoning, noting that the unqualified term of force is used only twice in the entire UN Charter and appears in its unqualified form in Article 44 but takes the qualified 'armed force' form in the context of Articles 41 and 46. Accordingly, she maintains that this suggests clearly 'that the force contemplated by the unqualified term is armed'. See Heather Harrison Dinniss, *Cyber Warfare and the Laws of War* (Cambridge University Press 2012) 41–2.
33 The notion of 'force', according to Hans Kelsen, 'is meant to include not only armed force, but any illegal action of one state which violates the legally protected interests of another'. Hans Kelsen, *Collective Security Under International Law* (Lawbook Exchange 2001) 55.
34 Charter of the United Nations (n 4) Art 51.
35 *Case Concerning Military and Paramilitary Activities in and Against Nicaragua* (n 2) 101.
36 See Vienna Convention on the Law of Treaties (n 20) Art 32.
37 See Randelzhofer (n 9) 118; Schmitt (n 15) 905.
38 Anthony C Arend and Robert J Beck, *International Law and the Use of Force: Beyond the UN Charter Paradigm* (Routledge 1993) 34.
39 UNGA Res 2625 (XXV) (24 October 1970) UN Doc A/RES/2625(XXV).
40 Schmitt (n 15) 907; UNGA Res 2625 (XXV) (n 39).
41 David J Harris, *Cases and Materials on International Law* (7th edn, Thomson Reuters 2010) 724. For a summary of the 'Socialist' interpretative position on the prohibition on the use of force, see Hanna Bokor-Szegö, 'The Attitude of Socialist States Towards the International Regulation of the Use of Force' in Antonio Cassese (ed), *The Current Legal Regulation of the Use of Force* (Martinus Nijhoff 1986) 455–8.
42 Antonio Tanca, 'The Prohibition of Force in the UN Declaration on Friendly Relations of 1970' in Antonio Cassese (ed), *The Current Legal Regulation of the Use of Force* (Martinus Nijhoff 1986) 400.
43 ibid.
44 Similarly, the 1987 Declaration on the Non-Use of Force (UNGA Res 42/22 (18 November 1987) UN Doc A/RES/42/22), with reference to both Article 2(4) and the 1970 Declaration on Friendly Relations, declares the duty of states to refrain from using force in their international relations and notes that states cannot make 'use of economic, political or any other type of measures to coerce another state' separately from the duty to refrain from using force. See Schmitt (n 15) 907. See also Dinniss (n 32) 48.

45 Thomas M Franck, 'Who Killed Article 2 (4)? or: Changing Norms Governing the Use of Force by States' (1970) 64(5) *American Journal of International Law* 809, 821.
46 Brownlie (n 9) 362.
47 *Legality of the Threat or Use of Nuclear Weapons (Advisory Opinion)* (n 9).
48 ibid 244.
49 Brownlie (n 9) 362–3.
50 ibid 376. See also Randelzhofer (n 9) 118.
51 Randelzhofer (n 9) 119.
52 ibid.
53 ibid.
54 Daniel B Silver, 'Computer Network Attack as a Use of Force Under Article 2(4) of the United Nations Charter' (2002) 76 *International Law Studies Series US Naval War College* 73, 83.
55 Farer (n 22) 408.
56 Clinton E Cameron, 'Developing a Standard for Politically Related State Economic Action' (1991) 13 *Michigan Journal of International Law* 218, 218.
57 See Malcolm N Shaw, *International Law* (7th edn, Cambridge University Press 2014) 815.
58 Jordan Paust and Albert Blaustein refer to the 1973 Arab oil embargo as 'the deliberate employment of an economic instrument of coercion (the oil "weapon") against other states'. Jordan J Paust and Albert P Blaustein, 'The Arab Oil Weapon: A Threat to International Peace' (1974) 68(3) *American Journal of International Law* 410, 412.
59 Cassandra LaRae-Perez, 'Economic Sanctions as a Use of Force: Re-evaluating the Legality of Sanctions from an Effects-Based Perspective' (2002) 20 *Boston University International Law Journal* 161, 162.
60 Paust and Blaustein (n 58) 439.
61 According to Malcolm Shaw, 'It does seem that there is at least a case to be made out in support of the view that such actions are contrary to the United Nations Charter, as interpreted in numerous resolutions and declarations. But whether such action constitutes a violation of Article 2(4) is dubious.' Shaw (n 57) 816.
62 *Case Concerning Military and Paramilitary Activities in and Against Nicaragua* (n 2).
63 ibid 123.
64 ibid 48, 50–1.
65 ibid 61.
66 ibid 124.
67 ibid 119.
68 Antonio Cassese, *International Law* (Oxford University Press 2005) 56; Randelzhofer (n 9) 117; Stephen Neff, 'Economic Warfare in Contemporary International Law: Three Schools of Thought, Evaluated According to an Historical Method' (1989) 26 *Stanford Journal of International Law* 67, 83; Dinstein (n 9) 81; Schmitt (n 15) 908.
69 Farer (n 22) 410.
70 Schachter (n 19) 1624.
71 See UNGA Res 2625 (XXV) (n 39).
72 The term is often used interchangeably with 'interference,' although 'interference' can be seen as a concept wider than 'intervention'. See Maziar Jamnejad and Michael Wood, 'The Principle of Non-Intervention' (2009) 22(2) *Leiden Journal of International Law* 345, 347 note 7; Terry D Gill, 'Non-Intervention in the Cyber Context' in Katharina Ziolkowski (ed), *Peacetime Regime for State Activities in Cyberspace: International Law, International Relations and Diplomacy* (NATO Cooperative Cyber Defence Centre of Excellence 2013) 217.

73 Robert Y Jennings and Arthur Watts (eds), *Oppenheim's International Law, Volume 1, Peace* (9th edn, Longman 1992) 430 cited in Harris (n 41) 743. See also Lori F Damrosch, 'Politics Across Borders: Nonintervention and Nonforcible Influence Over Domestic Affairs' (1989) 83 *American Journal of International Law* 1, 5.

74 According to Lori Damrosch, as with most scholarly literature at the time focusing only on forms of influence involving force, 'the prevailing viewpoint until well into the twentieth century was that the international legal concept of intervention concerned itself only with the use or threat of force against another state and not with lesser techniques'. Damrosch (n 73) 3 (citations omitted). Tom Farer also notes how, until the decolonization period, 'intervention was regarded as a principle feature of the normal intercourse of international life.' Tom J Farer, 'Problems of an International Law of Intervention' (1968) 3 *Stanford Journal of International Studies* 20, 21.

75 Article 3 of the proposed International Law Commission's Draft Articles on the Rights and Duties of States provided that, 'Every State has the duty to refrain from intervention in the internal or external affairs of any other State.' This declaration was never adopted by the UN General Assembly: see Sergio M Carbone and Lorenzo Schiano di Pepe, 'States, Fundamental Rights and Duties' in Rüdiger Wolfrum (ed), *Max Planck Encyclopedia of Public International Law* (Oxford University Press 2009).

76 Hans Kelsen, 'The Draft Declaration on Rights and Duties of States' (1950) 44(2) *American Journal of International Law* 259, 268. James Brierly, in discussing the duty of non-intervention in this context, also maintained that 'an act of intervention was an act of dictation by one State to another state with regard to its internal or external policy backed by the use or threat of force' emphasizing that actions without an element of force, 'however improper or unfriendly, could not be qualified as intervention.' Yearbook of the International Law Commission 1949, 'Summary Records and Documents of the First Session including the report of the Commission to the General Assembly' (United Nations, 1956) 90 <http://legal.un.org/ilc/publications/yearbooks/english/ilc_1949_v1.pdf> accessed 22 February 2018.

77 As Jamnejad and Wood maintain, 'nowadays the international law on the use of force is not generally thought of in terms of non-intervention but as a self-standing chapter of international law.' Jamnejad and Wood (n 72) 359.

78 Charter of the United Nations (n 4) Art 2(1).

79 See Goodrich and others (n 5) 37.

80 Charter of the United Nations (n 4) Art 2(7).

81 Jamnejad and Wood (n 72) 364.

82 UNGA Res 20/2132 (XX) (21 December 1965) UN Doc A/RES/20/2131(XX).

83 ibid 12.

84 UNGA Res 2625 (XXV) (n 39).

85 ibid 123 (emphasis added).

86 *Case Concerning Military and Paramilitary Activities in and Against Nicaragua* (n 2) 101, 106. The ICJ has also referred to the provisions of the 1970 Declaration on Friendly Relations as 'declaratory of customary international law'. *Armed Activities on the Territory of the Congo (Democratic Republic of the Congo v Uganda)* [2005] ICJ Rep 168, 226–7.

87 *Case Concerning Military and Paramilitary Activities in and Against Nicaragua* (n 2) 108.

88 Jamnejad and Wood (n 72) 347.

89 According to Cassese, it 'prohibits States from encroaching upon the internal affairs of other States. Thus, for instance, a State is not allowed to bring pressure to bear on *specific national bodies* of other countries'. Cassese (n 68) 53 (emphasis in original).

90 *Case Concerning Military and Paramilitary Activities in and Against Nicaragua* (n 2) 61.
91 ibid 124.
92 ibid 108. This was affirmed by the ICJ in *Armed Activities on the Territory of the Congo (Democratic Republic of the Congo v Uganda)* (n 86) 227.
93 *Case Concerning Military and Paramilitary Activities in and Against Nicaragua* (n 2) 101.
94 ibid 127.
95 The ICJ also goes on to list these as 'the choice of a political, economic, social and cultural system, and the formulation of foreign policy'. *Case Concerning Military and Paramilitary Activities in and Against Nicaragua* (n 2) 108.
96 Charter of the United Nations (n 4) Art 51.
97 ibid 108. David Harris has also noted that, 'An armed attack upon another State annexing its territory is the ultimate form of intervention.' Harris (n 41) 743.
98 Jamnejad and Wood (n 72) 381.
99 Richard Falk, *Legal Order in a Violent World* (Princeton University Press 1968) 159 cited in John R Vincent, *Nonintervention and International Order* (Princeton University Press 1974) 15.
100 Vincent (n 99) 15.
101 See, for example, John P Barlow, 'Declaration of the Independence of Cyberspace' (Electronic Frontier Foundation, 8 February 1996) <www.eff.org/cyberspace-independence> accessed 22 February 2018. He famously declared cyberspace as a realm outside state sovereignty and free from state governance.
102 UN Group of Governmental Experts on Developments in the Field of Information and Telecommunications in the Context of International Security, 'Report of the Group of Governmental Experts on Developments in the Field of Information and Telecommunications in the Context of International Security' (22 July 2015) UN Doc A/70/174, 12. However, the most recent UN GGE failed to reach agreement on this. See Owen Bowcott, 'Dispute along cold war lines led to collapse of UN cyberwarfare talks' *The Guardian* (23 August 2017) <www.theguardian.com/world/2017/aug/23/un-cyberwarfare-negotiations-collapsed-in-june-it-emerges> accessed 22 February 2018. Scott Shackelford also notes how cyberspace 'is far from the untamed digital Wild West that it is at times made out to be'. Scott J Shackelford, *Managing Cyber Attacks in International Law, Business, and Relations: In Search of Cyber Peace* (Cambridge University Press 2014) 311.
103 Scott J Shackelford, 'From Nuclear War to Net War: Analogizing Cyber Attacks in International Law' (2009) 27(1) *Berkeley Journal of International Law* 192, 218–19.
104 Oona A Hathaway and others, 'The Law of Cyber-Attack' (2012) 100(4) *California Law Review* 817, 866–8.
105 ibid 868–70.
106 Shackelford (n 103) 219–22; Hathaway and others (n 104) 870–2. See also Duncan B Hollis, 'Why States Need an International Law for Information Operations' (2007) 11(4) *Lewis & Clark Law Review* 1023, 1051.
107 Shackelford (n 103) 222–3.
108 ibid 227–8; Hathaway and others (n 104) 872–3. See also Hollis (n 106) 1051–2.
109 See, for example, Shackelford (n 102) 267–8.
110 Michael N Schmitt (ed), *Tallinn Manual 2.0 on the International Law Applicable to Cyber Operations* (2nd edn, Cambridge University Press 2017).
111 For the original *Tallinn Manual*, see Michael N Schmitt (ed), *Tallinn Manual on the International Law Applicable to Cyber Warfare* (Cambridge University Press 2013).

112 Schmitt (n 110) 329.
113 ibid 330.
114 For critical commentary on the Tallinn Manual in relation to the law on the use of force, see Dieter Fleck, 'Searching for International Rules Applicable to Cyber Warfare – A Critical First Assessment of the New Tallinn Manual' (2013) 18(2) *Journal of Conflict & Security Law* 331, 336–7; Oliver Kessler and Wouter Werner, 'Expertise, Uncertainty and International Law: A study of the Tallinn Manual on Cyberwarfare' (2013) 26(4) *Leiden Journal of International Law* 793, 807–9; Nicholas Tsagourias, 'The Tallinn Manual on the International Law Applicable to Cyber Warfare: A Commentary on Chapter II – The Use of Force' in Terry D Gill (ed), *Yearbook of International Humanitarian Law Volume 15, 2012* (Springer 2014).
115 Schmitt (n 110) 333.
116 Marco Roscini, *Cyber Operations and the Use of Force in International Law* (Oxford University Press 2014) 46–7; Hollis (n 106) 1041; Hathaway and others (n 104) 845–7; David E Graham, 'Cyber Threats and the Law of War' (2010) 4 *Journal of National Security Law and Policy* 87, 91.
117 Roscini (n 116) 49–50.
118 ibid 50.
119 William H Boothby, 'Methods and Means of Cyber Warfare' (2013) 89 *International Law Studies Series US Naval War College* 387, 389.
120 Schmitt (n 15) 909; Roscini (n 116) 46–7.
121 Schmitt (n 15) 909.
122 Hollis (n 106) 1041.
123 Dinniss (n 32) 68.
124 Reese Nguyen, 'Navigating *Jus Ad Bellum* in the Age of Cyber Warfare' (2013) 101(4) *California Law Review* 1079, 1127.
125 Boothby (n 119) 388–9. See also Brownlie (n 9) 362.
126 Boothby (n 119) 389.
127 Roscini (n 116) 47.
128 Silver (n 54) 88.
129 ibid.
130 Walter G Sharp, *CyberSpace and the Use of Force* (Aegis Research Corporation 1999) 129–30.
131 Roscini (n 116) 62.
132 ibid 63. Roscini thus argues that 'only cyber attacks that go beyond mere inconvenience and *significantly* disrupt the functioning of *critical* infrastructure that can potentially fall under the scope of Article 2(4)'. ibid 62 (emphasis in original).
133 Eric T Jensen, 'Computer Attack on Critical National Infrastructure: A Use of Force Invoking the Right of Self Defense' (2002) 38 *Stanford Journal of International Law* 207, 208–9.
134 Hollis (n 106) 1042.
135 Schmitt (n 110) 334. They also noted that the severity of an attack is influenced by its scope, duration and intensity.
136 Sharp (n 130) 133.
137 Jason Barkham, 'Information Warfare and International Law on the Use of Force' (2001) 34 *New York University Journal of International Law and Politics* 57, 72 citing Brownlie (n 9) 362–3.
138 Barkham (n 137) 80.
139 Schmitt (n 15) 913. See also Jack Goldsmith, 'How Cyber Changes the Laws of War' (2013) 24(1) *European Journal of International Law* 129, 133; Matthew Hoisington, 'Cyberwarfare and the Use of Force Giving Rise to the Right of Self-Defense' (2009) 32 *Boston College International and Comparative Law Review* 439, 447.

140 Dinniss (n 32) 74.
141 Herbert S Lin, 'Offensive Cyber Operations and the Use of Force' (2010) 4(1) *Journal of National Security Law and Policy* 63, 73.
142 Roscini (n 116) 53.
143 Katharina Ziolkowski, 'Computer Network Operations and the Law of Armed Conflict' 49(1–2) (2010) *Military Law and the Law of War Review* 47, 70.
144 Silver (n 54) 85.
145 Christopher Joyner and Catherine Lotrionte, 'Information Warfare as International Coercion: Elements of a Legal Framework' (2001) 12(5) *European Journal of International Law* 825, 850.
146 Yoram Dinstein, 'Computer Network Attacks and Self-Defense' (2002) 76 *International Law Studies Series US Naval War College* 99, 103.
147 Schmitt (n 110) 333.
148 ibid 334.
149 Schmitt (n 15) 914–15.
150 Georg Kerschischnig, *Cyberthreats and International Law* (Eleven International 2012) 133–9; Dinniss (n 32) 63–4; Roscini (n 116) 48; Silver (n 54) 89–92; Hoisington (n 139) 448; Nguyen (n 124) 1122–4; Michael Gervais, 'Cyber Attacks and the Laws of War' (2012) 30(2) *Berkeley Journal of International Law* 525, 539; David Weissbrodt, 'Cyber-Conflict, Cyber-Crime, and Cyber-Espionage' (2013) 22 *Minnesota Journal of International Law* 347, 359–60; Jack M Beard, 'Legal Phantoms in Cyberspace: The Problematic Status of Information as a Weapon and a Target Under International Humanitarian Law' (2014) 47 *Vanderbilt Journal of Transnational Law* 67, 119–22; Marco Benatar, 'The Use of Cyber Force: Need for Legal Justification?' (2009) 1(3) *Goettingen Journal of International Law* 375, 390–1; Hathaway and others (n 104) 847–8; Scott J Shackelford and Richard B Andres, 'State Responsibility for Cyber Attacks: Competing Standards for a Growing Problem' (2011) 42(4) *Georgetown Journal of International Law* 971, 997–8; Ziolkowski (n 143) 70. Waxman also refers to Schmitt's article as an 'influential' one: see Matthew C Waxman, 'Cyber-Attacks and the Use of Force: Back to the Future of Article 2(4)' (2011) 36 *Yale Journal of International Law* 421, 432.
151 Schmitt (n 110) 334–6.
152 Schmitt (n 15) 914.
153 Schmitt (n 110) 334–6; Schmitt (n 15) 914–15.
154 Schmitt (n 15) 915. For a critical discussion of these criteria, see Katharina Ziolkowski, '*Ius ad bellum* in Cyberspace: Some Thoughts on the "Schmitt Criteria" for Use of Force' in Christian Czosseck, Rain Ottis and Katharina Ziolkowski (eds), *2012 4th International Conference on Cyber Conflict* (NATO Cooperative Cyber Defence Centre of Excellence 2012) 301–8.
155 Dinniss (n 32) 68.
156 Barkham (n 137) 89.
157 ibid.
158 Shackelford (n 103) 231; see also Shackelford (n 102) 289.
159 Boothby (n 119) 389.
160 ibid 389–90.
161 Roscini (n 116) 55.
162 ibid citing Michael N Schmitt, 'Cyber Operations in International Law: The Use of Force, Collective Security, Self-Defense, and Armed Conflicts' in *Proceedings of a Workshop on Deterring Cyberattacks: Informing Strategies and Developing Options for US Policy* (National Academies Press 2010) 164.
163 Kerschischnig (n 150) 135.
164 ibid 135–6.
165 As Buchan argues, even where scholars recognize the 'potential application of this principle, they mention it only very briefly; crucially, these authors do not

engage in a sustained analysis of how the non-intervention principle may apply to cyber attacks, particularly those falling below the threshold of an unlawful use of force'. Russell Buchan, 'Cyber Attacks: Unlawful Uses of Force or Prohibited Interventions?' (2012) 17(2) *Journal of Conflict & Security Law* 211, 221.

166 ibid 226.

167 Schmitt (n 111) 44–5.

168 Schmitt (n 110) 312.

169 ibid 314.

170 ibid.

171 ibid 317 citing Jennings and Watts (n 73) 430–1. The Group of Experts distinguished coercion from other forms of pressures, such as 'persuasion, criticism, public diplomacy, propaganda ... retribution, mere maliciousness, and the like'. To amount to coercion, the act in question must amount to more than mere influence, as it 'must have the potential for compelling the target State to engage in an action that it would otherwise not take (or refrain from taking an action it would otherwise take)'. Schmitt (n 110) 318–19.

172 ibid 318.

173 Roscini (n 116) 115.

174 ibid 65 citing UNGA Res 2625 (XXV) (n 39).

175 Dinniss (n 32) 74.

176 Joyner and Lotrionte (n 145) 849.

177 Mary E O'Connell, 'Cyber Security without Cyber War' (2012) 17(2) *Journal of Conflict and Security Law* 187, 202.

178 Michael N Schmitt, 'Grey Zones in the International Law of Cyberspace' (2017) 42(2) *Yale Journal of International Law Online* 1, 20–1 <www.yjil.yale.edu/grey-zones-in-the-international-law-of-cyberspace> accessed 12 February 2018.

Bibliography

Arend AC and Beck RJ, *International Law and the Use of Force: Beyond the UN Charter Paradigm* (Routledge 1993)

Armed Activities on the Territory of the Congo (Democratic Republic of the Congo v Uganda) [2005] ICJ Rep 168

Barkham J, 'Information Warfare and International Law on the Use of Force' (2001) 34 *New York University Journal of International Law and Politics* 57

Barlow JP, 'Declaration of the Independence of Cyberspace' (Electronic Frontier Foundation, 8 February 1996) <www.eff.org/cyberspace-independence> accessed 22 February 2018

Beard JM, 'Legal Phantoms in Cyberspace: The Problematic Status of Information as a Weapon and a Target Under International Humanitarian Law' (2014) 47 *Vanderbilt Journal of Transnational Law* 67

Benatar M, 'The Use of Cyber Force: Need for Legal Justification?' (2009) 1(3) *Goettingen Journal of International Law* 375

Bokor-Szegö H, 'The Attitude of Socialist States Towards the International Regulation of the Use of Force' in Cassese A (ed), *The Current Legal Regulation of the Use of Force* (Martinus Nijhoff 1986)

Boothby WH, 'Methods and Means of Cyber Warfare' (2013) 89 *International Law Studies Series US Naval War College* 387

Bowcott O, 'Dispute Along Cold War Lines Led to Collapse of UN Cyberwarfare Talks' *The Guardian* (23 August 2017) <www.theguardian.com/world/2017/aug/23/un-cyberwarfare-negotiations-collapsed-in-june-it-emerges> accessed 22 February 2018

Brownlie I, *International Law and the Use of Force by States* (Oxford University Press 1963)
Buchan R, 'Cyber Attacks: Unlawful Uses of Force or Prohibited Interventions?' (2012) 17(2) *Journal of Conflict & Security Law* 211
Cameron CE, 'Developing a Standard for Politically Related State Economic Action' (1991) 13 *Michigan Journal of International Law* 218
Carbone SM and di Pepe LS, 'States, Fundamental Rights and Duties' in Wolfrum R (ed), *Max Planck Encyclopedia of Public International Law* (Oxford University Press 2009)
Case Concerning Military and Paramilitary Activities in and Against Nicaragua (Nicaragua v United States of America) (Merits) [1986] ICJ Rep 14
Cassese A, *International Law* (Oxford University Press 2005)
Charter of the United Nations (adopted 26 June 1945, entered into force 24 October 1945) [1945] ATS 1
Covenant of the League of Nations (adopted 28 June 1919, entered into force 10 January 1920) [1920] ATS 1
Crawford JR, *The Creation of States in International Law* (Oxford University Press 2006)
D'Amato A, 'The Invasion of Panama was a Lawful Response to Tyranny' (1990) 84(2) *American Journal of International Law* 516
Damrosch LF, 'Politics Across Borders: Nonintervention and Nonforcible Influence Over Domestic Affairs' (1989) 83 *American Journal of International Law* 1
Dinniss HH, *Cyber Warfare and the Laws of War* (Cambridge University Press 2012)
Dinstein Y, *War, Aggression and Self-Defence* (3rd edn, Cambridge University Press 2001)
——— 'Computer Network Attacks and Self-Defense' (2002) 76 *International Law Studies Series US Naval War College* 99
Falk R, *Legal Order in a Violent World* (Princeton University Press 1968)
Farer TJ, 'Problems of an International Law of Intervention' (1968) 3 *Stanford Journal of International Studies* 20
——— 'Political and Economic Coercion in Contemporary International Law' (1985) 79(2) *American Journal of International Law* 405
Fleck D, 'Searching for International Rules Applicable to Cyber Warfare: A Critical First Assessment of the New *Tallinn Manual*' (2013) 18(2) *Journal of Conflict & Security Law* 331
Franck TM, 'Who Killed Article 2(4)? or: Changing Norms Governing the Use of Force by States' (1970) 64(5) *American Journal of International Law* 809
General Treaty for the Renunciation of War as an Instrument of National Policy (adopted 27 August 1928, entered into force 24 July 1929) 94 LNTS 57
Gervais M, 'Cyber Attacks and the Laws of War' (2012) 30(2) *Berkeley Journal of International Law* 525
Gill TD, 'Non-Intervention in the Cyber Context' in Ziolkowski K (ed), *Peacetime Regime for State Activities in Cyberspace: International Law, International Relations and Diplomacy* (NATO Cooperative Cyber Defence Centre of Excellence 2013)
Goldsmith J, 'How Cyber Changes the Laws of War' (2013) 24(1) *European Journal of International Law* 129
Goodrich LM and others, *Charter of the United Nations: Commentary and Documents* (3rd rev edn, Columbia University Press 1969)

Graham DE, 'Cyber Threats and the Law of War' (2010) 4 *Journal of National Security Law and Policy* 87
Gray C, *International Law and the Use of Force* (Oxford University Press 2000)
Harris DJ, *Cases and Materials on International Law* (7th edn, Thomson Reuters 2010)
Hathaway OA and others, 'The Law of Cyber-Attack' (2012) 100(4) *California Law Review* 817
Hoisington M, 'Cyberwarfare and the Use of Force Giving Rise to the Right of Self-Defense' (2009) 32 *Boston College International and Comparative Law Review* 439
Hollis DB, 'Why States Need an International Law for Information Operations' (2007) 11(4) *Lewis & Clark Law Review* 1023
Jamnejad M and Wood M, 'The Principle of Non-Intervention' (2009) 22(2) *Leiden Journal of International Law* 345
Jennings RY and Watts A (eds), *Oppenheim's International Law, Volume 1: Peace* (9th edn, Longman 1992)
Jensen ET, 'Computer Attack on Critical National Infrastructure: A Use of Force Invoking the Right of Self Defense' (2002) 38 *Stanford Journal of International Law* 207
Joyner C and Lotrionte C, 'Information Warfare as International Coercion: Elements of a Legal Framework' (2001) 12(5) *European Journal of International Law* 825
Kelsen H, 'The Draft Declaration on Rights and Duties of States' (1950) 44(2) *American Journal of International Law* 259
——— *Collective Security Under International Law* (Lawbook Exchange 2001)
Kennedy D, *Of War and Law* (Princeton University Press 2006)
Kerschischnig G, *Cyberthreats and International Law* (Eleven International 2012)
Kessler O and Werner W, 'Expertise, Uncertainty and International Law: A study of the *Tallinn Manual on Cyberwarfare*' (2013) 26(4) *Leiden Journal of International Law* 793
LaRae-Perez C, 'Economic Sanctions as a Use of Force: Re-evaluating the Legality of Sanctions from an Effects-Based Perspective' (2002) 20 *Boston University International Law Journal* 161
Legality of the Threat or Use of Nuclear Weapons (Advisory Opinion) [1996] ICJ Rep 226
Lin HS, 'Offensive Cyber Operations and the Use of Force' (2010) 4(1) *Journal of National Security Law and Policy* 63
Montevideo Convention on Rights and Duties of States (adopted 26 December 1933, entered into force 26 December 1934) 136 LNTS 19
Neff SC, 'Economic Warfare in Contemporary International Law: Three Schools of Thought, Evaluated According to an Historical Method' (1989) 26 *Stanford Journal of International Law* 67
Nguyen R, 'Navigating *Jus Ad Bellum* in the Age of Cyber Warfare' (2013) 101(4) *California Law Review* 1079
O'Connell ME, 'Cyber Security Without Cyber War' (2012) 17(2) *Journal of Conflict and Security Law* 187
Paust JJ and Blaustein AP, 'The Arab Oil Weapon: A Threat to International Peace' (1974) 68(3) *American Journal of International Law* 410
Randelzhofer A, 'Article 2(4)' in Simma B and others (eds), *The Charter of the United Nations: A Commentary* (Oxford University Press 2002)

Röling BVA, 'The Ban on the Use of Force and the UN Charter' in Cassese A (ed), *The Current Legal Regulation of the Use of Force* (Martinus Nijhoff 1986)

Roscini M, *Cyber Operations and the Use of Force in International Law* (Oxford University Press 2014)

Schachter O, 'The Right of States to Use Armed Force' (1984) 82 *Michigan Law Review* 1620

Schmitt MN, 'Computer Network Attack and the Use of Force in International Law: Thoughts on a Normative Framework' (1999) 37 *Columbia Journal of Transnational Law* 885

——— 'Cyber Operations in International Law: The Use of Force, Collective Security, Self-Defense, and Armed Conflicts' in P*roceedings of a Workshop on Deterring Cyberattacks: Informing Strategies and Developing Options for US Policy* (National Academies Press 2010)

——— 'Grey Zones in the International Law of Cyberspace' (2017) 42(2) *Yale Journal of International Law Online* 1 <www.yjil.yale.edu/grey-zones-in-the-international-law-of-cyberspace> accessed 12 February 2018

——— (ed), *Tallinn Manual on the International Law Applicable to Cyber Warfare* (Cambridge University Press 2013)

——— (ed), *Tallinn Manual 2.0 on the International Law Applicable to Cyber Operations* (2nd edn, Cambridge University Press 2017)

Shackelford SJ, 'From Nuclear War to Net War: Analogizing Cyber Attacks in International Law' (2009) 27(1) *Berkeley Journal of International Law* 192

——— *Managing Cyber Attacks in International Law, Business, and Relations: In Search of Cyber Peace* (Cambridge University Press 2014)

Shackelford SJ and Andres RB, 'State Responsibility for Cyber Attacks: Competing Standards for a Growing Problem' (2011) 42(4) *Georgetown Journal of International Law* 971

Sharp WG, *CyberSpace and the Use of Force* (Aegis Research Corporation 1999)

Shaw MN, *International Law* (7th edn, Cambridge University Press 2014)

Silver DB, 'Computer Network Attack as a Use of Force Under Article 2(4) of the United Nations Charter' (2002) 76 *International Law Studies Series US Naval War College* 73

Stevenson A (ed), *Oxford Dictionary of English* (3rd edn, Oxford University Press 2010)

Tanca A, 'The Prohibition of Force in the U.N. Declaration on Friendly Relations of 1970' in Cassese A (ed), *The Current Legal Regulation of the Use of Force* (Martinus Nijhoff 1986)

Tsagourias N, 'The Tallinn Manual on the International Law Applicable to Cyber Warfare: A Commentary on Chapter II – The Use of Force' in Gill TD (ed), *Yearbook of International Humanitarian Law Volume 15* (Springer 2014)

UN Group of Governmental Experts on Developments in the Field of Information and Telecommunications in the Context of International Security, *Report of the Group of Governmental Experts on Developments in the Field of Information and Telecommunications in the Context of International Security* (22 July 2015) UN Doc A/70/174

UNGA Res 20/2132 (XX) (21 December 1965) UN Doc A/RES/20/2131(XX)

UNGA Res 2625 (XXV) (24 October 1970) UN Doc A/RES/2625(XXV)

UNGA Res 3314 (XXIX) (14 December 1974) UN Doc A/RES/29/3314

UNGA Res 42/22 (18 November 1987) UN Doc A/RES/42/22

Vienna Convention on the Law of Treaties (adopted 23 May 1969, entered into force 27 January 1980) [1974] ATS 2

Vincent JR, *Nonintervention and International Order* (Princeton University Press 1974)

Waxman MC, 'Cyber-Attacks and the Use of Force: Back to the Future of Article 2(4)' (2011) 36 *Yale Journal of International Law* 421

Weissbrodt D, 'Cyber-Conflict, Cyber-Crime, and Cyber-Espionage' (2013) 22 *Minnesota Journal of International Law* 347

Yearbook of the International Law Commission 1949, 'Summary Records and Documents of the First Session including the report of the Commission to the General Assembly' (United Nations, 1956) <http://legal.un.org/ilc/publications/yearbooks/english/ilc_1949_v1.pdf> accessed 22 February 2018

Ziolkowski K, 'Computer Network Operations and the Law of Armed Conflict' 49(1–2) (2010) *Military Law and the Law of War Review* 47

——— '*Ius ad bellum* in Cyberspace: Some Thoughts on the "Schmitt Criteria" for Use of Force' in Czosseck C, Ottis R, and Ziolkowski K (eds), *4th International Conference on Cyber Conflict* (NATO Cooperative Cyber Defence Centre of Excellence 2012)

5 The 2007 cyber attacks against Estonia

Introduction

In April and May 2007, Estonia became a victim of what the head of the US diplomatic mission to Estonia at the time described as 'the world's first cyber attacks against a nation state'.[1] In the media, the incident was widely described as a cyber war[2] and Estonia's president later referred to the incident as 'Web War One'.[3] Estonia was subjected to a series of cyber attacks in response to its government's decision to relocate a politically contentious war memorial statue. These attacks targeted a range of websites, including those of government departments and banks, as well as Internet Service Providers (ISPs) and the national Domain Name Service (DNS). The attacks were primarily disruptive, as a range of services were rendered temporarily unavailable, but they did not cause damage to physical objects or injury to human beings. Despite initial allegations by Estonian officials that Russia was responsible for the attacks, Russia has denied its involvement.[4]

This chapter considers the 2007 cyber attacks against Estonia to demonstrate that an informational approach offers a means by which to overcome the law's ontological constraints that limit its capacity to recognize non-material cyber attacks as a form of violence. The first section of the chapter examines the 2007 attacks against Estonia in detail, looking at the events, the methods of attack, the effects, Estonia's immediate responses to the attacks, and how Estonian officials characterized the incident. The chapter then considers existing legal analyses of the cyber attacks against Estonia in light of the law on the use of force. It demonstrates how the law's limited conception of violence is evident in the orthodox interpretation of the law on the use of force and its application to the incident. The final section adopts an informational approach, to consider Estonia as an information entity that was subject to cyber attacks causing entropy.

Events

Background and overview

The cyber attacks against Estonia occurred in the wake of the decision by the Estonian Government to relocate a Soviet-era war memorial statue (the

Bronze Soldier). Ultimately the statue was moved from a park in the Tallinn suburb of Tõnismägi to the Defence Forces Cemetery roughly 2 kilometers southeast from its original location. It was the decision to relocate the statue, as well as its actual relocation, that sparked the cyber attacks. The proposed relocation of the statue caused anger among Estonia's ethnic Russians and their supporters in Russia.[5] For the Russians, the statue was a memorial to the Soviet soldiers who died during World War II, whereas for Estonians it was a symbolic reminder of their oppression under the Soviets.[6] Preparations for the removal of the statue on 26 April were accompanied by protests, which led to violence and riots in the streets. The protestors were mostly Estonians of Russian descent, who account for about a quarter of Estonia's population.[7] Given the events of 26 April, the government decided to relocate the statue the following day ahead of schedule.[8] Protests were also held in Russia in response to the removal of the statue, with the Estonian embassy barricaded and ambassadors assaulted.[9] Besides the protests, riots, and violence[10] on the streets of Tallinn, the 'rioting' also spread into cyberspace.[11] Following this, there were numerous waves of cyber attacks lasting over three weeks in total.

Estonia was particularly vulnerable to cyber attacks, given the way it had embedded use of the Internet into public life: everything from communications between the state and its citizens, officials and private sector, to voting, filing of taxes and storage of public records occurred via the Internet. Estonia had also legislated to make access to the Internet a human right.[12] Given the extent to which the Internet and its use were already heavily integrated into public life in 2007, Estonia was considered an extremely wired society even by European standards.[13] Developments leading to this state of affairs began in the 1990s as a part of Estonia's 'Tiger Leap' program,[14] resulting in the creation of what could be described as an 'e-state' (electronic state).[15] This involved the promotion of Internet solutions by banks to reach Estonia's rural population, and efforts by the government to increase access to the Internet through free Internet stations, for example.[16] A digital national population registry system was also created, which stored information about Estonians digitally, whereas a state information system created a common service space that allowed the state to function in cyberspace.[17] The network connecting these services was known as the 'X-Road', and it allowed the online services of both the public and private sectors 'to link up and operate in harmony'.[18] Estonia had also introduced electronic identification cards (e-IDs) in 2002.[19] These were linked to each user's personal information in government databases and enabled people to file taxes, social security or other payment claims, and even in some instances vote online without the need to complete paper forms.[20] The state portal, in turn, provided a centralized online gateway through which these services could be accessed – 'a one-stop-shop for the hundreds of e-services offered by various government institutions'.[21] Therefore, by 2007 Estonia was an advanced state in terms of e-government and integration of the Internet into its people's everyday lives.

As the cyber attacks in the spring of 2007 demonstrated, however, Estonia's technological advancement also represented a vulnerability, effectively exposing its e-state to attack in and through cyberspace.

Events in April and May 2007

Following the removal of the Bronze Soldier and the protests and riots that ensued, Estonia became subject to cyber attacks that varied in intensity and sophistication, beginning in late April 2007 and lasting until the latter half of May 2007. By some accounts, the initial attacks began late on 26 April, the night prior to the removal of the statue.[22] Other accounts regard the first attacks as having occurred in the early hours of 27 April.[23] The first attacks are believed to have targeted the Minister of Foreign Affairs' website, followed by attacks against a wide range of government websites.[24] On 28 April, a number of websites, including that of the prime minister, parliament, government, and Ministry of Foreign Affairs, had been attacked and rendered unreachable to legitimate users.[25] The attacks that took place between 26 April and 29 April are regarded as the technologically less sophisticated 'emotional phase' of the attacks.[26] These attacks made use of quite simple techniques compared with the more sophisticated attacks that, according to cyber security experts, began to occur on 30 April.[27]

The attacks continued periodically between 1 and 8 May. On 2 May, one of Estonia's newspapers was forced to cut off international access to its website due to the volume of traffic that it was facing from the cyber attacks.[28] On 9 May, a significant spike in the attacks occurred. This was expected by the Estonians because it is a politically significant date for Russians, marking their victory over Germany in World War II.[29] The attacks began at midnight Moscow time and were the highest in intensity and duration of all the previous attacks.[30] It is believed that a large botnet was hired for this attack wave.[31] Between 9 and 18 May, government websites continued to be subjected to cyber attacks. Estonian banks were also increasingly targeted during this time – for example, Estonia's largest bank was forced to shut down its online services for one and half to two hours on both 9 and 10 May.[32] The last major attack had occurred by 18 May, although banks continued to experience some minor interruptions.[33]

Over these weeks in April and May 2007, a large number of Estonian websites came under attack, including the websites of the president, prime minister, parliament, most government departments,[34] political parties, media organizations, banks, and ISPs.[35] The attacks also targeted Estonia's Internet infrastructure and information systems, such as the national DNS and the DNSs operated by various ISPs.[36] They also affected the operation of government communication channels and caused slight interruptions to mobile networks[37] as well as to the emergency services line.[38] However, the critical information infrastructure of transportation and energy systems, for example, was not targeted.[39]

Attack methods

The cyber attacks that occurred in the immediate aftermath of the real-world protests and riots made use of relatively simple methods compared with the more sophisticated attacks that began to emerge on 30 April. The less sophisticated methods consisted of both pinging and malformed web queries.[40] In simple terms, pinging is the improper use of a troubleshooting program that is used in Microsoft Windows operating systems. Pinging generally is used when troubleshooting Internet communication problems, and can be done simply by entering a command into Windows' 'Command Prompt'.[41] Doing so sends Internet Control Message Protocol (ICMP) packets to the target address with the expectation that it will reply (provided the connection between the two is working). This method can be exploited when a large number of requests are sent and the target computer has a significantly lower bandwidth than the combination of incoming requests, creating a Denial-of-Service (DoS).[42] A DoS occurs when the target system is subjected to a volume of data that it cannot handle, therefore disrupting the ability of legitimate users to access it or its functions.[43] Files containing command lines allowing for automated commands were also made publicly available to attackers.[44] The use of these files minimized the amount of manual command input required of users, and further automated the process. Some websites were also hacked and defaced – for instance, an apparent apology in Russian was posted on the website of the prime minister's political party.[45] The early cyber attack methods used in the immediate aftermath of the removal of the statue were therefore relatively simple compared with the sophistication of the later attacks.

The more sophisticated attacks that began to appear on 30 April were Distributed Denial-of-Service (DDoS) attacks. A DDoS occurs when multiple computers are used to target one system simultaneously.[46] This is achieved through the use of botnets. A bot (short for robot) is a program designed to perform a certain action when it receives a command.[47] Bots can run in the background of compromised computers, waiting for commands from their controllers.[48] A computer can be compromised and made into a bot (or a 'zombie') without the awareness of its legitimate user, usually with the use of malicious software such as a Trojan.[49] A botnet, in turn, is a network of synchronized bots (a network of robots) performing the commands of their controllers.[50] Hundreds of thousands of compromised computers were involved in the attacks,[51] geographically located across 178 countries including the United States, Vietnam, Egypt, and Peru.[52] The aim of the DDoS attacks was to use the collective force of the botnet to subject the Estonian websites to a higher volume of data than they could handle, causing them to overload and become unreachable for legitimate users. From the information available on the volume of data used in the attacks against Estonia, most were either less than 10 megabits per second (Mbps) or between 10 Mbps and 30 Mbps, and lasted less than an hour. However, some of the attacks were made up of a significantly larger amount of data, reaching over 90 Mbps and lasting more than ten hours.[53] While even 90 Mbps is relatively small on a global scale, it was sufficient to be effective against Estonia, given the low amount of bandwidth it normally requires for its Internet infrastructure, which is relative to the size of its population.[54] In this context, the attacks over 90 Mbps were significant. The largest of these attacks occurred on 9 May, though they suddenly stopped the following day. It is believed that this is when the rental time for the specific botnet expired.[55] A number of different methods of DDoS attack were used, though their general aim was to prevent legitimate users from accessing the targeted websites and the services they provided.[56]

Effects of attacks

Collectively, the DDoS attacks were aimed at disrupting the functioning of the targeted computers and websites, and the services to which they provided access. Some maintain that, while the economic effect of the attacks is difficult to estimate, given that both the public and private sectors were reliant on ICTs and digital communications, the daily operations of various organizations, including banks, government departments and small businesses, were seriously impaired.[57] Other estimates quantify the economic impact of the attacks at between US$27.5 and US$40.5 million.[58] The broader societal effect resulted from a lack of access to information. With government department websites and communication channels inaccessible, the usual means and forms of communication between the government and Estonians were temporarily impaired.[59] Further, given the degree to which important public services were only accessible online, the attacks against the state portal had a 'discernible effect' on many people.[60] Additionally, the attacks also affected the flow of information about the events to the rest of the world. Especially given that most media sites were among the first to come under attack, Estonia was unable to rely on the usual online means for distribution of information.[61]

Estonian defenses

Estonia's defenses in response to the attacks came primarily from its Computer Emergency Response Team (CERT). This team involved cyber security experts from both the public and private sectors,[62] many of whom volunteered their assistance and expertise.[63] The team was also assisted by foreign CERTs and cyber security experts,[64] and both North Atlantic Treaty Organization (NATO) and US experts came to observe and assist with the situation.[65] The success of these experts in rapidly and flexibly responding to the crisis (in terms of information-sharing and decision-making) was due partly to the existing personal relationships between these people, which enabled them to work closely together without the hindrances of inter-agency bureaucracy.[66] For example, an online chat room was organized to provide a forum for information exchange between the various CERTs and cyber security experts across the region; this also provided Estonian authorities with real-time information on the attacks.[67] Some reports also add luck as a factor to their success in mitigating the attacks, given that a number of the cyber security experts were already in Tallinn at the time, due to a meeting of European network operators.[68]

Among the technical measures taken by the CERT was increasing the bandwidth of Estonia's state information system servers in order to handle a larger volume of traffic.[69] It also sought to filter malicious traffic – for example, all traffic originating from '.ru' (Russian) Internet addresses.[70] Other measures included applying security patches to update software, firewalling, attack-detection systems and blocking access.[71] In cooperation with ISPs, incoming traffic was filtered based on patterns that had been identified in the malicious traffic, and network operators were also contacted directly to request the blocking of the course of the traffic.[72] According to leaked diplomatic cables, Estonia's banks were better prepared to defend against the attacks than the government, given that they had the appropriate procedures and defense measures in place due to the prevalence of cyber crime in the region.[73]

Estonian responses and Russian involvement

As mentioned in the introduction to this chapter, the cyber attacks against Estonia marked the first time a state was subject to a large-scale cyber attack amounting to what Estonia's president later described as 'Web War One'.[74] While ultimately dealt with as a criminal matter – especially during the attacks and in their immediate aftermath – there was a degree of uncertainty about how to characterize this novel form of 'cyber violence'.[75] Estonia's immediate responses to the attacks reflected a fear that Estonia was under a partially virtual attack originating from Russia. On 1 May, Estonia's Minister of Foreign Affairs declared that, 'The European Union is under attack, as Russia is attacking Estonia.'[76] The attack was described as 'virtual, psychological and real – all at the same time.'[77] This was echoed the following day in a speech by the prime minister to the Riigikogu (the Estonian Parliament); he stated that the sovereign state of Estonia was 'under a heavy attack'.[78] According to the Minister of Foreign Affairs, the cyber attacks were being launched by cyber terrorists who were using Russian Internet Protocol (IP) addresses to attack Estonian sites and the Russian government was helping create an environment of hostility towards Estonia through its involvement in a propaganda campaign run by Russian state-owned television channels.[79] The Minister of Foreign Affairs assured that the government had 'plenty of evidence to support all of these statements'.[80] The prime minister's speech similarly placed the ongoing cyber attacks in the context of the real-world events that had occurred. He made specific mention of the assault of Estonia's ambassador to Moscow, the tearing of the Estonian flag at its Russian embassy and calls made for a change of government by the delegates of the Russian Duma. In this context, he claimed that Estonia's sovereignty was under attack.[81] Further, the prime minister said Estonia had turned to the European Union for immediate action as one of its member states was under attack.[82] On 3 May, it was reported that Estonia's president had also spoken to the NATO Secretary General, who had 'expressed serious concern about Russia's behavior toward its neighboring state'.[83]

Soon after these initial responses, Estonian officials moved away from describing the incident as an attack on its sovereignty. On 11 May the Minister of Foreign Affairs spoke at a Council of Europe committee meeting about the ongoing incident. While he continued to make reference to 'evidence that these [cyber] attacks are well-coordinated and a significant amount of them originate from Russia',[84] he framed this within the language of cyber crime and the Convention on Cybercrime framework. For example, the Minister of Foreign Affairs stated that, 'Current developments clearly confirm that we need to combat cyber crime in cooperation and international understanding';[85] he went on to strongly urge Russia to take measures against cyber criminals operating within its territory, due to the wider security threat they posed.[86] It was also reported that Estonia's Minister of Defence attended a meeting of EU defense ministers in Brussels on 14 May. The ministers discussed the need for rapid responses to future cyber attacks.[87] In the lead-up to the meeting, Estonia's Minister of Defence made a statement raising issues with whether cyber attacks could constitute military action under the NATO framework, which would allow for the invocation of the North Atlantic Treaty's collective security provisions.[88] In this context, he stated that 'not a single NATO defense minister would define a cyber attack as a clear military action at present; however, this matter needs to be resolved in the near future'.[89] Yet the Minister of Defence is reported to have stated prior to the meeting that the incident 'cannot be treated as hooliganism, but has to be treated as an attack against the state'.[90] A day after the meeting, the Estonian Minister of Defence compared the attacks to terrorism, stating that, given the 'scale of damage and the way these cyber-attacks have been organized, we can compare them to terrorist activities'.[91] The following month (June 2007), the Minister of Defence described the incident to have involved 'cyber-warfare and cyber-terrorism'.[92]

Despite these allegations of Russian state involvement, ultimately the only person officially held responsible has been a 20-year-old Estonian student who was fined for launching an attack against one of the targeted websites.[93] Though Estonian officials managed to track some of the attacks to Russian IP addresses (the assumed location of the computers), they lacked definitive information about the identity of the attackers (the identity of the people physically accessing those computers or doing so virtually from a different geographical location). For example, in response to Estonia's accusations of Russian involvement, a Russian official suggested that its IP addresses could have been used by professional hackers in an attempt to ruin relations between the two countries.[94] Another cyber security expert assisting Estonia in the situation noted that anyone could have been using a computer located there, 'from the son of some ministerial janitor upwards'.[95]

The prevailing view among experts is that no state actor, such as a Russian security agency, was responsible for the attacks, but they were in fact carried out by politically motivated non-state actors.[96] However, and adding to the uncertainty, in March 2009 a member of the Russian Duma maintained that his assistant, a member of a pro-Russian youth group, was responsible for launching the attacks with his associates.[97] This was consistent with some reports in 2007 that this group had admitted its involvement in the attacks.[98] Some note, however, that this account only explains some of the attacks used against Estonia.[99] Others suggest that despite the lack of concrete evidence to prove Russian involvement, given a range of factors relating to the timing, volume and organization of the attacks, the only plausible explanation is that Russian officials gave some degree of approval to the actions of those conducting the cyber attacks.[100] Other experts maintain that it is impossible to prove who was, or was not, responsible for the attacks, based on the technical information available.[101]

The relocation of the Bronze Soldier therefore triggered these cyber attacks against Estonia that lasted over three weeks in total. The cyber attacks did not result in damage to physical objects or injury to human beings, and they were not conducted by human actors wielding kinetic weapons. The DDoS attacks in particular involved unknown human actors controlling synchronized networks of computers, and the effects were felt primarily by Estonia's Internet infrastructure and information systems. The attacks were therefore mainly disruptive, impairing the functionality of a range of computers and services that were closely connected to the daily operation of Estonia's government and civil society.

The ontological constraints of the law

The 2007 cyber attacks against Estonia and the use of force threshold

This section considers the Estonia incident in light of international law on the use of force, with a focus on the use of force threshold. It seeks to show how the limited conception of violence embodied in Article 2(4) undermines its capacity to adequately recognize the harm caused by the cyber attacks against Estonia, and how the incident is equated to a form of non-violence outside of its scope.

Given that the Estonia incident was the first large-scale cyber attack against a nation state, it is widely discussed in international legal scholarship on the legal issues surrounding cyber attacks. A prominent issue raised by the incident was whether attacks of this kind could amount to a use of force under Article 2(4).[102] However, the prevailing view is that the incident would not qualify as a use of force largely because the attacks did not result in material effects, such as damage to computer hardware or injury to human beings. Illustrative of this position is Russel Buchan's argument that because the cyber attacks against Estonia did not cause any physical damage and were merely disruptive, they cannot amount to a use of force: 'a violation of Article 2(4) will only occur where a weapon is used that produces physical damage'.[103] He therefore argues that 'in the absence of physical damage … the cyber attacks committed against Estonia cannot be regarded as an unlawful use of force for the purposes of Article 2(4)'.[104]

Nicholas Tsagourias also questions whether the attacks against Estonia would constitute a use of force. Commenting on the incident in light of the *Tallinn Manual* criteria, he maintains in relation to the attacks that:

> Their severity (in view of the duration and scope of the attack) was limited, and their harmful effect was limited and containable; the invasiveness of the attack was superficial and whereas there were some direct consequences, other consequences – economic or financial – were rather remote.[105]

Others also argue that the Estonian incident would not amount to a use of force even under the *Tallinn Manual* criteria. Michael Gervais, for example, maintains that the 'severity' of the cyber attacks against Estonia falls short of a use of force, as the consequences were minimal and, 'There was no physical damage or measurable suffering.'[106]

Michael Schmitt also adopts the position that under existing law the cyber attacks against Estonia would not amount to a use of force. He argues, however, that the incident could be viewed as such under the *Tallinn Manual* criteria – or at least this is the likely direction in which the law will develop.[107] In relation to the *Tallinn Manual* criteria, he writes in relation to the severity of the incident that, while no deaths, injury or physical damage resulted, the attacks 'fundamentally affected the operation of the entire Estonian society'.[108] This was evident in the severe disruption of government functions and services, and the negative effects on the economy and the daily life of the Estonian people. As to the immediacy of the consequences, he maintains that the impact on the confidence in government and economic activity was more than merely an inconvenience, and had an immediate effect that was widespread and long term in nature. The consequences of the attacks were also direct, as people were unable to access funds and government benefits, and invasive because some of the targeted systems were designed to be secure. In relation to their measurability, Schmitt maintains that it is hard to quantify this because the consequences mainly involved denial of service opposed to the destruction of data. Finally, in relation to presumptive legitimacy (assuming the requirement for Russian state responsibility is satisfied), he maintains that the attacks were more than political or economic pressure (which would fall outside the traditional use of force analysis), as they 'involved intentionally frustrating governmental and economic functions'.[109] Therefore, considering the *Tallinn Manual* criteria in relation to the Estonia incident, he argues that, according to this approach, the cyber attacks collectively would amount to what is regarded (or should be regarded) as a use of force by the international community.[110] However, he emphasizes that these criteria only suggest the probable direction in which the law will develop in the future; the position in existing law remains intact.[111] Therefore, under existing law according to Schmitt, the cyber attacks against Estonia would not amount to a use of force.

As the cyber attacks against Estonia are considered to be below the use of force threshold mainly because no material harm or destruction was caused, the incident is treated as a potential breach of the non-intervention principle. Buchan argues that even though no physical damage was caused, given the duration and severity of the attacks, they 'crossed the threshold of exerting influence and amounted to the intentional application of coercion against the Estonian government, seeking to force it to reverse its policy to relocate the statue of the Bronze Solider'.[112] He maintains, therefore, that the cyber attacks constituted a violation of Estonia's sovereignty and breached the non-intervention principle.[113] Tsagourias takes a similar position, arguing that even if the attacks were not a use of force, 'they could amount to unlawful intervention because their aim was to change the Estonian government's decision to relocate a Soviet era statue, provided however that they were attributed to a state'.[114] Similarly, Anders Henriksen maintains that while the incident did not reach a threshold triggering the right to self-defense,[115] if Russia was responsible and 'intended to coerce the Estonia[n] politicians to undo their decision to remove the war memorial', then it would amount to a breach of the non-intervention principle.[116] Consequently, because the cyber attacks – despite their duration and severity – did not cause material damage, they cannot be regarded as a use of force under existing law. Instead, they are at best viewed as a breach of the non-intervention principle.

In making this distinction primarily on the basis of the whether or not the cyber attacks had material effects, these legal analyses of the Estonia incident reveal the law's limited conception of violence. The conception of violence underpinning Article 2(4) is inherently anthropocentric and materialist in the sense that there is a need for injury or death of human beings, or damage or destruction of material objects, for the law to be capable of recognizing the harm caused by cyber attacks as real. As a result, mainly disruptive non-material cyber attacks like those against Estonia cannot be recognized sufficiently by the law. Further, by depicting the incident as a potential breach of the non-intervention principle alone, these analyses of the incident effectively liken the attacks to a form of non-violence outside the scope of law on the use of force. This rests on the problematic assumption that, despite the degree to which states such as Estonia rely on the functioning of ICTs in the proper operation of their governmental and societal functions, disrupting these processes is not sufficiently serious to constitute a potential violation of Article 2(4). The Estonia incident therefore demonstrates how Article 2(4) is underpinned by an outdated conception of violence, as states can be harmed even where the functioning of processes and networks is undermined, and merely viewing such attacks as potential breaches of the non-intervention principle does not account sufficiently for this reality.[117] Accordingly, under existing law, non-material cyber attacks escape the doctrinal and conceptual bounds of the law seeking to regulate interstate violence. As demonstrated in Chapters 3 and 4, the reasons are ontological as the harm caused by non-material attacks is to virtual entities and processes – such as to data and to the operation of computer systems – and hence the violence associated with cyber attacks is different from traditional warfare. Consequently, as the next section will demonstrate, an informational reconceptualization of violence offers a means by which to overcome these limitations, and provides a way to consider non-material cyber attacks as a form of informational violence against the state.

An informational approach

This section considers the cyber attacks against Estonia through an informational approach to demonstrate how such an approach provides an alternative means to consider and assess the impact of the attacks in the informational environment in which the Estonian government and civil society functioned. Drawing on the way the state was re-described as an information entity and how the notion of violence was reconceptualized through the notion of entropy in Chapter 3, this section first describes the Estonian entity as an information system, then considers the cyber attacks against Estonia in April and May 2007 in terms of the entropy they produced. It is argued that the cyber attacks – particularly the DDoS attacks that disrupted the functioning of Estonia's government and civil society – produced significant increases in entropy. In addition to infringing on Estonia's autonomy and ability to interact, these attacks infringed its essence as an entity by threatening its ability to care for and protect the entities within its region of the infosphere.

The Estonian entity

As a dynamic entity, in its usual state Estonia is subject to continuous flows of information moving in and out of it. Within its region of the infosphere, approximately 82 per cent of households have Internet access,[118] there is a growing number of Internet users,[119] the levels of access to ICTs are high, the ICT infrastructure is well developed and there is a high level of use of ICTs across society.[120] In terms of the economic impact of ICTs, Estonia also ranks high globally, reflecting a shift towards knowledge-intensive activities in its economy.[121] Similarly, there are continuous capital flows in and out of its economy.[122] In addition to these information flows, when viewed informationally, all potential entities can be seen as information patterns or structures moving in and out of Estonia's region of the infosphere. Everything from the migration of humans to trade in goods can therefore be seen as part of the changing flow of the informational substance of Estonia. This entity is situated within a particular region of the infosphere – both in its territory and in the virtual environment of cyberspace. Therefore, particularly given its developed ICT infrastructure and the continuous flows of information that it continuously receives, processes and communicates, Estonia can be seen as a dynamic entity with a continuously changing informational substance.

The systematic features of Estonia as an information system – its ability to interact, its autonomy and its ability to adapt – delineate it as an entity separate from other entities. Its autonomy as an information system – that is, its ability to act independently from other entities – was re-established in 1991 when it regained its political independence from the Soviet Union. As an entity, it is capable of interaction – both with its internal sub-entities and sub-systems (humans, corporations, government institutions) and externally with regional organizations like the European Union and NATO. Similarly, its ability to adapt as an entity and interact with other entities is highlighted by its decision to become a component of the larger EU information system, which it joined in 2004. Its adaptability is also highlighted by the measures it took in response to the cyber attacks, as will be shown below.

The form or pattern of Estonia as an information system is evident in its information structures. Its unicameral parliament (the Riigikogu), Supreme Court and lower courts, executive government including the offices of the prime minister and president, and various government departments can all be seen as the informational structures through which Estonia as an information system was configured. While the humans occupying various positions within these sub-systems or components of Estonia can change, as can their exact configuration, the persisting form or pattern of the organization of these information structures delineates Estonia.

The protocols governing the information exchanges between these components and other entities within Estonia's region of the infosphere come from its internal laws, policies and procedures. In addition to the constitution and other protocols configuring these sub-systems and their functions and tasks, there are also protocols according to which the people of Estonia can interact with these entities. In terms of the everyday operation of Estonia's government and civil society, the information exchanges that take place involve a range of interactions between Estonian government institutions, the private sector and individuals. Government communications with citizens, voting in elections, filing of social security applications, the filing of taxes, banking and so forth all increasingly occur online, captured by the notion of 'e-Stonia' or 'e-state' that Estonia had become.[123] The relationship between Estonians and the government became one integrated with ICTs – by verifying their digital identities with e-IDs through computer interfaces, Estonians can access various services linked to databases storing information about them, all connected by the X-Road, or what is described as the 'backbone of e-Estonia'.[124] These processes involve interaction between various entities – humans, computer hardware and software, and public and private sector organizations. ICTs are at the core of these interactions, as are the various protocols enabling these interactions and the information exchanges between these entities.

The purpose of Estonia as an information system is to care for and protect its region of the infosphere. This means protecting itself as an entity from entropy from other entities, and caring for the well-being of this region to minimize increases in entropy. Consequently, its ultimate purpose as an entity is to protect the natural environment (from environmental pollution, for example), its physical territory (from traditional military threats) and the virtual environment of cyberspace (from cyber threats such as DDoS attacks). Therefore, the flourishing or well-being of Estonia as an information system depends on its ability to care for and protect its region of the infosphere, and its ability to prevent increases in entropy.

The cyber attacks against Estonia and entropy

Against this account of Estonia as an information system, the harm caused by the cyber attacks can be viewed in terms of the increases in entropy that they produced. Unlike the usual information flows into Estonia, the cyber attacks were different, as they sought to disrupt the proper functioning of its government and civil society. As such, they constituted hostile information flows seeking to increase entropy within Estonia. The cyber attacks produced entropy as they infringed on Estonia's ability to interact, its autonomy and its very essence as an information system. However, the increases in entropy that were produced varied in degree when comparing the initial 'emotional phase' of the attacks with the later DDoS attacks.

The 'emotional phase' of the attacks from 26 April to 29 April, which involved unsophisticated methods such as pinging and defacement of websites, can be said to have caused only minor increases in entropy. These information flows primarily affected access to these sites and changed the content of some of them.[125] These attacks did not disrupt the interactions between the components integral to the functioning of Estonia, such as access to government services and banking, or the communications channels of government officials. The impact of these attacks was minor in terms of infringing on Estonia's ability to interact and its autonomy, as it was mainly access to websites that was affected. Also, given the lack of sophistication in attack methods, Estonia was easily capable of adapting to these attacks by increasing bandwidth, for example. Similarly, these attacks did not significantly infringe upon Estonia's ability to fulfil its purpose of caring for and protecting the entities within its region of the infosphere. Therefore, while these attacks did cause some increases in entropy, the increases were only temporary and minimal, and did not significantly disrupt the functioning of Estonia as an information system. Further, given its adaptability as a system, it was able to take measures to manage these information flows and prevent them from causing significant increases in entropy.

In contrast, the more sophisticated attacks resulted in more significant increases in entropy. Instead of merely rendering some websites inaccessible, these attacks had a more significant and wide effect on Estonia's informational infrastructure, impacting interactions between its components for a prolonged period of time. Consequently, these attacks affected the very essence of Estonia as an information system, challenging its purpose as an entity, its ability to interact and its autonomy, but also demonstrating its adaptability as a system. The DDoS attacks involved hundreds of thousands of computers that had been compromised by malicious software. The properties of these entities had been corrupted, meaning they were able to be used as slaves to cause significant increases in the amount of information flowing into Estonia. The corruption of these computers itself can be seen to have produced entropy on a global level, as it meant that the integrity of hundreds of thousands of entities had been undermined. However, only when this botnet was used against Estonia can it be said to have sought to cause entropy within Estonia specifically. When used in the DDoS attack, the information requests that were sent by this collective of corrupted computers were aimed at disrupting the functioning of Estonia's information infrastructure. As such, they were different from the legitimate requests that would come from human users seeking to utilize a single computer as a means to access and interact with websites or the information and services to which they provide access. Instead of many individual users sending malicious requests to Estonian information systems, as in the initial phase of the attacks, the virtually organized network of artificial entities allowed human users to significantly multiply the amount of information sent into Estonia. The systematic and sustained flow of information caused by these attacks resulted in more significant increases in entropy as they disrupted Estonia's proper functioning as an information system.

By exploiting a range of information exchange channels that normally enabled the natural flow of information in and out of Estonia, the DDoS attacks subjected Estonian information networks to more data than it had the processing power and bandwidth to handle under normal conditions. These attacks impacted the availability of services provided by various sub-systems, from banking to government emails, limiting human access to information and services, and preventing various computers and networks from functioning properly. They thus resulted in more significant increases in entropy than the 'emotional phase' of the attacks. They disrupted the availability of government and commercial services integral to the functioning of Estonian civil society, and therefore also disrupted the functioning of Estonia as an information system. For example, the DDoS attacks on 1 May that resulted in ISPs needing to reboot their systems – albeit only for 20 seconds[126] – disrupted the functioning of a range of computer systems and the services to which they provided access. This also affected human users reliant on the ISP for their Internet connections. Similarly, the attacks on Estonia's largest banks – Hansabank on 9 May and 10 May, and SEB Eesti Ühispank on 15 May – required the banks to shut down online services for at least one and a half hours on each occasion. While some of the attacks on a range of government websites throughout the first weeks of May lasted for under an hour, many of them lasted up to five hours, and some attacks lasted for more than ten hours.[127] Even though some of these attacks were short in duration, together they resulted in a sustained attack against government networks.[128] For example, the Estonian parliament's email service was down for twelve hours as a result of the attacks.[129] Similarly, the attacks disrupted the online availability of public services, particularly for Estonians overseas.[130]

Collectively, the DDoS attacks that began to appear on 30 April and lasted into the second half of May resulted in more significant increases in entropy than the initial 'emotional phase' of the attacks. While they did not cause any known material damage, they undermined Estonia's ability to interact, its autonomy and its essence as an entity. Its autonomy in deciding the location of physical structures within its territory (such as war memorial statues) was challenged. The interactions of its internal components and entities within its region of the infosphere – including its citizens, government departments and services, and banking – were disrupted over numerous occasions for long periods of time, also affecting those Estonians outside of its region of the infosphere, who were unable to access these services. These attacks also undermined the very essence of Estonia as an information system, as the disruptions to the functioning of its government and civil society undermined its ability to care for and protect the entities within its region of the infosphere. Therefore, in contrast to the 'emotional phase' of the attacks, the DDoS attacks caused a more significant degree of entropy, disrupting the proper functioning of Estonia and its society.

Estonia's efforts to mitigate the effects of the attacks also demonstrated that, as an information system, it regarded these information flows as capable of increasing entropy, and that they needed to be minimized or prevented. Its ability to respond to the attacks, however, also demonstrated its adaptability as an information system. A range of virtual entities such as software patches were utilized to remove vulnerabilities in computers, firewalls were set up to filter and block malicious data, and attack-detection systems were used to monitor and assist in detecting attacks. Similarly, by increasing server bandwidth, Estonia was able to increase the capacity of its systems to function, and thus prevent the increases in entropy that would otherwise have been caused by the high volume of traffic. Also, to prevent hostile data from entering Estonia, large parts of the network were closed to people outside its region of the infosphere, meaning Estonians overseas could not access their bank accounts[131] or public services.[132] To preserve its own functioning and well-being as an information system, Estonia to a degree disconnected itself from parts of the infosphere so that it could better protect the interactions between its internal components. All these measures were taken in order to minimize and undermine the ability of the DDoS attacks to cause further increases in entropy within Estonia. By taking these measures, Estonia demonstrated that it was not operating under the usual conditions in which information flowed in and out of its system, but that it was being subject to information flows capable of causing increases in entropy. Additionally, through these measures it sought to prevent further increases in entropy and protect its proper functioning, and this also demonstrated its adaptability as an information system.

Conclusion

Accordingly, an informational approach provides a means through which to reimagine the state as an entity subject to violence, and the harm caused by cyber attacks in terms of the entropy they produce. Estonia can be seen as an information system – a dynamic but systematic entity that is constituted by information structures and protocols, located within a particular region of the infosphere. The cyber attacks to which it was subject in April and May 2007 caused various degrees of increases in entropy. The DDoS attacks in particular, by disrupting the operation of government and civil society, constituted hostile information flows into the Estonian entity and undermined its ability to function properly. These attacks undermined its ability to interact, its autonomy and its capacity to care for and protect its region of the infosphere. They thus constituted a form of informational violence against the Estonian entity, despite the lack of material damage to physical objects or injury to human beings.

This is in contrast to the way in which existing legal analyses consider the harm caused by the attacks against Estonia, particularly given the fixation on damage to physical objects or injury to human beings evident within the use of force analysis. Effectively, the law is limited to regulating only certain forms of entropy that involve an entity's material degradation or destruction. As the Estonia incident demonstrated, increasingly ICT-dependent information societies can be subject to novel forms of violence that, while capable of seriously disrupting the functioning of those societies, escape the central doctrines of international law regulating interstate violence. Had the cyber attacks directly caused damage to hardware or injury to human beings, they would more readily have fallen within the understanding of violence embodied in the law, and been considered to have constituted a use of force under existing law. As this was not the case, the non-intervention principle is deemed to be applicable, meaning the incident effectively is depicted as a form of non-violence below the use of force threshold. However, this characterization does not take incidents such as the incident that occurred in Estonia sufficiently seriously, and fails to account adequately for the new ways in which states rely on the functioning of ICTs for the proper operation of their governmental and societal functions.[133]

By reconceptualizing violence through the notion of entropy and viewing the state entity in informational terms, a broader ontological spectrum of violence can be recognized by the law. As the Estonia incident demonstrated, this is warranted given the changing nature of violence in a world of increasingly ICT-dependent information societies that exist not simply in a physical, territorial space, but also virtually in cyberspace and as part of the infosphere. Yet non-material cyber attacks effectively are reduced to something outside the dominant legal doctrines regulating interstate violence, as evidenced by the depiction of such attacks as a form of non-violence below the use of force threshold. Instead, by adopting an informational approach, the cyber attacks against Estonia can be regarded as constituting a form of informational violence against the state.

Notes

1. Jeff Goldstein, 'Estonia's Cyber Attacks: Lessons Learned' (Wikileaks Cable, 6 June 2007) <https://wikileaks.org/plusd/cables/07TALLINN375_a.html> accessed 2 March 2018.
2. The *Washington Post* described it as 'cyber-warfare' (see 'Pushback for Mr. Putin', *Washington Post* (19 May 2007) <www.washingtonpost.com/wp-dyn/content/article/2007/05/18/AR2007051801722.html> accessed 2 March 2018, as did *The Guardian*: see Ian Traynor, 'Russia Accused of Unleashing Cyberwar to Disable Estonia' *The Guardian* (17 May 2007) <www.theguardian.com/world/2007/may/17/topstories3.russia> accessed 2 March 2018. *The New York Times* depicted it as 'the first war in cyberspace': see Mark Landler and John Markoff, 'Digital Fears Emerge After Data Siege in Estonia' *New York Times* (29 May 2007) <www.nytimes.com/2007/05/29/technology/29estonia.html?_r=0> accessed 2 March 2018.
3. Toomas H Ilves, 'Address by the President of Estonia' (speech at the 67th Session of the United Nations General Assembly, New York, 26 September 2012) <https://vp2006-2016.president.ee/en/official-duties/speeches/7991-address-by-h-e-toomas-hendrik-ilves-president-of-estonia-to-the-67th-session-of-the-united-nations-general-assembly-un-headquarters-new-york-september-2012> accessed 2 March 2018.
4. Charles Clover, 'Kremlin-backed group behind Estonia cyber blitz' *Financial Times* (11 March 2009) <www.ft.com/intl/cms/s/0/57536d5a-0ddc-11de-8ea3-0000779fd2ac.html> accessed 15 November 2016.
5. Traynor (n 2); Landler and Markoff (n 2).
6. 'Estonia urges firm EU, NATO response to new form of warfare: cyber-attacks' *Sydney Morning Herald* (17 May 2007) <www.smh.com.au/technology/estonia-urges-firm-eu-nato-response-to-new-form-of-warfare-cyberattacks-20070516-d1h.html> accessed 2 March 2018.
7. ibid.
8. Steven L Myers, 'Russia Rebukes Estonia for Moving Soviet Statue' *New York Times* (27 April 2007) <www.nytimes.com/2007/04/27/world/europe/27cnd-estonia.html> accessed 2 March 2018.
9. Ian Traynor, 'EU Protests Over Russian Attacks on Ambassadors' *The Guardian* (3 May 2007) <www.theguardian.com/world/2007/may/03/russia.eu> accessed 2 March 2018.

10 Dozens were injured and one person died: see Myers (n 8).

11 Traynor (n 2); 'A Cyber Riot' *The Economist* (10 May 2007) <www.economist.com/node/9163598> accessed 2 March 2018.

12 *Telecommunications Act* (Estonia) Art 5(2).

13 Traynor (n 2).

14 Pille Runnell and others, 'The Estonian Tiger Leap from Post-Communism to the Information Society: From Policy to Practice' (2009) 40(1) *Journal of Baltic Studies* 29, 29–30.

15 Eneken Tikk and Reet Oorn, *Legal and Policy Evaluation: International Coordination of Prosecution and Prevention of Cyber Terrorism* (IOS Press 2008) 93.

16 ibid.

17 Republic of Estonia Information System Authority, 'State information system in Estonia' (2007) 1 <www.ria.ee/public/publikatsioonid/state_IS.pdf> accessed 2 March 2018.

18 'X-Road' (*E-Estonia*) <https://e-estonia.com/solutions/interoperability-services/x-road> accessed 2 March 2018.

19 'The Estonian ID Card' (Republic of Estonia Information System Authority) <www.ria.ee/en/id-card.html> accessed 2 March 2018.

20 Republic of Estonia Information System Authority, 'The State Portal «eesti.ee»' (2007) 2 <www.ria.ee/public/publikatsioonid/State_portal.pdf> accessed 2 March 2018.

21 'State e-Services Portal' (*E-Estonia*) <https://e-estonia.com/solutions/e-governance/state-e-services-portal> accessed 2 March 2018.

22 Gadi Evron, 'Battling Botnets and Online Mobs: Estonia's Defense Efforts During the Internet War' (2008) 9(1) *Georgetown Journal of International Affairs* 121, 123; Landler and Markoff (n 2).

23 Rain Ottis, 'Analysis of the 2007 Cyber Attacks Against Estonia from the Information Warfare Perspective' in Dan Remenyi (ed), *Proceedings of the 7th European Conference on Information Warfare and Security* (Academic Publishing 2008) 164; Miska Rantanen, 'Virtual Harassment, but for Real' *Helsingin Sanomat* (6 May 2007) <www.hs.fi/english/article/Virtual+harassment+but+for+real+/1135227099868> accessed 24 June 2016; Tikk and Oorn (n 15) 96; Eneken Tikk, Kadri Kaska and Liis Vihul, *International Cyber Incidents: Legal Considerations* (NATO Cooperative Cyber Defence Centre of Excellence 2010) 18.

24 Rantanen (n 23).

25 F-Secure, 'Declaration of Cyber War I: Distributed Denial of Service (DDoS) Attacks in Estonia' in *Threat Summaries Volume 2 2011–2007* (F-Secure Labs, 2012) 49 <www.f-secure.com/documents/996508/1030743/threat_summaries_2011_2007.pdf> accessed 2 March 2018.

26 Tikk, Kaska and Vihul (n 23) 18.

27 Peter Finn, 'Cyber Assaults on Estonia Typify a New Battle Tactic' *Washington Post* (19 May 2007) <www.washingtonpost.com/wp-dyn/content/article/2007/05/18/AR2007051802122.html> accessed 2 March 2018.

28 Joshua Davis, 'Hackers Take Down the Most Wired Country in Europe' *Wired* (21 August 2007) <www.wired.com/2007/08/ff-estonia> accessed 2 March 2018.

29 Landler and Markoff (n 2).

30 Jose Nazario, 'Estonian DDoS Attacks – A Summary to Date' (*Arbor Networks*, 17 May 2007) <www.arbornetworks.com/blog/asert/estonian-ddos-attacks-a-summary-to-date> accessed 2 March 2018.

31 Iain Thomson, 'Russia "Hired Botnets" for Estonia Cyber-war' *ITnews* (1 June 2007) <www.itnews.com.au/news/russia-hired-botnets-for-estonia-cyber-war-82600> accessed 2 March 2018; Landler and Markoff (n 2). A botnet is a network of externally controlled 'robot' computers.

32 Landler and Markoff (n 2); Finn (n 27).

33 Landler and Markoff (n 2).
34 For a list, see Nazario (n 30).
35 Landler and Markoff (n 2); Finn (n 27).
36 Tikk, Kaska and Vihul (n 23) 21.
37 ibid 22.
38 'Marching Off to Cyberwar' *The Economist* (4 December 2008) <www.economist.com/node/12673385> accessed 2 March 2018.
39 Tikk, Kaska and Vihul (n 23) 21.
40 ibid 18–19.
41 Mitch Tulloch, *Microsoft Encyclopedia of Security* (Microsoft Press 2003) 246.
42 ibid.
43 Jelena Mirkovic et al, *Internet Denial of Service: Attack and Defense Mechanisms* (Prentice-Hall 2005) 2.
44 Tikk, Kaska and Vihul (n 23) 19.
45 ibid 21.
46 Mirkovic et al (n 63) 3.
47 Bots commonly operate in Internet Relay Chat (IRC) client programs. IRC is a network of servers that relay text chat messages to each other or their users (clients) that are connected to an IRC server. See ibid 294–5.
48 ibid 62.
49 Trojans are malicious software 'designed to reach a target stealthily and to be executed inadvertently'. Alan Calder and Steve G Watkins, 'Trojan' in *ISO27000 and Information Security: A Combined Glossary* (IT Governance 2010). These computers can then be centrally controlled and form a botnet, see Evron (n 22) 124.
50 Mirkovic and others (n 63) 291.
51 Landler and Markoff (n 2).
52 Clover (n 4); Davis (n 28); Landler and Markoff (n 2).
53 Nazario (n 30).
54 Steve Mansfield-Devine, 'Estonia: What Doesn't Kill You Makes You Stronger' [2012] (7) *Network Security* 12, 14.
55 Thomson (n 31); Landler and Markoff (n 2).
56 See Nazario (n 30); Ottis (n 23) 165.
57 Tikk, Kaska and Vihul (n 23) 24.
58 Sheng Li, 'When Does Internet Denial Trigger the Right of Armed Self-Defense?' (2013) 38(1) *Yale Journal of International Law* 179, 200.
59 Tikk, Kaska and Vihul (n 23) 25.
60 ibid.
61 ibid.
62 ibid 24.
63 Evron (n 22) 123.
64 ibid 124.
65 Tikk, Kaska and Vihul (n 23) 24; Finn (n 27).
66 Goldstein (n 1).
67 Evron (n 22) 124.
68 Davis (n 28).
69 Tikk, Kaska and Vihul (n 23) 24.
70 Finn (n 27).
71 Tikk, Kaska and Vihul (n 23) 24.
72 ibid.
73 Goldstein (n 1).
74 Ilves (n 3).
75 Estonia's President Toomas Hendrik Ilves used this vocabulary to describe the threat posed by cyber attacks. See Toomas H Ilves, 'Address by the President

of Estonia' (Speech at the 62nd Session of the United Nations General Assembly, New York, 25 September 2007) <www.un.org/webcast/ga/62/2007/pdfs/estonia-eng.pdf> accessed 2 March 2018.

76 Republic of Estonia Government, 'Declaration of the Minister of Foreign Affairs of the Republic of Estonia' (Media Release, 1 May 2007) <www.valitsus.ee/en/news/declaration-minister-foreign-affairs-republic-estonia> accessed 2 March 2018.

77 ibid.

78 Republic of Estonia Government, 'Prime Minister Andrus Ansip's speech in Riigikogu' (Media Release, 2 May 2007) <www.valitsus.ee/en/news/prime-minister-andrus-ansips-speech-riigikogu> accessed 2 March 2018.

79 The TV channels reported that Estonian defence forces had been ordered to shoot at Russians: see Republic of Estonia Government, 'Declaration of the Minister of Foreign Affairs of the Republic of Estonia' (n 96).

80 ibid.

81 Republic of Estonia Government, 'Prime Minister Andrus Ansip's speech in Riigikogu' (n 98).

82 ibid.

83 Office of the President of the Republic of Estonia, 'NATO Secretary General to the President of the Republic: The Alliance Supports Estonia' (Media Release, 3 May 2007) <https://vp2006-2016.president.ee/en/media/press-releases/1387-nato-secretary-general-to-the-president-of-the-republic-the-alliance-supports-estonia/index.html> accessed 2 March 2018.

84 Republic of Estonia Ministry of Foreign Affairs, 'Address by Minister of Foreign Affairs of Estonia Urmas Paet' (Media Release, 11 May 2007) <http://vm.ee/en/news/address-minister-foreign-affairs-estonia-urmas-paet> accessed 2 March 2018.

85 ibid.

86 ibid.

87 Republic of Estonia Ministry of Defence, 'Minister Addresses Cyber Attacks at Meeting of EU Defence Ministers' (Media Release, 14 May 2007) <www.kaitseministeerium.ee/en/news/minister-addresses-cyber-attacks-meeting-eu-defence-ministers> accessed 2 March 2018.

88 Republic of Estonia Ministry of Defence, 'Minister to Attend Meeting of EU Defence Ministers in Brussels' (Media Release, 13 May 2007) <www.kaitseministeerium.ee/en/news/minister-attend-meeting-eu-defence-ministers-brussels> accessed 2 March 2018.

89 ibid.

90 'US Warns Cyber-attacks will Increase' *Financial Times* (17 May 2007) <www.ft.com/intl/cms/s/0/324fa472-049e-11dc-80ed-000b5df10621.html> accessed 2 March 2018.

91 'Estonia Urges Firm EU, NATO Response to New Form of Warfare: Cyber-attacks' (n 6).

92 Jaak Aaviksoo, 'Cyber-Defense: Estonia's Recent Experience of this Unnoticed Third World War' (Speech at the Center for Strategic Decision Research 24th International Workshop on Global Security, Paris, 2007) <www.csdr.org/2007book/aaviksoo07.htm> accessed 2 March 2018.

93 'Estonia Fines Man for "Cyber War"' *BBC News* (25 January 2008) <http://news.bbc.co.uk/2/hi/technology/7208511.stm> accessed 2 March 2018.

94 Finn (n 27).

95 Rantanen (n 23).

96 Shaun Waterman, 'Analysis: Who Cyber Smacked Estonia?' United Press International (11 June 2007) <www.upi.com/Defense-News/2007/06/11/Analysis-Who-cyber-smacked-Estonia/26831181580439> accessed 2 March 2018; Jose

Nazario, 'Politically Motivated Denial of Service Attacks' in Christian Czosseck and Kenneth Geers (eds), *The Virtual Battlefield: Perspectives on Cyber Warfare* (IOS Press 2009); Gadi Evron, 'Authoritatively, Who was Behind the Estonian Attacks?' (*Dark Reading*, 17 May 2009) <www.darkreading.com/risk/authoritatively-who-was-behind-the-estonian-attacks/d/d-id/1130584> accessed 2 March 2018. See also Tikk, Kaska and Vihul (n 23) 23–4.

97 Clover (n 4); Noah Shachtman, 'Kremlin Kids: We Launched the Estonian Cyber War' *Wired* (11 March 2009) <www.wired.com/2009/03/pro-kremlin-gro> accessed 2 March 2018.

98 Evron (n 96).

99 Tikk, Kaska and Vihul (n 23) 23–4.

100 Ottis (n 23).

101 Evron (n 96).

102 Among the authors expressly taking a view on this are Michael N Schmitt, 'Cyber Operations and the *Jus Ad Bellum* Revisited' (2011) 56(3) *Villanova Law Review* 569, 577; Russell Buchan, 'Cyber Attacks: Unlawful Uses of Force or Prohibited Interventions?' (2012) 17(2) *Journal of Conflict & Security Law* 211, 219; Terry D Gill and Paul AL Ducheine, 'Anticipatory Self-Defense in the Cyber Context' (2013) 89 *International Law Studies Series US Naval War College* 438, 458–9; Li (n 78) 182.

103 Buchan (n 102) 219.

104 ibid.

105 Nicholas Tsagourias, 'The *Tallinn Manual on the International Law* Applicable to Cyber Warfare: A Commentary on Chapter II – The Use of Force' in Terry D Gill (ed), *Yearbook of International Humanitarian Law Volume 15* (Springer 2014) 25.

106 Michael Gervais, 'Cyber Attacks and the Laws of War' (2012) 30(2) *Berkeley Journal of International Law* 525, 540. Gervais goes on to discuss the cyber attack disrupting emergency services, and maintains that this specific incident should amount to a use of force under the *Tallinn Manual* criteria.

107 Schmitt (n 102) 605.

108 ibid 577.

109 ibid.

110 ibid.

111 ibid 605. Other commentators, such as Sheng Li, also note the existing law's limtations and develop alternate arguments about to how the incident could be seen as a use of force. Li likens the cyber attacks to an information blockade that, like a naval blockade, should constitute a use of force as it threatened the welfare of a state and its people, who were 'heavily dependent upon access to digital information for their physical and material well-being'. Li (n 78) 196.

112 Buchan (n 102) 226.

113 ibid.

114 Tsagourias (n 105) 25.

115 Anders Henriksen, 'Lawful State Responses to Low-Level Cyber-Attacks' (2015) 84(2) *Nordic Journal of International Law* 323, 327.

116 ibid 340.

117 These limitations arguably are also recognized by others, such as Schmitt and Li, who seek to make arguments for how the cyber attacks against Estonia could be considered a use of force – or at least that the law should develop in that direction. See Schmitt (n 102) 577; Li (n 78) 196.

118 International Telecommunication Union, *Measuring the Information Society Report* (ITU, 2015) 219 <www.itu.int/en/ITU-D/Statistics/Documents/publications/misr2015/MISR2015-w5.pdf> accessed 2 March 2018.

119 'Individuals using the Internet (% of population)' (The World Bank) <https://data.worldbank.org/indicator/IT.NET.USER.ZS?locations=EE> accessed 2 March 2018.
120 International Telecommunication Union (n 118) 46.
121 Silja Baller, Soumitra Dutta and Bruno Lanvin (eds), *The Global Information Technology Report 2016* (World Economic Forum, 2016) 92 <www3.weforum.org/docs/GITR2016/GITR_2016_full%20report_final.pdf> accessed 2 March 2018.
122 'Economy in Numbers' (Republic of Estonia Ministry of Foreign Affairs, 16 June 2017) <http://vm.ee/en/economy-numbers> accessed 2 March 2018.
123 On a range of components of Estonia's digital society, ranging from e-government to e-health and e-education initiatives in Estonia, see 'Building Blocks of E-Estonia' (*E-Estonia*) <https://e-estonia.com/solutions> accessed 2 March 2018.
124 'X-Road' (n 18).
125 For example, the website of Prime Minister Andrus Ansip's political party was hacked and an apparent apology in Russian was posted. See Tikk, Kaska and Vihul (n 23) 21.
126 Finn (n 27).
127 Nazario (n 30).
128 ibid.
129 Finn (n 27).
130 Tikk, Kaska and Vihul (n 23) 25.
131 Landler and Markoff (n 2).
132 Tikk, Kaska and Vihul (n 23) 25.
133 Li, for example, is also critical of this tendency in the literature to consider non-material cyber attacks as a breach of the non-intervention principle instead of Article 2(4), as it would essentially permit states to launch cyber attacks short of physical effects without triggering the consequences that flow from uses of force. See Li (n 78) 214.

Bibliography

Aaviksoo J, 'Cyber-Defense: Estonia's Recent Experience of this Unnoticed Third World War' (Speech at the Center for Strategic Decision Research 24th International Workshop on Global Security, Paris, 2007) <www.csdr.org/2007book/aaviksoo07.htm> accessed 2 March 2018

Baller S, Dutta S and Lanvin B (eds), *The Global Information Technology Report 2016* (World Economic Forum, 2016) <www3.weforum.org/docs/GITR2016/GITR_2016_full%20report_final.pdf> accessed 2 March 2018

Buchan R, 'Cyber Attacks: Unlawful Uses of Force or Prohibited Interventions?' (2012) 17(2) *Journal of Conflict & Security Law* 211

'Building Blocks of E-Estonia' (*E-Estonia*) <https://e-estonia.com/solutions> accessed 2 March 2018

Calder A and Watkins SG, 'Trojan' in *ISO27000 and Information Security: A Combined Glossary* (IT Governance 2010)

Clover C, 'Kremlin-Backed Group Behind Estonia Cyber Blitz' *Financial Times* (11 March 2009) <www.ft.com/intl/cms/s/0/57536d5a-0ddc-11de-8ea3-0000779fd2ac.html> accessed 15 November 2016

'A Cyber Riot' *The Economist* (10 May 2007) <www.economist.com/node/9163598> accessed 2 March 2018

Davis J, 'Hackers Take Down the Most Wired Country in Europe' *Wired* (21 August 2007) <www.wired.com/2007/08/ff-estonia> accessed 2 March 2018

'Economy in Numbers' (Republic of Estonia Ministry of Foreign Affairs, 16 June 2017) <http://vm.ee/en/economy-numbers> accessed 2 March 2018

'Estonia Fines Man for "Cyber War"' *BBC News* (25 January 2008) <http://news.bbc.co.uk/2/hi/technology/7208511.stm> accessed 2 March 2018

'Estonia Urges Firm EU, NATO Response to New Form of Warfare: Cyber-attacks' *Sydney Morning Herald* (17 May 2007) <www.smh.com.au/technology/estonia-urges-firm-eu-nato-response-to-new-form-of-warfare-cyberattacks-20070516-d1h.html> accessed 2 March 2018

'The Estonian ID Card' (Republic of Estonia Information System Authority) <www.ria.ee/en/id-card.html> accessed 2 March 2018

Evron G, 'Battling Botnets and Online Mobs: Estonia's Defense Efforts During the Internet War' (2008) 9(1) *Georgetown Journal of International Affairs* 121

——— 'Authoritatively, Who was Behind the Estonian Attacks?' (*Dark Reading*, 17 May 2009) <www.darkreading.com/risk/authoritatively-who-was-behind-the-estonian-attacks/d/d-id/1130584> accessed 2 March 2018

Finn P, 'Cyber Assaults on Estonia Typify a New Battle Tactic' *Washington Post* (19 May 2007) <www.washingtonpost.com/wp-dyn/content/article/2007/05/18/AR2007051802122.html> accessed 2 March 2018

F-Secure, 'Declaration of Cyber War I: Distributed Denial of Service (DDoS) Attacks in Estonia' in *Threat Summaries Volume 2 2011–2007* (F-Secure Labs, 2012) <www.f-secure.com/documents/996508/1030743/threat_summaries_2011_2007.pdf> accessed 2 March 2018

Gervais M, 'Cyber Attacks and the Laws of War' (2012) 30(2) *Berkeley Journal of International Law* 525

Gill TD and Ducheine PAL, 'Anticipatory Self-Defense in the Cyber Context' (2013) 89 *International Law Studies Series US Naval War College* 438

Goldstein J, 'Estonia's Cyber Attacks: Lessons Learned' (WikiLeaks Cable, 6 June 2007) <https://wikileaks.org/plusd/cables/07TALLINN375_a.html> accessed 2 March 2018

Henriksen A, 'Lawful State Responses to Low-Level Cyber-Attacks' (2015) 84(2) *Nordic Journal of International Law* 323

Ilves TH, 'Address by the President of Estonia' (Speech at the 62nd Session of the United Nations General Assembly, New York, 25 September 2007) <www.un.org/webcast/ga/62/2007/pdfs/estonia-eng.pdf> accessed 2 March 2018

——— 'Address by the President of Estonia' (Speech at the 67th Session of the United Nations General Assembly, New York, 26 September 2012) <https://vp2006-2016.president.ee/en/official-duties/speeches/7991-address-by-h-e-toomas-hendrik-ilves-president-of-estonia-to-the-67th-session-of-the-united-nations-general-assembly-un-headquarters-new-york-september-2012> accessed 2 March 2018

'Individuals Using the Internet (% of population)' (World Bank) <https://data.worldbank.org/indicator/IT.NET.USER.ZS?locations=EE> accessed 2 March 2018

International Telecommunication Union, *Measuring the Information Society Report* (ITU, 2015) <www.itu.int/en/ITU-D/Statistics/Documents/publications/misr2015/MISR2015-w5.pdf> accessed 2 March 2018

Landler M and Markoff J, 'Digital Fears Emerge after Data Siege in Estonia' *New York Times* (29 May 2007) <www.nytimes.com/2007/05/29/technology/29estonia.html?_r=0> accessed 2 March 2018

Li S, 'When Does Internet Denial Trigger the Right of Armed Self-Defense?' (2013) 38(1) *Yale Journal of International Law* 179

Mansfield-Devine S, 'Estonia: What Doesn't Kill You Makes You Stronger' [2012] (7) *Network Security* 12

'Marching Off to Cyberwar' *The Economist* (4 December 2008) <www.economist.com/node/12673385> accessed 2 March 2018

Mirkovic J and others, *Internet Denial of Service: Attack and Defense Mechanisms* (Prentice-Hall 2005)

Myers SL, 'Russia Rebukes Estonia for Moving Soviet Statue' *New York Times* (27 April 2007) <www.nytimes.com/2007/04/27/world/europe/27cnd-estonia.html> accessed 2 March 2018

Nazario J, 'Estonian DDoS Attacks: A Summary to Date' (Arbor Networks, 17 May 2007) <www.arbornetworks.com/blog/asert/estonian-ddos-attacks-a-summary-to-date> accessed 2 March 2018

——— 'Politically Motivated Denial of Service Attacks' in Czosseck C and Geers K (eds), *The Virtual Battlefield: Perspectives on Cyber Warfare* (IOS Press 2009)

Office of the President of the Republic of Estonia, 'NATO Secretary General to the President of the Republic: The Alliance Supports Estonia' (Media Release, 3 May 2007) <https://vp2006-2016.president.ee/en/media/press-releases/1387-nato-secretary-general-to-the-president-of-the-republic-the-alliance-supports-estonia/index.html> accessed 2 March 2018

Ottis R, 'Analysis of the 2007 Cyber Attacks Against Estonia from the Information Warfare Perspective' in Remenyi D (ed), *Proceedings of the 7th European Conference on Information Warfare and Security* (Academic Publishing 2008)

'Pushback for Mr Putin', *Washington Post* (19 May 2007) <www.washingtonpost.com/wp-dyn/content/article/2007/05/18/AR2007051801722.html> accessed 2 March 2018

Rantanen M, 'Virtual Harassment, but for Real' *Helsingin Sanomat* (6 May 2007) <www.hs.fi/english/article/Virtual+harassment+but+for+real+/1135227099868> accessed 24 June 2016

Republic of Estonia Government, 'Declaration of the Minister of Foreign Affairs of the Republic of Estonia' (Media Release, 1 May 2007) <www.valitsus.ee/en/news/declaration-minister-foreign-affairs-republic-estonia> accessed 2 March 2018

——— 'Prime Minister Andrus Ansip's Speech in Riigikogu' (Media Release, 2 May 2007) <www.valitsus.ee/en/news/prime-minister-andrus-ansips-speech-riigikogu> accessed 2 March 2018

Republic of Estonia Information System Authority, 'State Information System in Estonia' (2007) <www.ria.ee/public/publikatsioonid/state_IS.pdf> accessed 2 March 2018

——— 'The State Portal «eesti.ee»' (2007) <www.ria.ee/public/publikatsioonid/State_portal.pdf> accessed 2 March 2018

Republic of Estonia Ministry of Defence, 'Minister to Attend meeting of EU Defence Ministers in Brussels' (Media Release, 13 May 2007) <www.kaitseministeerium.ee/en/news/minister-attend-meeting-eu-defence-ministers-brussels> accessed 2 March 2018

——— 'Minister Addresses Cyber Attacks at Meeting of EU Defence Ministers' (Media Release, 14 May 2007) <www.kaitseministeerium.ee/en/news/minister-addresses-cyber-attacks-meeting-eu-defence-ministers> accessed 2 March 2018

Republic of Estonia Ministry of Foreign Affairs, 'Address by Minister of Foreign Affairs of Estonia Urmas Paet' (Media Release, 11 May 2007) <http://vm.ee/en/news/address-minister-foreign-affairs-estonia-urmas-paet> accessed 2 March 2018

Runnell P et al, 'The Estonian Tiger Leap from Post-Communism to the Information Society: From Policy to Practice' (2009) 40(1) *Journal of Baltic Studies* 29

Schmitt MN, 'Cyber Operations and the *Jus Ad Bellum* Revisited' (2011) 56(3) *Villanova Law Review* 569

Shachtman N, 'Kremlin Kids: We Launched the Estonian Cyber War' *Wired* (11 March 2009) <www.wired.com/2009/03/pro-kremlin-gro> accessed 2 March 2018

'State e-Services Portal' (*E-Estonia*) <https://e-estonia.com/solutions/e-governance/state-e-services-portal> accessed 2 March 2018

Telecommunications Act (Estonia)

Thomson I, 'Russia "Hired Botnets" for Estonia Cyber-war' *ITnews* (1 June 2007) <www.itnews.com.au/news/russia-hired-botnets-for-estonia-cyber-war-82600> accessed 2 March 2018

Tikk E and Oorn R, *Legal and Policy Evaluation: International Coordination of Prosecution and Prevention of Cyber Terrorism* (IOS Press 2008)

——— Kaska K and Vihul L, *International Cyber Incidents: Legal Considerations* (NATO Cooperative Cyber Defence Centre of Excellence 2010)

Traynor I, 'EU Protests Over Russian Attacks on Ambassadors' *The Guardian* (3 May 2007) <www.theguardian.com/world/2007/may/03/russia.eu> accessed 2 March 2018

——— 'Russia Accused of Unleashing Cyberwar to Disable Estonia' *The Guardian* (17 May 2007) <www.theguardian.com/world/2007/may/17/topstories3.russia> accessed 2 March 2018

Tsagourias N, 'The *Tallinn Manual on the International Law Applicable to Cyber Warfare*: A Commentary on Chapter II – The Use of Force' in Gill TD (ed), *Yearbook of International Humanitarian Law Volume 15* (Springer 2014)

Tulloch M, *Microsoft Encyclopedia of Security* (Microsoft Press 2003)

'US Warns Cyber-attacks will Increase' *Financial Times* (17 May 2007) <www.ft.com/intl/cms/s/0/324fa472-049e-11dc-80ed-000b5df10621.html> accessed 2 March 2018

Waterman S, 'Analysis: Who Cyber Smacked Estonia?' *United Press International* (11 June 2007) <www.upi.com/Defense-News/2007/06/11/Analysis-Who-cyber-smacked-Estonia/26831181580439> accessed 2 March 2018

'X-Road' (*E-Estonia*) <https://e-estonia.com/solutions/interoperability-services/x-road> accessed 2 March 2018

6 Stuxnet

Introduction

In 2012 in Fordo, close to the city of Qom in northern Iran, an object that looked like a rock exploded.[1] The examination of the object's remains revealed that it was not a rock, but instead a 'device capable of intercepting data' from the computers located at a nearby uranium-enrichment facility in Fordo.[2] The origins of this device remain unknown; however, media reports have linked it to similar technologies developed by the US National Security Agency (NSA) as revealed in the course of the Edward Snowden investigation.[3] These technologies have the capacity to transmit data through radio frequencies from computers that are not connected to the Internet, provided they have been connected to hardware that makes this possible.[4] Approximately 200 kilometers away from the Fordo uranium-enrichment facility is the uranium-enrichment facility of Natanz. This facility was at the center of what was revealed to be a joint US–Israeli operation called 'Olympic Games'.[5] It was aimed at sabotaging the operation of Iran's uranium-enrichment facility in Natanz and involved a sophisticated piece of malicious software (malware) named by those who discovered it as Stuxnet.[6] Originally discovered in June 2010,[7] Stuxnet has been described as the 'malware of the century'.[8] It managed to penetrate computer systems within Iran's Natanz uranium-enrichment facility that, like the computers at the aforementioned Fordo facility, were not connected to the Internet. Stuxnet's design demonstrated that its ultimate aim was to adjust the frequency settings responsible for the rotation speeds of nuclear centrifuges, causing physical damage to the centrifuges and effectively undermining Iran's ability to successfully enrich uranium. In contrast to the 2007 DDoS attacks on Estonia, Stuxnet was therefore not aimed simply at disrupting the functioning of ICTs, but was intended to cause physical damage to nuclear centrifuges.

This chapter considers the Stuxnet incident in order to argue that an informational approach offers a more in-depth account of the harm caused by Stuxnet beyond simply its material effects. Stuxnet is widely regarded as having amounted to a use of force primarily because it resulted in physical damage to material objects. Given its effects, it largely subscribed to the conception of violence that underpins Article 2(4). However, this chapter argues that this is a one-dimensional account of the harm caused by Stuxnet, and it fails to adequately account for the non-material harm Stuxnet caused to countless virtual entities and processes in disrupting the operation of the Natanz facility. This is particularly evident in the idea that, had Stuxnet simply disrupted the operation of the centrifuges without causing physical damage, it would not be seen to constitute a use of force under existing law.

The chapter begins by providing a detailed examination of Stuxnet, including its technical design, overall purpose and effects on the nuclear centrifuges at Natanz. It then considers existing analyses of Stuxnet in relation to the law on the use of force, demonstrating that Stuxnet is almost universally considered to have crossed the use of force threshold – it effectively constituted a form of violence that the law is capable of recognizing because it caused material damage to centrifuges. Finally, an informational approach is adopted to consider the increases in entropy caused by Stuxnet against the Natanz facility within Iran's region of the infosphere.

Events

Media reports on Stuxnet

Stuxnet was first discovered in June 2010 by a Belarussian Internet security firm working for a client in Iran.[9] It was described as a 'turning point' in the design and purpose of malicious software.[10] Unlike other computer viruses or worms, which commonly are designed for financial gain, Stuxnet was designed specifically for sabotage.[11] It appeared that it was tailored to target the computer systems used to control important infrastructure, as the hardware and software configurations it targeted were those used to operate a range of industrial equipment found in power grids, power plants, pipelines, and dams.[12]

Initially, when it was first discovered in June 2010, the exact purpose of Stuxnet and those responsible for its creation were not known. However, particularly given its technical sophistication, it was widely believed that a group of hackers could not have been able to create it, and instead a nation-state was responsible for its development.[13] Stuxnet's design, for example, showed that its creation required a sophisticated team of programmers and an organization with 'substantial financial resources to develop, test and then release such a program'.[14] Similarly in relation to its purpose, while later revelations in 2012 appeared to confirm that the United States and Israel had created Stuxnet to target Iran's uranium-enrichment facility at Natanz,[15] the primary target or purpose of Stuxnet was not immediately known when it was initially discovered.[16]

Stuxnet was reported to have spread to computers across the world.[17] According to Siemens, the manufacturer of the computers it ultimately targeted, Stuxnet was found in fifteen industrial plants around the world, including five located in Germany.[18] However, none of these sites' operations were affected.[19] Globally over 100,000 computers had been infected, but over 60 per cent of these were located in Iran.[20] Iran therefore appeared to be the general or primary target of the attacks; however, at first there was only speculation about the specific target of the attacks within Iran.[21] For example, given reports that a computer worm had infected the personal computers of workers at Iran's Bushehr nuclear plant, it was suggested that the Bushehr plant was potentially Stuxnet's target.[22] However, later analysis of Stuxnet's code revealed that this was not the case.[23]

In September 2010 there was already some speculation that the enrichment facility at Natanz was the target.[24] In November 2010, only days after it was revealed by the computer security company Symantec that Stuxnet targeted specific frequency converter drives operating in a very particular way, reports from the International Atomic Energy Agency (IAEA) noted that Iran had 'stopped feeding hot uranium gas into its thousands of centrifuges'.[25] As Iranian officials did not provide any reason for this, it led some to believe that it was as a result of the operators of the Natanz facility disconnecting computers and restoring systems to ensure that all traces of Stuxnet were removed.[26] In late December 2010, the Institute for Science and International Security (ISIS)[27] released a report in which it had compiled data from the IAEA's quarterly reports on Iran.[28] Combined with Symantec's technical analysis of Stuxnet, these findings effectively confirmed that the Natanz facility was Stuxnet's target and that it was responsible for a fall in the number of working centrifuges there during late 2009 and early 2010.[29] An estimated 900 to 1000 centrifuges were reported to have been broken.[30]

In January 2011, the *New York Times* reported that Stuxnet was a joint US–Israeli effort targeting the Natanz facility.[31] The following year, in June 2012, the *New York Times* reported that the name of this operation was Olympic Games.[32] Interviews with current and former US, European, and Israeli officials revealed that Stuxnet was part of an operation originally started during President George W. Bush's administration and later intensified under President Barack Obama's administration. It involved an extensive development program that required in-depth knowledge of the 'structure and daily rhythms' of the Natanz enrichment facility.[33] Stuxnet also had to be tested at what was described as a 'virtual replica of Natanz', equipped with the same centrifuges (which were of an older design) as those used at the Natanz facility.[34] According to these reports, given that Stuxnet needed to be physically introduced into the Natanz facility (that is, it could not be done across the Internet), they relied on engineers and maintenance workers with physical access to the facility to unknowingly infect the computers.[35] USB thumb drives were reported to have been 'critical in spreading the first variants of the worm', while more sophisticated methods were used to further spread and deliver the code to the computers it targeted. Originally Stuxnet was not meant to spread outside the computers at the Natanz facility, and its spread was attributed to an error in its code, which was reported to most likely have been a later modification by the Israelis.[36]

Technical design

In addition to the media attention the incident received, the cyber security community also examined Stuxnet carefully. In late September 2010, Symantec released a dossier containing the company's technical analysis of Stuxnet. Symantec had reverse engineered Stuxnet to properly understand its purpose and design.[37] The company had gathered 3280 samples of Stuxnet in its three variants, and these samples contained timestamps and other information providing a history of the computers it had infected.[38] Based on these data, Symantec was also able to determine a range of factors including the different organizations to and from which Stuxnet had spread, when these infections occurred and how long it took to spread.[39] In 2013, Symantec also released a follow-up to its earlier report entitled *Stuxnet 0.5: The Missing Link*.[40] Stuxnet 0.5 was the oldest known version of Stuxnet that had been analysed.[41] It is believed to have begun its operation as early as November 2007, although it was designed to stop compromising computers on 4 July 2009 and stop communicating with its command-and-control servers on 11 January 2009.[42] Compared to the 'full' version of Stuxnet, Stuxnet 0.5 had some different and less-developed features, and a different attack strategy.[43] The full version of Stuxnet infected computers in three different attack waves: in June 2009, March 2010 and April 2010.[44] Overall, Stuxnet's technical sophistication was evident in a range of its features, which enabled it to reach the facility at Natanz and deliver its payload to the computers used to operate the nuclear centrifuges. Among these features were four zero-day vulnerabilities;[45] two stolen digital certificates; multiple propagation methods enabling it to spread across computers not connected to the Internet; a sophisticated payload delivered only to computers configured in a particular way; the ability to disable digital alarm systems; and the use of a 'man-in-the-middle' attack to make it appear that its target computers were operating normally while it delivered its payload. These features will be examined in detail below; however, what follows is first an overview of the international context of Iran's nuclear program and then a basic overview of how the uranium-enrichment process operates.

The non-proliferation treaty and the uranium-enrichment process

Stuxnet's ultimate goal was to undermine Iran's ability to develop nuclear weapons. Under the Treaty on the Non-Proliferation of Nuclear Weapons (NPT)[46] regime, to which Iran is a party,[47] except for those states that had a nuclear weapons capability in the late 1960s (the United States, the United

Kingdom, France, Russia, and China), other member states such as Iran are permitted to use nuclear technology only for peaceful purposes.[48] Additionally, pursuant to the NPT,[49] non-nuclear weapon states such as Iran have entered into safeguard agreements with the IAEA to ensure the transparency of their nuclear programs, allowing the IAEA to monitor and verify their compliance.[50] Iran claims that its nuclear program is for peaceful purposes; however, the United States, other Western states, and the IAEA maintain that Iran intends to develop a nuclear weapons capability.[51] For example, until 2002 the existence of Iran's uranium-enrichment facility at Natanz had not been disclosed contrary to Iran's commitments under the NPT safeguard obligations,[52] and in 2003 the IAEA found traces of highly enriched uranium at the Natanz facility.[53] Consequently, the UN Security Council (UNSC) has, through various resolutions, authorized and imposed sanctions against Iran aiming to limit its capacity to obtain the technology and materials that contribute to its development of nuclear weapons technologies.[54] Therefore, while Iran is permitted to develop, research, produce, and use nuclear energy for peaceful purposes under the NPT, given the dual-use nature of this technology, the concern is that if it develops an effective ability to enrich uranium for peaceful purposes, it will also be able to further enrich uranium for weapons purposes.[55]

The primary difference in the production process used to enrich uranium for either 'peaceful' or 'weapons' purposes is minor, lying 'only in the extent and duration of the application of those processes to the uranium'.[56] The uranium-enrichment process involves increasing the concentration of the uranium-235 (U-235) isotope which only makes up 0.7 per cent of natural uranium. Uranium enriched for energy production requires about 3.5–5 per cent of the U-235 isotope, and as this is below 20 per cent purity, it is regarded as low-enriched uranium.[57] Where the concentration of U-235 is over 20 per cent, it is considered highly enriched uranium, whereas weapons grade uranium requires approximately 90 per cent of U-235.[58] Therefore, the uranium that can be used for energy or weapons purposes mainly differs in terms of the concentration of U-235. The process used to enrich uranium is also largely the same, as '[t]he essential difference in the production process for material of weapons grade purity, as opposed to reactor fuel purity, lies only in the extent and duration of the application of those processes to the uranium.'[59] There are also various methods of uranium enrichment, however, the gas centrifuge process used at the uranium-enrichment facility at Natanz involves large rotating cylinders (centrifuges) that are connected to form cascades (groups of centrifuges). The enrichment process involves feeding uranium in its gas form as uranium hexafluoride (UF_6) into the centrifuge, which is being spun by a rotor inside. The rapid rotation of the UF_6 results in a higher concentration of U-238 (the unwanted uranium isotope that forms 99.3 per cent of natural uranium) in the outer edge of the cylinder because of its heavier molecules.[60] This means the U-235 molecules are concentrated in the center of the cylinder, and they are drawn from one end of the cylinder.[61] Provided there is sufficient UF_6, this process can be used to enrich uranium for either energy or weapons purposes.[62]

The centrifuge cascades (forming modules) used in the enrichment process are operated by special computers called programmable logic controllers (PLCs). A PLC is a 'controller that uses programmable memory to store instructions and to implement functions such as logic, sequencing, timing, counting, and arithmetic in order to control machines and processes'.[63] PLCs are special computers that are 'optimized for control tasks and the industrial environment'.[64] They can be programmed by engineers, for example, using personal computers such as laptops to input instructions into the memory of the PLC, and the PLC uses these inputs to carry out the functions for which it is programmed.[65] Siemens PLCs specifically are controlled with computers installed with Step 7 software. Using this software, a PLC can be programmed so that once the computer used to program it is disconnected, the PLC functions independently.[66] In the case of uranium enrichment, PLCs are used to configure the operation of the centrifuges cascades, including the speed at which the rotors inside the centrifuges are spun. Stuxnet's goal was to first spread across personal computers installed with Microsoft's Windows operating system with the aim of reaching a computer used by an engineer or programmer to input instructions into the PLCs. It first spread across these personal computers with the aim of eventually reaching the PLCs that were used to control the centrifuges.

Propagation methods

The PLCs and the personal computers used to program PLCs are generally non-networked or 'air gapped', meaning that they are not connected to the Internet or even a Local Area Network (LAN).[67] To infect the computers used to control the centrifuges at Natanz, Stuxnet had to first be physically carried into Natanz on an infected computer or USB drive.[68] It has been suggested that the original introduction of Stuxnet into Natanz was through five separate Iranian companies understood to have been involved with its nuclear program,[69] and these companies' computers could have been infected through a removable drive or an email attachment by either an insider or an unsuspecting third party.[70] Once the computer or USB drive of a contractor or programmer was infected with Stuxnet, it was capable of crossing the air gap into the Natanz facility.

In order to spread across Windows computers in an effort to ultimately reach the PLCs, Stuxnet utilized numerous features. The main propagation method used was removable USB drives.[71] Stuxnet was also able to spread across computers that shared a printer over a LAN,[72] and it was capable of using peer-to-peer (P2P) methods to communicate with other infected computers within a LAN.[73] Additionally, Stuxnet spread across Windows computers using Step 7 software (the software used to control PLCs) by infecting the project files used by this software that are stored in a database. By infecting these project files, each time the project was opened from a different computer, Stuxnet would be able to infect that computer too.[74]

When Stuxnet installed itself onto a Windows computer, it escalated its privileges so it had administrator rights, allowing it to perform any action it wanted on those computers.[75] It also gathered information about each computer and transmitted it to its command and control servers if (or when) it had Internet connectivity.[76] Based on information obtained from monitoring traffic to Stuxnet's command and control servers, Symantec discovered that by 20 September 2010 there were approximately 100,000 infected host computers, and over 60,000 of these were in Iran.[77]

By using these techniques to spread across Windows computers, Stuxnet ultimately was able to spread to the specific PLCs it targeted. It targeted the S7–315 and S7–417 models of Siemens PLCs that were operated by Step 7 software.[78] While the full version of Stuxnet contained the attack code for both of these models, the code targeting S7–417 models was disabled, meaning that only the code targeting S7–315 models was active.[79] This was in contrast to Stuxnet 0.5, which only contained the S7–417 attack code and targeted the valves used to control the flow of UF_6 into the centrifuges.[80] The attack code used in the full version of Stuxnet targeting S7–315 PLCs therefore targeted frequency converter drives as opposed to valves. Specifically, it targeted S7–315 PLCs that were used to operate frequency converter drives that were manufactured by either Fararo Paya, an Iranian company, or Vacon, a Finnish company.[81] It determined its target by checking, for example, the System Data Blocks (SDBs) of a PLC to determine how it was configured and what hardware was connected to it.[82] As part of this process, Stuxnet searched for specific part numbers found in frequency converter drives manufactured by either Fararo Paya or Vacon.[83] Depending on the manufacturer of the frequency converter drive that the PLC was used to operate, Stuxnet could then use a slightly different infection sequence.[84]

Another check that Stuxnet performed was to monitor these devices to ensure they were running between 807 Hz and 1210 Hz, as this was the frequency range it expected from its target.[85] While it has not been confirmed that the facility at Natanz used the frequency converters manufactured by these companies, this frequency range corresponded to that at which the IR-1 centrifuges known to be used at the Natanz facility are operated.[86] Additionally, there were values within the disabled part of the code targeting S7–417 PLCs that indicated IR-1 centrifuges were being targeted. An IR-1 centrifuge cascade contains 164 centrifuges, and the attack sequence of this part of the code was 'grouped in six arrays of 164 each', and this was believed to represent 'six cascades, each with 164 centrifuges'.[87] This part of the code, therefore, was searching for PLCs with 164 peripherals, and this corresponded with the number of centrifuges in each cascade.[88] Given 'that this array is identical to an IR-1 centrifuge cascade' used at the Natanz facility, it has been described as 'perhaps the strongest evidence' that Stuxnet targeted the Natanz facility specifically.[89] These factors indicated that the PLCs that Stuxnet targeted were those used to control centrifuges used in the uranium-enrichment process at the Natanz facility.

The payload

Once Stuxnet found its targets, another part of its code would become active that would deliver the payload. According to Ralph Langer, an expert on industrial control systems, while Stuxnet's propagation methods were complex, its payload was 'rocket science' in comparison.[90] Stuxnet's payload was delivered in almost 27-day cycles, and it involved adjusting the settings of the frequency converter responsible for the rotation speed of the rotors inside the centrifuges.[91] Essentially, Stuxnet effectively sought to 'sabotage the system by slowing down or speeding up the motor to different rates at different times'.[92]

While delivering its payload, Stuxnet also utilized what is known as a 'man-in-the-middle' attack. This term is used to describe 'an unseen relay that intercepts, understands, alters, and retransmits a message for the purpose of deception'.[93] It used the data it had gathered, and played it back to the monitoring system of the PLCs to make it appear that the frequency converters were operating normally.[94] Additionally, it prevented an automatic safety mechanism capable of stopping any dangerous process being run by the PLC from operating during its sabotage routine.[95] This is assumed to have prevented any shutdown that would normally occur during catastrophic events.[96]

Stuxnet therefore adjusted the settings of the frequency converter drives responsible for the speed of the rotors within the centrifuges. When the rotation speed was raised, the effect was to disrupt the enrichment process and probably also destroy the centrifuges.[97] In contrast, when the rotation speed was lowered, this is likely to have degraded the uranium-enrichment process, meaning a lower amount of uranium was enriched.[98] The combination of the two, however, was likely done 'with the intention of inducing excessive vibrations or distortions that would destroy the centrifuge'.[99] Given its technical design, Stuxnet is understood to have been intended mainly to physically destroy the centrifuges and not simply, for instance, manipulate the 'parameters of the centrifuge cascades so as to lower the production of low enriched uranium (LEU) on a sustained basis'.[100]

Iran's responses

The design and purpose of Stuxnet are well understood from a technical perspective, and the 2011 and 2012 revelations by the *New York Times* confirmed earlier suspicions that the United States and Israel created Stuxnet. Versions of events about Stuxnet's effects – that is, whether it was responsible for the broken centrifuges – vary depending on whether Iranian or IAEA accounts are believed.

Iran has not confirmed that Stuxnet was the cause of the broken centrifuges at Natanz; however, Iranian officials have confirmed that some of their computers were infected by a computer virus. In September 2010, an Iranian official from the Ministry of Industry and Mines admitted that a computer 'worm had infected more than 30,000 computers, including personal computers owned by employees of the nuclear power plant near Bushehr'.[101] This worm was described as a form of 'electronic warfare' against Iran.[102] Another official from the Ministry of Communications and Information Technology, however, maintained that 'the effect and damage of this spy worm in government systems is not serious', and that it had largely been halted.[103] In November 2010, coinciding with IAEA reports that indicated Iran was having problems with its centrifuges at the Natanz facility, there were conflicting reports about whether Stuxnet was responsible for these problems. It was reported that, despite the aforementioned acknowledgements by Iranian officials in September 2010 that over 30,000 computers had been infected with a virus, Iran denied that this virus had 'infected the operating systems at any nuclear site'.[104] However, according to reports in November 2010, Iran's President Mahmoud Ahmadinejad had stated that Iran's enemies 'had been successful in making problems for a limited number of our centrifuges, with software they had installed in electronic devices'.[105] He also maintained that the source of the problems had been located and the problems solved.[106] When asked specifically about Stuxnet and whether it had been responsible, President Ahmadinejad's response was one of silence.[107] However, around the same time Iran's Vice President Ali Akbar Salehi, who is also the head of the Iranian Atomic Energy Organization, maintained that, 'One year and several months ago, Westerners sent a virus to [our] country's nuclear sites', and that 'with the help of God', the virus was discovered and prevented from causing harm to Iran's progress in the nuclear field.[108]

While Iran did not admit that Stuxnet had managed to cause damage to its nuclear centrifuges, it did acknowledge that it had experienced issues with a computer virus. In particular, the statement made by Iran's vice president indicating that Iran had experienced issues with a computer virus in late 2009 indicates that Iranian computers were infected by a computer virus around the same time that Stuxnet is believed to have been active. The timing of this infection, alongside IAEA reports indicating a decrease in the amount of active centrifuges around this time, suggests that Stuxnet was responsible for the broken centrifuges at the Natanz facility.

The IAEA's reports

The IAEA releases quarterly reports on Iran's implementation of NPT safeguards and UNSC resolutions. According to data compiled from these reports by ISIS, between the November 2009 and February 2010 reports, the number of cascades enriching uranium decreased.[109] As mentioned, this timeframe refers specifically to when Stuxnet is known to have been active based on the timestamps in its log file, and the statement made by Iran's vice president regarding a virus sent by Westerners. According to the authors of the ISIS report, this means that between November 2009 and January 2010, one of the nuclear centrifuge cascade modules (A26) at the Natanz facility suffered problems requiring the decommission and replacement of about 1000 IR-1 centrifuges.[110] The authors of the ISIS report maintain that the module in question 'suffered a major problem with at least eleven cascades directly affected'.[111] This was evident in the sudden drop of centrifuge cascades under vacuum (a drop from twelve in the November 2009 report to one in the February 2010 report), and in the number of cascades with disconnected centrifuges (a rise from zero out of eighteen in the November 2009 report to eleven out of eighteen in the February 2010 report).[112] By August 2010, the number of centrifuge cascades under vacuum and being fed with UF_6 still had not returned to the November 2009 levels.[113]

In addition to this information from the IAEA's reports corresponding with the statements by Iranian officials that their computer systems were infected with a virus, the IAEA's video footage from the Natanz facility also shows that Iran was having problems there. The IAEA has surveillance cameras at the facility in order to monitor Iran's compliance with NPT safeguards and UNSC resolutions. While these cameras only monitor the perimeter of the cascade areas and not the area itself,[114] it has been reported that the footage shows that Iran had 'dismantled more than 10 percent of the Natanz plant's 9000 centrifuge machines used to enrich uranium'.[115] This occurred in the six-month period following late 2009.[116] IAEA officials who later examined the machines could not determine why they failed; however, according to reports from European diplomats, the operators of the plant 'worked frantically to replace each piece of equipment they removed' in what was described as a determination to hide any sign of a drop in production from the IAEA safeguard reports.[117]

Stuxnet's effects

Based on this information, it is generally believed that Stuxnet destroyed about 1000 of about 9000 IR-1 centrifuges at Natanz.[118] This damage is understood to have been caused by the first (June 2009) variant of Stuxnet, as the exact effects of the 2010 variants (March 2010 and April 2010) remain unclear.[119] Some, drawing on the technical design of Stuxnet, maintain that it destroyed 984 centrifuges,[120] however, the IAEA has not provided such a specific number as it is unable to monitor every single cascade going in and out of the cascade area.[121] In addition to these direct effects – particularly before Stuxnet was publicly revealed – it has been suggested that Iran was unlikely to have known the cause of the broken centrifuges.[122] This, in turn, would have caused a degree of uncertainty and challenged its quality assurance program.[123]

The ontological constraints of the law

As demonstrated in Chapter 5, the Estonia incident highlighted the ontological constraints of the law, as the incident generally is not considered a use of force – particularly because the DDoS attacks against Estonia did not cause material damage. In contrast, Stuxnet is generally considered to have constituted a use of force. As this section illustrates, according to existing legal analyses of Stuxnet in relation to the use of force threshold, especially given that Stuxnet caused physical damage to centrifuges, it can easily be regarded as a use of force. Stuxnet therefore involved a form of violence that the law has the capacity to recognize. It can be argued, however, that this only provides a one-dimensional account of violence that does not adequately capture the non-material or informational harm that Stuxnet caused.

Stuxnet and the use of force threshold

Stuxnet is widely considered in relation to questions surrounding when a cyber attack crosses the use of force threshold. The majority of authors, accepting that Stuxnet was the cause of the destruction of approximately 1000 centrifuges, maintain that it constituted a use of force – particularly as it caused material damage to physical objects. For example, Gary Brown points to the fact that Stuxnet was 'intentionally designed malware directed against a nation-state [and] resulted in the physical destruction of state-owned equipment. The centrifuges were destroyed as effectively as if someone had taken a hammer to them.'[124] He therefore maintains that the incident violated the general prohibition on the use of force.[125] Heather Harrison Dinniss also notes how, in contrast to the Estonia incident, in which 'no loss of life, physical injury or destruction of property was suffered' due to the cyber attacks, Stuxnet 'purportedly resulted in significant destruction of property'.[126] As a result, she takes the position that Stuxnet 'would undoubtedly amount to a use of force'.[127] David Fidler maintains that 'a plausible argument can be made' that Stuxnet constituted an illegal use of force because its design reflected an intention 'to cause physical damage – and the worm reportedly caused significant damage – to specific tangible objects in a particular location in one country: the uranium-enrichment centrifuges at Natanz, Iran'.[128] Also, according to a number of authors including William Boothby and Michael Schmitt, Stuxnet qualifies as a use of force because 'the facilities suffered physical damage'.[129] For these authors, given that Stuxnet caused material damage to physical objects, it clearly constituted a use of force.

A number of authors also consider Stuxnet in relation to the *Tallinn Manual* criteria.[130] In this context, most authors highlight the physical damage caused by Stuxnet in relation to the 'severity' criterion. For example, David Weissbrodt argues that, 'Stuxnet, at minimum, is considered to be a use of force.'[131] In relation to the severity criterion, he notes that 'the Stuxnet attack was severe because it caused physical harm to property. Stuxnet caused the centrifuges to speed up and slow down their rotation causing them to break.'[132] Similarly, others argue that the *Tallinn Manual* criteria support the conclusion that Stuxnet constituted a use of force, especially as there was severe harm to property.[133] Finally, the *Tallinn Manual*'s Group of Experts unanimously took the view that Stuxnet amounted to a use of force.[134]

Given that Iran has not confirmed the destruction of centrifuges and the consequent degree of uncertainty around whether Stuxnet was responsible for their destruction, some authors question whether the incident in fact amounted to a use of force. According to Katharina Ziolkowski, for example, whether Stuxnet constituted a use of force within the meaning of Article 2(4) depends on whether it 'caused a non-trivial destruction of property'.[135] She argues that if indeed Stuxnet 'did not cause any damage of physical nature, it appears not to reach the threshold of illegality pursuant to public international law and thus to be a "legal masterpiece"'.[136] Russell Buchan also questions the conflicting reports on whether or not there was in fact physical damage, and explicitly notes the difference this makes for the use of force analysis. He maintains that if Stuxnet simply 'prevented the centrifuges from rotating at the correct speed' – meaning that uranium could not be enriched without the actual destruction of centrifuges – then Stuxnet 'cannot be regarded as an unlawful use of force because no damage to physical property was caused'.[137] However, if the reports that Stuxnet did cause the physical destruction of centrifuges are correct, he argues that 'this would constitute the requisite physical damage in order for a violation of Article 2(4) to be established'.[138]

As these analyses of Stuxnet in light of Article 2(4) highlight, the law requires known physical damage for a cyber attack to constitute a use of force. Stuxnet generally is considered to have crossed this threshold. This is almost exclusively because it caused damage to approximately 1000 centrifuges or, alternatively, the primary obstacle for making this determination is the lack of sufficient certainty that it in fact had this effect. For example, as Andrew Foltz suggests (and Buchan also alludes to), had Stuxnet only disrupted the operation of the uranium-enrichment process and not destroyed centrifuges, it is unlikely it would have been considered a use of force.[139] Hypothetically, if Stuxnet's payload only involved the second sequence of the attack that sent instructions to the frequency converter drives to decrease the speed at which the rotors inside the centrifuges were spun (and did not both decease and increase their speed as it did), this is likely only to have affected the amount of enriched uranium.[140] This would have undermined the ability of those centrifuges to enrich uranium, but potentially not caused the destruction of the centrifuges. Yet there would have been little real difference in its overall effect in undermining Iran's ability to properly enrich uranium with those centrifuges, even if the centrifuges remained physically intact.

This near-exclusive focus of existing legal analyses on physical effects demonstrates the law's limited conception of violence. Particularly in relation to Stuxnet, this highlights that the law is underpinned by a one-dimensional account of violence that fails to adequately capture the non-material harm that Stuxnet caused. Despite the range of ways in which Stuxnet undermined the integrity of thousands of computers within Iran and disrupted the proper operation of the computers within the Natanz enrichment facility, the primary focus of these analyses is the physical damage to centrifuges. Further, had Stuxnet not resulted in material effects, it would have likely been considered to fall below the use of force threshold and amounted to a breach of the non-intervention principle alone.[141] It would effectively have been cast outside the scope of what Article 2(4) is capable of recognizing as violence amounting to a form of non-violence considered through the non-intervention principle. This is problematic on a conceptual level, as it rests on the assumption that states must be subject to some kind of material harm for a cyber attack to constitute a prohibited form of interstate violence under Article 2(4); otherwise, such cyber attacks are seen only to affect the legal personality of the state. However, given the degree to which states are increasingly reliant on ICTs, this does not sufficiently account for the harm that can be caused through cyber attacks. Therefore, while the existing law has the capacity to recognize Stuxnet as a form of violence, it only offers a one-dimensional account that does not adequately capture the informational harm that Stuxnet caused.

An informational approach

This section adopts an informational approach to Stuxnet to demonstrate that this offers a means to appreciate both the informational and physical forms of harm that Stuxnet caused, instead of primarily focusing on its material effects that dominate existing legal analyses of the incident. It will be shown that Stuxnet was not simply an example of physical violence causing entropy, but instead that it can be seen as a combination of physical and informational forms of violence causing entropy within the Natanz facility and in Iran's region of the infosphere.

The Iranian entity and the Natanz facility

In contrast to the Estonian entity, the Iranian entity is a less developed information society. For example, within its region of the infosphere, only approximately 44 per cent of households have Internet access;[142] there is a smaller but growing number of Internet users at under 40 per cent of the population;[143] and the levels of access to ICTs, the level of development of its ICT infrastructure, and the level of use of ICTs across society are slightly below the global average.[144] Iran has also begun to develop its e-government services,[145] although a developing ICT infrastructure means Iran is also faced with technological barriers in this effort.[146] Nonetheless, Iran is a dynamic entity, as its informational substance continuously changes over time with various flows of information moving in and out of it.

Like Estonia, Iran is autonomous, as it has a degree of independence from its environment and from other entities. Despite structural reconfigurations in 1979 when it transitioned from a monarchy to a republic, Iran has political independence and continues to operate as an independent state separate from other states. It is also capable of interacting with other entities, including other states in the physical proximity of its region of the infosphere, and international organizations such as the United Nations and the IAEA. It is an adaptable entity capable of changing its policies and strategies depending on the information it receives from its environment. As a state entity, its inherent purpose is to care for and protect its region of the infosphere, including the various entities and processes – such as its nuclear program – within this region.

The form or pattern of Iran is also evident in its structural configuration. Its information structures are, for instance, evident in the organization of its executive, legislative, and judicial institutions. Its executive includes the offices of the Supreme Leader and President and the Council of Ministers (cabinet). The Islamic Consultative Assembly in turn performs the legislative functions, whereas the Supreme Courts and lower courts are organized and structured to perform judicial functions. The overall structural configuration of these entities and their basic tasks and functions are in turn set out in the Constitution of the Islamic Republic of Iran, which provides the overarching protocol governing the interactions of these entities, and embeds a particular value system into Iran.[147] Among other key internal protocols governing the interactions of these entities and their relationships to the environments within Iran's region of the infosphere are public and administrative law, and environmental law. These structures and protocols delineate Iran from other states, and give it a degree of internal coherence.

Given Iran's nuclear program, an important external protocol governing the interactions between Iran and the majority of other states is the NPT. The NPT regime's protocols are aimed at regulating the proliferation of nuclear weapons, promoting the peaceful use of nuclear energy and disarmament of nuclear weapons stockpiles.[148] In effect, the NPT protocols are designed to restrict the spread and development of nuclear technologies, given the capability of these technologies to cause the large-scale destruction of information entities and parts of the infosphere. Since 1968, Iran has agreed to operate according to the NPT protocols. It is therefore bound by the safeguard agreements pursuant to which it has authorized the IAEA to monitor its nuclear program. However, the international system considers Iran's nuclear program to be for non-peaceful purposes and contrary to the operational limitations of states provided by the NPT protocols. Iran's nuclear program, which includes the enrichment facility at Natanz, is therefore considered a potentially hostile and malicious process within Iran's region of the infosphere. This is because it is operated contrary to the external protocols governing the interactions between Iran and other states within the international system.

This is illustrated by various decisions made by the entity responsible for maintaining international peace and security within the infosphere: the UNSC, the decisions of which constitute protocols according to which all states are bound in their interactions. In several of its decisions, the UNSC has recognized that Iran's nuclear program is a process in contravention of the NPT protocols. As a result, it has imposed restrictions on various information flows in and out of Iran. For example, in 2006 the UNSC passed a resolution recognizing the potential military dimension to Iran's nuclear program contrary to the NPT, and demanded that Iran suspend 'all enrichment-related and reprocessing activities'.[149] The same year, the UNSC imposed sanctions on Iran limiting the ability of all states to supply, sell or transfer any 'items, materials, equipment, goods and technology which could contribute to Iran's enrichment-related, reprocessing or heavy water-related activities, or to the development of nuclear weapon delivery systems'.[150] This resolution also required other states to inform the sanctions committee about the movement of any individuals within their territories 'who are engaged in, directly associated with or providing support for Iran's proliferation sensitive nuclear activities or for the development of nuclear weapon delivery systems'.[151] Further, the UNSC decided that all states should freeze any funds within their territories 'owned or controlled by the persons or entities' associated with or supporting Iran's nuclear program.[152] Numerous other resolutions relating to Iran's nuclear program have also been passed since 2006.[153] For example, in 2008 the UNSC decided that other states should 'take the necessary measures to prevent the entry into or transit through their territories' of designated persons associated with Iran's nuclear program.[154] The UNSC, as the entity responsible for international peace and security within the infosphere, therefore has deemed Iran's nuclear program to be a malicious process, given its operation contrary to the NPT protocols. As a result of this and in an effort to ensure Iran ends this malicious process and recommences operation according to the NPT protocols, it has restricted various flows of information (ranging from goods, services, and technologies to humans and financial activities) in and out of Iran's region of the infosphere.

As part of Iran's state-run nuclear program, the Natanz facility can be considered a component of the Iranian entity that is also located within its region of the infosphere. Iran continues to operate the Natanz facility and its nuclear program generally, and adapt its operation to the external protocols restricting information flows in and out of its region of the infosphere, maintaining its autonomy and adaptability as an entity. Maintaining the operation of this process enables it to provide energy and security to entities within its region of the infosphere, and it is regarded by Iran as essential to maintaining its ability to care for and protect the well-being of its region of the infosphere.[155] This is despite the officials responsible for the operation of Iran knowing that the continued operation of this process is contrary to the external protocols according to which Iran has agreed to operate. Nonetheless, its internal protocols continue to authorize the operation of this process which the international system regards as malicious. As such, given its responsibility to care for and protect all entities within its region of the infosphere, Iran has also sought to protect the integrity of the Natanz facility as a component of its nuclear program. For example, to protect the integrity of the enrichment process at the Natanz facility, it has been disconnected from digital flows of information from the rest of the infosphere as a means to protect it from potential threats capable of causing increases in entropy.

Stuxnet and entropy

Stuxnet was a technically sophisticated piece of malicious software and demonstrated that its designers had extensive knowledge of the Natanz facility. It was specifically designed to undermine the operation of Iran's nuclear program by causing increased entropy within the Natanz facility. However, the degrees of entropy produced by various parts of Stuxnet varied, ranging from undermining the integrity of computers and exploiting the communication protocols between computers to delivering a payload causing physical damage to approximately 1000 centrifuges.

Propagation methods

The original infection method and propagation methods used by Stuxnet allowing the introduction and spread of Stuxnet into and throughout Iran resulted in various degrees of increases in entropy. While it remains unknown exactly how and when Stuxnet 0.5 was introduced into Natanz, from the information obtained from Stuxnet's log file, the June 2009, March 2010, and April 2010 variants first infected the computers of five separate companies.[156] Through these computers, Stuxnet then spread into the Natanz facility. The initial infection of the first computers within these companies can only be considered a very minor increase in entropy. However, over time approximately 12,000 computers within these corporate entities were infected, leading to a larger increase in entropy given the total amount of infected computer systems. Stuxnet ultimately spread and infected over 100,000 computers around the world, which in turn can be regarded as a more significant increase in entropy. Over 60,000 of these were located within Iran's region of the infosphere. While these computers continued to operate normally, their integrity was compromised. Stuxnet would, for example, check which anti-virus software was installed on a computer and choose the most appropriate injection process into that computer, and if necessary also utilize one of its zero-day vulnerabilities to inject itself into an active process run by the computer.[157] Also without the authorization of the legitimate users, Stuxnet granted itself administrator rights through the exploitation of zero-day vulnerabilities.[158] It was therefore capable of bypassing the security mechanisms of each computer system, which were designed to protect these entities from threats capable of causing increases in entropy.

Further, given that Stuxnet had administrator rights on each computer, it was capable of taking any action it wanted.[159] While it only delivered its payload to very specific computer configurations, and only sent basic information about the other computers it infected to the command and control servers, it is understood to have had the ability to download additional features from these servers.[160] While it did not disrupt the operation of these computers, it had undermined their integrity and was able to communicate with other computers infected by Stuxnet and the command and control servers, update itself, and even potentially obtain additional features. In addition to the entropy caused in undermining the integrity of these computers in the above ways, Stuxnet thus also had further potential to cause more increases in entropy in the over 100,000 entities it had infected.

The computers used within the Natanz facility to program the PLCs (and the PLCs themselves) were specifically configured so as to protect them from entropy and keep them secure from potential threats that could come through the Internet. Through an air gap limiting the flows of digital information into these computers, Iran sought to protect the integrity of these computers and the processes they used to operate within the Natanz facility. The Natanz facility's interactions with other entities, even within Iran's region of the infosphere, were thus limited to those with physical access to it. Consequently, the attackers exploited other information flows into the Natanz facility in order infect it with Stuxnet. These included, for example, programmers and engineers with physical access to the Natanz facility. Stuxnet was able to copy itself onto USB drives using a driver file which was signed with a stolen digital certificate, meaning it would be trusted by the system as a safe file.[161] One of the methods it used in this process of spreading to and from USB drives was the exploitation of a zero-day vulnerability in .LNK files.[162] This allowed Stuxnet to execute automatically whenever the USB drive containing Stuxnet was inserted and the folder displaying the contents of the USB was viewed.[163] In order to mask that these entities were the source of Stuxnet's infection, Stuxnet was able to hide its files on the USB drives, and it also deleted itself from them once it had been used to infect three computers.[164] As the main propagation method used, by spreading to and from USB drives, Stuxnet was able to spread across the computers of humans working for corporate entities involved with Iran's nuclear program and consequently obtain access to the secured Natanz facility. Therefore, while the Natanz facility was disconnected from the Internet, Stuxnet exploited other information flows into the Natanz facility. In this context, it produced entropy by undermining the integrity of the Natanz facility, and by doing so it also undermined Iran's ability to care for and protect the Natanz facility from entropy.

In addition to the entropy caused by Stuxnet in the process of undermining the integrity of the Natanz facility, the various other propagation methods used to further spread and reach the PLCs also caused increases in entropy. In addition to USB drives, the propagation methods also made use of P2P connectivity and LANs, and involved the exploitation of information exchanges between entities. For example, by exploiting the print-spooler vulnerability of computers connected to a shared printed through a LAN, Stuxnet enabled unauthorized information exchanges between these computers and used these exchanges to spread.[165] Also, by infecting Step 7 project files located in a database, Stuxnet was able to spread to computers using the Step 7 software and to those computers used to configure PLCs.[166] Therefore, Stuxnet caused increases in entropy by undermining and degrading the integrity of the normal information exchange processes between computers sharing a printer on a LAN, and between computers using Step 7 software to access project files. Finally, by exploiting P2P connectivity within a LAN, Stuxnet enabled information exchanges to and from computers that had been configured to be secure and disconnected from the Internet.[167] In this way, Stuxnet could communicate with computers not connected to the Internet and relay information about these computers to the command and control servers. In addition to causing increases in entropy by undermining the integrity of these computers, Stuxnet also caused increases in entropy by undermining the non-networked configuration of these computers. Through these propagation methods, Stuxnet was able to undermine the integrity of these computers and their interactions, and it ultimately undermined the integrity of the PLCs it reached using these methods, causing increases in entropy within the infected computer systems and within the Natanz facility as a whole.

The man-in-the-middle attack

Besides the entropy produced by Stuxnet's propagation methods, the man-in-the-middle attack also produced increases in entropy. Stuxnet replaced the legitimate library file that is used by the Step 7 software to communicate with PLCs with its own version.[168] This allowed Stuxnet to monitor the data sent to and from the PLC, to send its own data or replace existing data being sent to and from the PLC, and to hide the fact that the PLC was infected.[169] As a result, Stuxnet was capable of intercepting and manipulating the data that was communicated between the computer operating Step 7 software and the PLC used to configure the operation of the centrifuge cascades. Using the data that Stuxnet had obtained during its monitoring phase, the man-in-the-middle attack allowed it to feed data showing the normal operation of the frequency controllers to the operators of the Natanz facility and prevented them from receiving 'the anomalous operating frequency data'[170] that otherwise would have been sent while it delivered its payload. This undermined the integrity of the information that was being relayed from the Step 7 software to the PLC used to operate centrifuge machines, and the information relayed to and relied upon by the human operators of the Natanz facility. Also by replacing the library file with a malicious version, Stuxnet undermined the integrity of relationship between the Step 7 software and the PLC it was used to configure. By doing so and undermining the integrity of this information exchange process, Stuxnet caused further increases in entropy. Additionally, by infecting a particular data block used by the PLC as a safety mechanism for when it is faced with catastrophic events, Stuxnet prevented the operation of digital alarm systems that would have otherwise been triggered. Stuxnet prevented the PLC from executing this data block during its sabotage routine, and this is understood to have prevented the system's automatic shutdown that would normally occur during catastrophic events.[171] Stuxnet therefore disabled a protective function that would have otherwise indicated that a component of the Natanz facility was threatened by an entity capable of causing increased entropy.

The payload

In addition to the various degrees of entropy caused by Stuxnet's propagation methods and its man-in-the-middle attack, the most significant amount of entropy was caused by its payload. Among the necessary conditions required by Stuxnet before it delivered its payload was that it had found a S7–315 PLC used to operate a frequency converter drive manufactured by either Fararo Paya or Vacon[172] which was operating at between 807 Hz and 1210 Hz.[173] Then, during the third and fourth states of its 27-day attack cycle, Stuxnet sent bursts of data containing instructions determining the operation of the frequency converter drives used to control the rotation speed of the centrifuges. In the first cycle, Stuxnet adjusted the frequency of the frequency converter drive to 1410 Hz for fifteen minutes and then back to 1064 Hz.[174] This resulted in an increase in the rotation speed of the centrifuge that is believed to have been sufficient to both disrupt the enrichment process and destroy the centrifuge.[175] Approximately 27 days later, in the third and fourth states of the second cycle, Stuxnet sent another burst of data adjusting the frequency to 2 Hz for 50 minutes then back to 1064 Hz, meaning the centrifuge rotors were slowed down.[176] This is believed to have degraded the uranium-enrichment process, meaning a lower amount of uranium was enriched.[177] As such, Stuxnet altered the information sent from the PLC to the frequency converter drives, and, as the normal operation frequency of these devices is between 807 Hz and 1210 Hz,[178] it corrupted the normal properties of these entities when used for uranium enrichment. The combined result of the two cycles demonstrated that Stuxnet was intended to induce 'excessive vibrations or distortions' capable of physically damaging the centrifuge.[179] Instead of simply instructing the frequency converter drives or the PLC to shut down, for example, Stuxnet's payload involved a more subtle adjustment of the settings of these devices for fifteen- and 50-minute periods at approximately 27-day intervals. In addition to the entropy caused by the corruption of the frequency converter drives and the consequent disruption of the normal operation of the centrifuges, Stuxnet is believed to have caused material damage to approximately 1000 IR-1 centrifuges. Therefore, its payload resulted in a significant degree of increased entropy within the Natanz facility. This was also evident from the IAEA's reports, demonstrating that there was a sudden drop in the number of centrifuges under vacuum and a rise in the number of cascades with disconnected centrifuges,[180] as well as video footage showing that a similar number of centrifuges were dismantled.[181] In effect, these reports indicated that the Natanz facility was not operating normally and that, given the timing, Stuxnet was the likely cause of these increases in entropy.

Iran's responses

The exact measures taken by Iran's officials in response to Stuxnet are unknown; however, statements by some of its officials about the incident reflect a recognition that Iran was under threat. These statements effectively show that Iran's capacity to care for and protect the entities within its region of the infosphere was undermined by Stuxnet and the increases in entropy it is believed to have caused. For example, in September 2010 an official from the Ministry of Industry and Mines admitted that 30,000 computers had been infected by a hostile entity, including the computers of those working at the nuclear facility near Bushehr.[182] Similarly, in November 2010, Iran's president acknowledged that Iran's enemies had been successful in creating problems for its centrifuges using software, even though he maintained that the problem had been solved.[183] Finally, Iran's vice president also acknowledged that a hostile entity had infected its nuclear program, but that it was 'discovered and prevented from causing harm' to the operation of this program.[184] These senior officials within Iran explicitly recognized the hostile nature of Stuxnet and its ability to cause increased entropy within its region of the infosphere. These statements also demonstrate that Iran was taking measures to prevent Stuxnet from causing further entropy within its nuclear program so that it could continue the operation of this process. As an entity responsible for the care and protection of entities within its region of the infosphere, Iran recognized that Stuxnet was a hostile entity capable of causing increases in entropy within the Natanz facility and undermining its nuclear program.

Conclusion

An informational approach to the Stuxnet incident therefore demonstrates how, in addition the physical damage to approximately 1000 centrifuges, Stuxnet also undermined the integrity, or disrupted the operation, of thousands of entities associated with the functioning of the enrichment facility at Natanz. The harm to most of these entities did not involve physical damage, and instead mainly involved the disruption of their proper operation. Stuxnet undermined the integrity of over 100,000 computers around the world, and approximately 60,000 of these were within Iran. It exploited the interactions between these computers to ultimately access the PLCs used to operate uranium-enrichment centrifuges at the Natanz facility. In this process, it undermined the information exchanges between these entities and altered their properties, and undermined the functioning of the uranium-enrichment process, causing physical damage to approximately 1000 centrifuges.

Existing analyses of Stuxnet and the law on the use of force highlight the law's ontological constraints, as the law is largely incapable of recognizing the non-material harm to these entities. The near-exclusive focus on Stuxnet's material effects that dominates these analyses marginalizes Stuxnet's non-material effects. This is most strongly evident in the position that, had Stuxnet merely disrupted the operation of the centrifuges without causing material damage, it could be regarded as a 'legal masterpiece'.[185] Had this been the case, Stuxnet would have been seen as something below the use of force threshold and as a potential breach of the non-intervention principle. Essentially, even if it had largely the same effect of disrupting the operation of the enrichment facility at Natanz without causing physical damage, it would have fallen outside the scope of what is considered a use of force under Article 2(4). It would not have involved a form of violence that Article 2(4) has the capacity to recognize, and instead, it would have been equated with a form of non-violence only affecting the personality of the state. This distinction, based on whether a cyber attack results in material effects, is especially problematic, as Stuxnet highlights, because it implies that non-material effects are not taken sufficiently seriously in the use of force analysis. Given the degree to which states increasingly rely on ICTs for their proper functioning and are vulnerable to seemingly 'non-violent' cyber attacks that are considered outside the scope of Article 2(4), simply focusing on damage to physical objects is insufficient when considering the harm caused by cyber attacks.

By viewing Stuxnet's effects in terms of the increases in entropy they produced, the harm caused to a broader ontological range of entities can be recognized. In undermining the integrity of the uranium-enrichment facility at Natanz and disrupting the operation of various entities involved in the operation of the facility, as well as the uranium-enrichment process itself, Stuxnet can be seen to have effected both physical and informational violence against Iran. Detailed consideration of the various ways in which Stuxnet spread, compromised computers, and ultimately adjusted the rotation speed of nuclear centrifuges provides a more in-depth account of the harm caused by Stuxnet and how it occurred. The entropy caused by the payload resulting in physical damage to centrifuges, while significant in degree, was only part of the overall increases in entropy caused by Stuxnet. Stuxnet also corrupted the properties of over 60,000 entities within Iran's region of the infosphere, undermined the integrity of the Natanz facility, and disrupted and damaged the operation of centrifuges used in the enrichment process.

Notes

1 Uzi Mahnaimi, '"Flintstone" Spy Device Explodes at Iranian Nuclear Site' *The Australian* (23 September 2012) <www.theaustralian.com.au/news/world/flintstone-spy-device-explodes-at-iranian-nuclear-site/story-fnb64oi6-1226479668976> accessed 6 March 2018.
2 ibid.
3 David E Sanger and Thom Shanker, 'NSA Devises Radio Pathway into Computers' *New York Times* (15 January 2014) <www.nytimes.com/2014/01/15/us/nsa-effort-pries-open-computers-not-connected-to-internet.html> accessed 6 March 2018.
4 These technologies, in operation from at least 2008, rely 'on a covert channel of radio waves that can be transmitted from tiny circuit boards and USB cards inserted surreptitiously into the computers'. However, these transceivers have to be physically inserted into the computers, enabling them then to receive and transmit data through radio frequencies. See ibid.
5 David E Sanger, 'Obama Order Sped Up Wave of Cyberattacks Against Iran' *New York Times* (1 June 2012) <www.nytimes.com/2012/06/01/world/middleeast/obama-ordered-wave-of-cyberattacks-against-iran.html> accessed 6 March 2018.
6 ibid.
7 John Markoff, 'A Code for Chaos' *New York Times* (2 October 2010) <www.nytimes.com/2010/10/03/weekinreview/03markoff.html> accessed 6 March 2018.
8 Ellen Nakashima, 'Stuxnet Malware is Blueprint for Computer Attacks on US' *Washington Post* (2 October 2010) <www.washingtonpost.com/wp-dyn/content/article/2010/10/01/AR2010100106981.html> accessed 6 March 2018.
9 Josh Halliday and Julian Borger, 'Iranian Nuclear Plants Likely Target of Foiled Cyber Sabotage' *The Guardian* (25 September 2010) <www.theguardian.com/world/2010/sep/25/iran-cyber-hacking-nuclear-plants> accessed 6 March 2018.
10 Dylan Welch, 'Cyber Soldiers' *Sydney Morning Herald* (9 October 2010) <www.smh.com.au/technology/technology-news/cyber-soldiers-20101008-16c7e> accessed 6 March 2018.
11 Halliday and Borger (n 9).
12 Riva Richmond, 'Malware Hits Computerized Industrial Equipment' *New York Times* (24 September 2010) <https://bits.blogs.nytimes.com/2010/09/24/

malware-hits-computerized-industrial-equipment> accessed 6 March 2018; Markoff (n 7).
13 Richmond (n 12).
14 Markoff (n 7).
15 Sanger (n 5).
16 Richmond (n 12).
17 ibid.
18 ibid; John Markoff, 'A Silent Attack, but Not a Subtle One' *New York Times* (26 September 2010) <www.nytimes.com/2010/09/27/technology/27virus.html> accessed 6 March 2018.
19 Markoff (n 18); Sagar Meghani and Nasser Karimi, 'Anti-Iran Computer Bug had Powerful Backers' *The Guardian* (27 September 2010) <www.theguardian.com/education/2010/sep/26/iran-computer-bug-attcks-nuclear-plants> accessed 6 March 2018.
20 Halliday and Borger (n 9); Meghani and Karimi (n 19).
21 Richmond (n 12).
22 Markoff (n 18); Halliday and Borger (n 9); Meghani and Karimi (n 19).
23 David Albright, Paul Brannan and Christina Walrond, 'Stuxnet Malware and Natanz: Update of ISIS December 22, 2010 Report' (Institute for Science and International Security, 15 February 2011) 2 <http://isis-online.org/uploads/isis-reports/documents/stuxnet_update_15Feb2011.pdf> accessed 6 March 2018.
24 John Markoff and David E Sanger, 'In a Computer Worm, a Possible Biblical Clue' *New York Times* (29 September 2010) <www.nytimes.com/2010/09/30/world/middleeast/30worm.html?scp=2&sq=stuxnet&st=cse> accessed 6 March 2018.
25 Glenn Kessler, 'Centrifuges in Iran Were Shut Down, IAEA Report Says' *Washington Post* (24 November 2010) <www.washingtonpost.com/wp-dyn/content/article/2010/11/23/AR2010112306964.html> accessed 6 March 2018.
26 Kim Zetter, *Countdown to Zero Day: Stuxnet and the Launch of the World's First Digital Weapon* (Crown 2014) 237–8.
27 ISIS is a non-profit think tank focused on issues surrounding the proliferation of nuclear weapons technologies.
28 David Albright, Paul Brannan and Christina Walrond, 'Did Stuxnet Take Out 1,000 Centrifuges at the Natanz Enrichment Plant?' (ISIS, 22 December 2010) <http://isis-online.org/uploads/isis-reports/documents/stuxnet_FEP_22Dec2010.pdf> accessed 6 March 2018.
29 ibid 2, 8.
30 Joby Warrick, 'Iran's Natanz Nuclear Facility Recovered Quickly from Stuxnet Cyberattack' *Washington Post* (16 February 2011) <www.washingtonpost.com/wp-dyn/content/article/2011/02/15/AR2011021505395.html> accessed 6 March 2018.
31 William J Broad, John Markoff and David E Sanger, 'Israeli Test on Worm Called Crucial in Iran Nuclear Delay' *New York Times* (15 January 2011) <www.nytimes.com/2011/01/16/world/middleeast/16stuxnet.html> accessed 6 March 2018.
32 Sanger (n 5).
33 ibid.
34 ibid. This was also reported the previous year: see Broad, Markoff and Sanger (n 31).
35 Sanger (n 5).
36 ibid.
37 The final version of this dossier was released in February 2011 (version 1.4). Nicolas Falliere, Liam O'Murchu L and Eric Chien, *W32.Stuxnet Dossier. Version 1.4* (Symantec, February 2011) <www.symantec.com/content/en/us/enterprise/media/security_response/whitepapers/w32_stuxnet_dossier.pdf> accessed 6 March 2018.

38 ibid 53–54.
39 ibid 7.
40 Geoff McDonald and others, *Stuxnet 0.5: The Missing Link* (Symantec, 26 February 2013) <www.symantec.com/content/en/us/enterprise/media/security_response/whitepapers/stuxnet_0_5_the_missing_link.pdf> accessed 6 March 2018.
41 ibid 1.
42 ibid 2. Stuxnet's development appears to have begun as early as May 2006, see Zetter (n 26) 321–2.
43 McDonald and others (n 40) 2–4, 9.
44 Falliere, O'Murchu and Chien (n 37) 8–11.
45 David Kushner, 'The Real Story of Stuxnet' (2013) 50(3) *IEEE Spectrum* 48, 51. These are vulnerabilities in software unknown to the developers, meaning that where such vulnerabilities are exploited, the developers of the software have 'zero days' (in terms of time) to develop fixes for the vulnerability.
46 Treaty on the Non-Proliferation of Nuclear Weapons (adopted 1 July 1968, entered into force 5 March 1970) [1973] ATS 3.
47 Iran signed the NPT in 1968 and ratified it in 1970. On the history of Iran's nuclear program, see Gawdat Bahgat, 'Nuclear Proliferation: The Islamic Republic of Iran' (2006) 39(3) *Iranian Studies* 307, 308–12.
48 Article IV of the NPT recognizes 'the inalienable right of all the Parties to the Treaty to develop research, production and use of nuclear energy for peaceful purposes', and pursuant to Article II those states without an existing weapons capability agree not, by any means, to receive or develop nuclear weapons. Treaty on the Non-Proliferation of Nuclear Weapons (n 46).
49 Treaty on the Non-Proliferation of Nuclear Weapons (n 46) Art III.
50 Jansen Calamita, 'Sanctions, Countermeasures, and the Iranian Nuclear Issue' (2009) 42(5) *Vanderbilt Journal of Transnational Law* 1393, 1399–1400.
51 Saira Khan, *Iran and Nuclear Weapons: Protracted Conflict and Proliferation* (Routledge 2009) 51.
52 Calamita (n 50) 1400; Bahgat (n 47) 310.
53 Khan (n 51) 13.
54 See, for example, UNSC Res 1696 (31 July 2006) UN Doc S/RES/1696; UNSC Res 1737 (23 December 2006) UN Doc S/RES/1737; UNSC Res 1803 (3 March 2008) UN Doc S/RES/1803. See also Dina Esfandiary and Mark Fitzpatrick 'Sanctions on Iran: Defining and Enabling "Success"' (2011) 53(5) *Survival* 143, 144.
55 Khan (n 51) 51–2.
56 Daniel Joyner, *Interpreting the Nuclear Non-Proliferation Treaty* (Oxford University Press 2011) 6.
57 ibid 4.
58 ibid; 'Uranium Enrichment' (World Nuclear Association, May 2017) <www.world-nuclear.org/information-library/nuclear-fuel-cycle/conversion-enrichment-and-fabrication/uranium-enrichment.aspx> accessed 6 March 2018; 'How Uranium Ore is Made into Nuclear Fuel' (World Nuclear Association) <www.world-nuclear.org/nuclear-basics/how-is-uranium-ore-made-into-nuclear-fuel.aspx> accessed 6 March 2018.
59 Joyner (n 56) 6.
60 'Uranium Enrichment' (n 58).
61 ibid.
62 Joyner (n 56) 5.
63 William Bolton, *Programmable Logic Controllers* (5th edn, Newnes 2009) 3.
64 ibid.
65 ibid.
66 Falliere, O'Murchu and Chien (n 37) 36.

67 ibid 3; Kim Zetter, 'Hacker Lexicon: What is an Air Gap?' *Wired* (8 December 2014) <www.wired.com/2014/12/hacker-lexicon-air-gap> accessed 6 March 2018.
68 Zetter (n 67).
69 Albright, Brannan and Walrond (n 23) 2.
70 Falliere, O'Murchu and Chien (n 37) 3. See also Zetter (n 26) 322–3.
71 Falliere, O'Murchu and Chien (n 37) 29.
72 Zetter (n 26) 90.
73 Falliere, O'Murchu and Chien (n 37) 25–6.
74 ibid 25, 33.
75 ibid 14–16.
76 ibid 21.
77 ibid 5.
78 Albright, Brannan and Walrond (n 23) 6.
79 Zetter (n 26) 236–7. See also Falliere, O'Murchu and Chien (n 37) 45–8.
80 McDonald and others (n 40) 9.
81 Falliere, O'Murchu and Chien (n 37) 39.
82 ibid.
83 ibid.
84 ibid.
85 ibid 41.
86 Albright, Brannan and Walrond (n 28) 3–4.
87 Albright, Brannan and Walrond (n 23) 6.
88 Falliere, O'Murchu and Chien (n 37) 47. As mentioned, this part of the code was only active in Stuxnet 0.5 and it was disabled in the full version of Stuxnet.
89 Albright, Brannan and Walrond (n 23) 6.
90 Ralph Langer, 'Cracking Stuxnet, a 21st-Century Cyber Weapon' (TED Talk, March 2011) 3:25 <www.ted.com/talks/ralph_langner_cracking_stuxnet_a_21st_century_cyberweapon?language=en> accessed 6 March 2018.
91 Falliere, O'Murchu and Chien (n 37) 41–3.
92 ibid 43.
93 Richard E Blahut, *Cryptography and Secure Communication* (Cambridge University Press 2014) 511.
94 Falliere, O'Murchu and Chien (n 37) 48–9.
95 ibid 38–9, 49; Zetter (n 26) 123.
96 Falliere, O'Murchu and Chien (n 37) 49.
97 Albright, Brannan and Walrond (n 28) 4–5.
98 Zetter (n 26) 343.
99 Albright, Brannan and Walrond (n 28) 6.
100 Albright, Brannan and Walrond (n 23) 1.
101 Thomas Erdbrink and Ellen Nakashima, 'Iran Struggling to Contain "Foreign-made" Computer Worm' *Washington Post* (28 September 2010) <www.washingtonpost.com/wp-dyn/content/article/2010/09/27/AR2010092706606.html> accessed 6 March 2018; David E Sanger, John Markoff and William Yong, 'Iran Fights Malware Attacking Computers' *New York Times* (26 September 2010) <www.nytimes.com/2010/09/26/world/middleeast/26iran.html> accessed 6 March 2018.
102 Erdbrink and Nakashima (n 101); Sanger, Markoff and Yong (n 101).
103 Sanger, Markoff and Yong (n 101).
104 'Iran "briefly halted enrichment"' *Al Jazeera* (23 November 2010) <www.aljazeera.com/news/middleeast/2010/11/20101123193667 3748.html> accessed 6 March 2018.
105 Thomas Erdbrink, 'Ahmadinejad: Iran's Nuclear Program Hit by Sabotage' *Washington Post* (29 November 2010) <www.washingtonpost.com/wp-dyn/content/article/2010/11/29/AR2010112903468.html> accessed 6 March 2018.

106 ibid.
107 When specifically asked whether Stuxnet was responsible, President Ahmadinejad responded by saying, 'The Iranian president's answer to this question is: silence. That's it.' ibid.
108 Kessler (n 25).
109 Albright, Brannan and Walrond (n 28) 2, 8.
110 ibid 1–2.
111 ibid 2.
112 ibid 2, 8.
113 ibid 6, 8.
114 Albright, Brannan and Walrond (n 23) 3.
115 Warrick (n 30).
116 ibid.
117 ibid.
118 Albright, Brannan and Walrond (n 23) 4.
119 See Zetter (n 26) 354–7.
120 Broad, Markoff and Sanger (n 31).
121 Albright, Brannan and Walrond (n 23) 4.
122 ibid 1.
123 ibid 4.
124 Gary D Brown, 'Why Iran Didn't Admit Stuxnet was an Attack' (2011) 63 *Joint Force Quarterly* 70, 71 (citations omitted).
125 ibid.
126 Heather Harrison Dinniss, *Cyber Warfare and the Laws of War* (Cambridge University Press 2012) 81.
127 ibid.
128 David P Fidler, 'Was Stuxnet an Act of War? Decoding a Cyberattack' (2011) 9(4) *IEEE Security & Privacy* 56, 57.
129 William H Boothby and others, 'When is a Cyberattack a Use of Force or an Armed Attack?' (2012) 45(8) *Computer* 82, 83. A number of other authors also take this view, emphasizing the destruction of physical property in determining whether Stuxnet constituted a use of force. See Christopher D DeLuca, 'The Need for International Laws of War to Include Cyber Attacks Involving State and Non-State Actors' (2013) 3(9) *Pace International Law Review Online Companion* 278, 298; Andrew Moore, 'Stuxnet and Article 2(4)'s Prohibition Against the Use of Force: Customary Law and Potential Models' (2015) 64 *Naval Law Review* 1, 1; Marco Roscini, *Cyber Operations and the Use of Force in International Law* (Oxford University Press 2014) 53.
130 Some of these authors consider the *Tallinn Manual* criteria specifically, whereas others consider Schmitt's criteria (which formed the basis for the *Tallinn Manual* criteria) before the *Tallinn Manual* was published.
131 David Weissbrodt, 'Cyber-Conflict, Cyber-Crime, and Cyber-Espionage' (2013) 22 *Minnesota Journal of International Law* 347, 376.
132 ibid.
133 See Priyanka Dev, 'Use of Force and Armed Attack Thresholds in Cyber Conflict: The Looming Definitional Gaps and the Growing Need for Formal UN Response' (2015) 50(2) *Texas International Law Journal* 381, 398–9; Andrew C Foltz, 'Stuxnet, Schmitt Analysis, and the Cyber Use-of-Force Debate' (2012) 67 *Joint Force Quarterly* 40, 44; Charles C Poché, This Means War! (Maybe?) – Clarifying Casus Belli in Cyberspace' (2013) 15 *Oregon Review of International Law* 413, 432–4.
134 Michael N Schmitt (ed), *Tallinn Manual 2.0 on the International Law Applicable to Cyber Operations* (2nd edn, Cambridge University Press 2017) 342. Some in the Group of Experts also maintained it constituted an armed attack.

135 Katharina Ziolkowski, 'Stuxnet – Legal Considerations' (2012) 25(3) *Humanitäres Völkerrecht – Informationsschriften /Journal of International Law of Peace and Armed Conflict* 139, 142.
136 ibid 147.
137 Russell Buchan, 'Cyber Attacks: Unlawful Uses of Force or Prohibited Interventions?' (2012) 17(2) *Journal of Conflict & Security Law* 211, 220.
138 ibid 220–1.
139 Foltz (n 133) 45. See also Buchan (n 137) 220.
140 As mentioned, according to the ISIS report, Stuxnet was designed to damage the centrifuges and not to manipulate the 'parameters of the centrifuge cascades so as to lower the production of low enriched uranium (LEU) on a sustained basis'. See Albright, Brannan and Walrond (n 23) 1.
141 Terry Gill, for example, while not taking a definitive position on whether Stuxnet constituted a use of force, nonetheless maintains that Stuxnet definitely qualified as an 'intervention', given that it involved coercive means to prevent a state from 'pursuing a particular course of action'. See Terry D Gill, 'Non-Intervention in the Cyber Context' in Katharina Ziolkowski (ed), *Peacetime Regime for State Activities in Cyberspace. International Law, International Relations and Diplomacy* (NATO Cooperative Cyber Defence Centre of Excellence 2013) 235.
142 International Telecommunication Union, 'Measuring the Information Society Report' (ITU, 2015) 219 <www.itu.int/en/ITU-D/Statistics/Documents/publications/misr2015/MISR2015-w5.pdf> accessed 6 March 2018.
143 'Individuals Using the Internet (% of population)' (The World Bank) <https://data.worldbank.org/indicator/IT.NET.USER.ZS?locations=IR> accessed 6 March 2018.
144 International Telecommunication Union (n 142) 44–6.
145 For an overview of the laws and policies since 2000 relating to Iran's development of e-government, see Alinaghi Ziaee Bigdeli and Sergio de Cesare, 'Barriers to e-Government Service Delivery in Developing Countries: The Case of Iran' in Andrea Carugati and Cecilia Rossignoli (eds), *Emerging Themes in Information Systems and Organization Studies* (Springer 2011) 308–9. For an overview of the history of the implementation of ICTs into Iran's administrative and government communications, see Hossein Sharifi and Behrouz Zarei, 'An Adaptive Approach for Implementing e-Government in I.R. Iran' (2004) 30(5) *Journal of Government Information* 600, 605–6.
146 Bigdeli and de Cesare (n 145) 314.
147 For example, Homa Katouzian describes Iran's 1979 constitution as having both theocratic and secular/democratic elements. See Homa Katouzian, *The Persians: Ancient, Mediaeval, and Modern Iran* (Yale University Press 2009) 335–7. Similarly, Saïd Arjomand describes it as an 'ideological constitution', as all laws have to be in accordance with Islamic standards. See Saïd A Arjomand, 'Shi'ite Jurists and the Iranian Law and Constitutional Order in the Twentieth Century' in Saïd A Arjomand and Nathan J Brown (eds), *The Rule of Law, Islam, and Constitutional Politics in Egypt and Iran* (SUNY Press 2013) 31–2.
148 Joyner (n 56) 19–20.
149 UNSC Res 1696 (n 54) 2.
150 UNSC Res 1737 (n 54) 2.
151 ibid 4.
152 ibid.
153 See, for example, Pierre-Emmanuel Dupont, 'Countermeasures and Collective Security: The Case of the EU Sanctions Against Iran' (2012) 17(3) *Journal of Conflict and Security Law* 301, 303–6.
154 UNSC Res 1803 (n 54) 3.

155 According to Gawdat Bahgat, Iran's nuclear policy is driven by the dynamics of its security environment, domestic political and economic concerns, and its national pride in developing a self-sufficient nuclear program. See Bahgat (n 47) 313–24.
156 Falliere, O'Murchu and Chien (n 37) 8–11.
157 ibid 14.
158 ibid 16.
159 ibid.
160 ibid 22.
161 ibid 24.
162 ibid 29.
163 ibid 30; Zetter (n 26) 10.
164 Falliere, O'Murchu and Chien (n 37) 24, 29.
165 ibid 27–8; Zetter (n 26) 90.
166 Falliere, O'Murchu and Chien (n 37) 25, 33.
167 ibid 26.
168 ibid 37–8.
169 ibid 36.
170 ibid 49.
171 ibid.
172 ibid 39.
173 ibid 41.
174 ibid 42–3.
175 Albright, Brannan and Walrond (n 28) 4–5.
176 Falliere, O'Murchu and Chien (n 37) 42–3.
177 Zetter (n 26) 343.
178 Falliere, O'Murchu and Chien (n 37) 43.
179 Albright, Brannan and Walrond (n 28) 6.
180 ibid 2, 8.
181 Warrick (n 30).
182 Erdbrink and Nakashima (n 101); Sanger, Markoff and Yong (n 101).
183 Erdbrink (n 105).
184 Kessler (n 25).
185 Ziolkowski (n 135) 147. Similarly, Foltz suggests that it is unlikely to have been considered a use of force by the international community. See Foltz (n 133) 45. This point is also made by Buchan, see Buchan (n 137) 220.

Bibliography

Albright D, Brannan P and Walrond C, 'Did Stuxnet Take Out 1,000 Centrifuges at the Natanz Enrichment Plant?' (Institute for Science and International Security, 22 December 2010) <http://isis-online.org/uploads/isis-reports/documents/stuxnet_FEP_22Dec2010.pdf> accessed 6 March 2018

——— *Stuxnet Malware and Natanz: Update of ISIS December 22, 2010 Report* (Institute for Science and International Security, 15 February 2011) <http://isis-online.org/uploads/isis-reports/documents/stuxnet_update_15Feb2011.pdf> accessed 6 March 2018

Arjomand SA, 'Shi'ite Jurists and the Iranian Law and Constitutional Order in the Twentieth Century' in Arjomand SA and Brown NJ (eds), *The Rule of Law, Islam, and Constitutional Politics in Egypt and Iran* (SUNY Press 2013)

Bahgat G, 'Nuclear Proliferation: The Islamic Republic of Iran' (2006) 39(3) *Iranian Studies* 307

Bigdeli AZ and de Cesare S, 'Barriers to e-Government Service Delivery in Developing Countries: The Case of Iran' in Carugati A and Rossignoli C (eds), *Emerging Themes in Information Systems and Organization Studies* (Springer 2011)
Blahut RE, *Cryptography and Secure Communication* (Cambridge University Press 2014)
Bolton W, *Programmable Logic Controllers* (5th edn, Newnes 2009)
Boothby WH and others, 'When is a Cyberattack a Use of Force or an Armed Attack?' (2012) 45(8) *Computer* 82
Broad WJ, Markoff J and Sanger DE, 'Israeli Test on Worm Called Crucial in Iran Nuclear Delay' *New York Times* (15 January 2011) <www.nytimes.com/2011/01/16/world/middleeast/16stuxnet.html> accessed 6 March 2018
Brown GD, 'Why Iran Didn't Admit Stuxnet was an Attack' (2011) 63 *Joint Force Quarterly* 70
Buchan R, 'Cyber Attacks: Unlawful Uses of Force or Prohibited Interventions?' (2012) 17(2) *Journal of Conflict & Security Law* 211
Calamita J, 'Sanctions, Countermeasures, and the Iranian Nuclear Issue' (2009) 42(5) *Vanderbilt Journal of Transnational Law* 1393
DeLuca CD, 'The Need for International Laws of War to Include Cyber Attacks Involving State and Non-State Actors' (2013) 3(9) *Pace International Law Review Online Companion* 278
Dev P, 'Use of Force and Armed Attack Thresholds in Cyber Conflict: The Looming Definitional Gaps and the Growing Need for Formal UN Response' (2015) 50(2) *Texas International Law Journal* 381
Dinniss HH, *Cyber Warfare and the Laws of War* (Cambridge University Press 2012)
Dupont PE, 'Countermeasures and Collective Security: The Case of the EU Sanctions Against Iran' (2012) 17(3) *Journal of Conflict and Security Law* 301
Erdbrink T, 'Ahmadinejad: Iran's Nuclear Program Hit by Sabotage' *Washington Post* (29 November 2010) <www.washingtonpost.com/wp-dyn/content/article/2010/11/29/AR2010112903468.html> accessed 6 March 2018
Erdbrink T and Nakashima E, 'Iran Struggling to Contain "Foreign-made" Computer Worm' *Washington Post* (28 September 2010) <www.washingtonpost.com/wp-dyn/content/article/2010/09/27/AR2010092706606.html> accessed 6 March 2018
Esfandiary D and Fitzpatrick M, 'Sanctions on Iran: Defining and Enabling "Success"' (2011) 53(5) *Survival* 143
Falliere N, O'Murchu L and Chien E, 'W32.Stuxnet Dossier. Version 1.4' (Symantec, February 2011) <www.symantec.com/content/en/us/enterprise/media/security_response/whitepapers/w32_stuxnet_dossier.pdf> accessed 6 March 2018
Fidler DP, 'Was Stuxnet an Act of War? Decoding a Cyberattack' (2011) 9(4) *IEEE Security & Privacy* 56
Foltz AC, 'Stuxnet, Schmitt Analysis, and the Cyber Use-of-Force Debate' (2012) 67 *Joint Force Quarterly* 40
Gill TD, 'Non-Intervention in the Cyber Context' in Ziolkowski K (ed), *Peacetime Regime for State Activities in Cyberspace: International Law, International Relations and Diplomacy* (NATO Cooperative Cyber Defence Centre of Excellence 2013)
Halliday J and Borger J, 'Iranian Nuclear Plants Likely Target of Foiled Cyber Sabotage' *The Guardian* (25 September 2010) <www.theguardian.com/world/2010/sep/25/iran-cyber-hacking-nuclear-plants> accessed 6 March 2018

'How Uranium Ore is Made into Nuclear Fuel' (World Nuclear Association) <www.world-nuclear.org/nuclear-basics/how-is-uranium-ore-made-into-nuclear-fuel.aspx> accessed 6 March 2018

'Individuals Using the Internet (% of Population)' (World Bank) <https://data.worldbank.org/indicator/IT.NET.USER.ZS?locations=IR> accessed 6 March 2018

International Telecommunication Union, *Measuring the Information Society Report* (ITU, 2015) <www.itu.int/en/ITU-D/Statistics/Documents/publications/misr2015/MISR2015-w5.pdf> accessed 6 March 2018

'Iran "Briefly Halted Enrichment"' *Al Jazeera* (23 November 2010) <www.aljazeera.com/news/middleeast/2010/11/20101123193667374 8.html> accessed 6 March 2018

Joyner D, *Interpreting the Nuclear Non-Proliferation Treaty* (Oxford University Press 2011)

Katouzian H, *The Persians: Ancient, Mediaeval, and Modern Iran* (Yale University Press 2009)

Kessler G, 'Centrifuges in Iran were Shut Down, IAEA Report Says' *Washington Post* (24 November 2010) <www.washingtonpost.com/wp-dyn/content/article/2010/11/23/AR2010112306964.html> accessed 6 March 2018

Khan S, *Iran and Nuclear Weapons: Protracted Conflict and Proliferation* (Routledge 2009)

Kushner D, 'The Real Story of Stuxnet' (2013) 50(3) *IEEE Spectrum* 48

Langer R, 'Cracking Stuxnet, a 21st-Century Cyber Weapon' (TED Talk, March 2011) <www.ted.com/talks/ralph_langner_cracking_stuxnet_a_21st_century_cyberweapon?language=en> accessed 6 March 2018

Mahnaimi U, '"Flintstone" Spy Device Explodes at Iranian Nuclear Site' *The Australian* (23 September 2012) <www.theaustralian.com.au/news/world/flintstone-spy-device-explodes-at-iranian-nuclear-site/story-fnb64oi6-1226479668976> accessed 6 March 2018

Markoff J, 'A Code for Chaos' *New York Times* (2 October 2010) <www.nytimes.com/2010/10/03/weekinreview/03markoff.html> accessed 6 March 2018

——— 'A Silent Attack, but Not a Subtle One' *New York Times* (New York, 26 September 2010) <www.nytimes.com/2010/09/27/technology/27virus.html> accessed 6 March 2018

Markoff J and Sanger DE, 'In a Computer Worm, a Possible Biblical Clue' *New York Times* (29 September 2010) <www.nytimes.com/2010/09/30/world/middleeast/30worm.html?scp=2&sq=stuxnet&st=cse> accessed 6 March 2018

McDonald G and others, 'Stuxnet 0.5: The Missing Link' (Symantec, 26 February 2013) <www.symantec.com/content/en/us/enterprise/media/security_response/whitepapers/stuxnet_0_5_the_missing_link.pdf> accessed 6 March 2018

Meghani S and Karimi N, 'Anti-Iran Computer Bug had Powerful Backers' *The Guardian* (27 September 2010) <www.theguardian.com/education/2010/sep/26/iran-computer-bug-attcks-nuclear-plants> accessed 6 March 2018

Moore A, 'Stuxnet and Article 2(4)'s Prohibition Against the Use of Force: Customary Law and Potential Models' (2015) 64 *Naval Law Review* 1

Nakashima E, 'Stuxnet Malware is Blueprint for Computer Attacks on US' *Washington Post* (2 October 2010) <www.washingtonpost.com/wp-dyn/content/article/2010/10/01/AR2010100106981.html> accessed 6 March 2018

Poché CC, 'This Means War! (Maybe?): Clarifying Casus Belli in Cyberspace' (2013) 15 *Oregon Review of International Law* 413

Richmond R, 'Malware Hits Computerized Industrial Equipment' *New York Times* (24 September 2010) <https://bits.blogs.nytimes.com/2010/09/24/malware-hits-computerized-industrial-equipment> accessed 6 March 2018

Roscini M, *Cyber Operations and the Use of Force in International Law* (Oxford University Press 2014)

Sanger DE, 'Obama Order Sped up Wave of Cyberattacks against Iran' *New York Times* (1 June 2012) <www.nytimes.com/2012/06/01/world/middleeast/obama-ordered-wave-of-cyberattacks-against-iran.html> accessed 6 March 2018

Sanger DE, Markoff J and Yong W, 'Iran Fights Malware Attacking Computers' *New York Times* (26 September 2010) <www.nytimes.com/2010/09/26/world/middleeast/26iran.html> accessed 6 March 2018

Sanger DE and Shanker T, 'NSA Devises Radio Pathway into Computers' *New York Times* (15 January 2014) <www.nytimes.com/2014/01/15/us/nsa-effort-pries-open-computers-not-connected-to-internet.html> accessed 6 March 2018

Schmitt MN (ed), *Tallinn Manual 2.0 on the International Law Applicable to Cyber Operations* (2nd edn, Cambridge University Press 2017)

Sharifi H and Zarei B, 'An Adaptive Approach for Implementing e-Government in I.R. Iran' (2004) 30(5) *Journal of Government Information* 600

Treaty on the Non-Proliferation of Nuclear Weapons (adopted 1 July 1968, entered into force 5 March 1970) [1973] ATS 3

UNSC Res 1696 (31 July 2006) UN Doc S/RES/1696

UNSC Res 1737 (23 December 2006) UN Doc S/RES/1737

UNSC Res 1803 (3 March 2008) UN Doc S/RES/1803

'Uranium Enrichment' (World Nuclear Association, May 2017) <www.world-nuclear.org/information-library/nuclear-fuel-cycle/conversion-enrichment-and-fabrication/uranium-enrichment.aspx> accessed 6 March 2018

Warrick J, 'Iran's Natanz Nuclear Facility Recovered Quickly from Stuxnet Cyber-attack' *Washington Post* (16 February 2011) <www.washingtonpost.com/wp-dyn/content/article/2011/02/15/AR2011021505395.html> accessed 6 March 2018

Weissbrodt D, 'Cyber-Conflict, Cyber-Crime, and Cyber-Espionage' (2013) 22 *Minnesota Journal of International Law* 347

Welch D, 'Cyber Soldiers' *Sydney Morning Herald* (9 October 2010) <www.smh.com.au/technology/technology-news/cyber-soldiers-20101008-16c7e> accessed 6 March 2018

Zetter K, *Countdown to Zero Day: Stuxnet and the Launch of the World's First Digital Weapon* (Crown 2014)

——— 'Hacker Lexicon: What is an Air Gap' *Wired* (8 December 2014) <www.wired.com/2014/12/hacker-lexicon-air-gap> accessed 6 March 2018

Ziolkowski K, 'Stuxnet: Legal Considerations' (2012) 25(3) *Humanitäres Völkerrecht – Informationsschriften/Journal of International Law of Peace and Armed Conflict* 139

7 Russian interference in the 2016 US presidential election

Introduction

During the 2016 US presidential election, the US Democratic National Committee's (DNC) network was compromised by cyber attacks believed to have been conducted by two groups affiliated with Russian intelligence agencies.[1] This led to the release of tens of thousands of private emails and attachments to the public through WikiLeaks, DCLeaks.com, and an online persona identifying himself as 'Guccifer 2.0'.[2] Electoral boards were compromised by similar attacks, and there was a broader influence campaign by Russian state-owned media and paid social media users.[3] According to an Intelligence Community Assessment (ICA) report by the Central Intelligence Agency (CIA), the Federal Bureau of Investigation (FBI), and the National Security Agency (NSA), Russia had developed a preference for Donald Trump, and through this campaign, it had sought to 'undermine public faith in the US democratic process, denigrate Secretary Clinton, and harm her electability and potential presidency'.[4] These intelligence agencies assessed 'with high confidence' that the influence campaign was ordered by Russian President Vladimir Putin.[5] The ICA report also noted that, compared with previous operations directed towards US elections, Russian actions 'represented a significant escalation in directness, level of activity, and scope of effort'.[6] The incident was described by prominent US politicians such as Senator John McCain as an 'act of war';[7] US House of Representatives member Jackie Speier described it as 'an act of hybrid warfare'.[8]

This chapter considers the cyber attacks[9] used as part of the Russian interference in the 2016 US presidential election and international law on the use of force and non-intervention. It demonstrates that an informational approach enables an analysis of the incident that takes into account how the cyber attacks impacted a range of entities – human beings, computer systems, and the electoral process – and their interactions, and how the incident amounted to a form of informational violence against the United States. The first section provides an overview of the Russian interference in the 2016 US presidential election, with a focus on the cyber attacks used in this context. The chapter then considers whether and to what extent the non-use of force and non-intervention principles apply to the incident. Generally the incident is considered to fall outside the scope of Article 2(4) and is regarded as a possible violation of the non-intervention principle. This is mainly because the cyber attacks that were used involved obtaining unauthorized access to computers and networks, and resulted in the release of data obtained from those networks. The harm caused is therefore not something Article 2(4) is capable of recognizing within its conception of violence. The chapter demonstrates that through an informational approach to the incident, the spear-phishing attacks against US political and electoral organizations, and the subsequent release of information obtained from DNC networks, can be considered in terms of the increases in entropy they produced. Given the harm caused, particularly by the systematic and strategic release of information, the incident can be seen as a form of informational violence warranting concern with regard to Article 2(4). Essentially, the attacks sought to disrupt the proper operation of the election process and the autonomy of the United States as an entity.

Overview of events

There were two separate attacks through which the DNC's networks were compromised – one in mid-2015 and another in early 2016.[10] The actor believed responsible for the first attack was known as Advanced Persistent Threat 29 (APT29), or Cozy Bear, and the actor believed to have been responsible for the second attack was known as APT28, or Fancy Bear.[11] Fancy Bear is understood to have been directed by Russia's Main Intelligence Directorate (GRU).[12] Most reports link Cozy Bear to the GRU's competing intelligence agency, the Federal Security Service (FSB),[13] although according to Dutch sources, it is also linked to the GRU.[14] No collaboration has been identified between these groups, and they are understood to have compromised the same systems separately without awareness of each other.[15]

Both Cozy Bear and Fancy Bear made use of spear-phishing attacks – a form of social engineering involving emails targeted at those affiliated with particular organizations, with the aim of misleading human users into activating links or providing their user credentials to the attackers.[16] Social engineering is a form of 'cognitive hacking', which involves obtaining unauthorized access to 'a computer information system for the purpose of modifying certain behaviors of a human user in a way that violates the integrity of the overall user-information system'.[17] Cognitive hacking therefore involves efforts that seek to undermine the integrity of the wider information system of which the human user is also regarded as a part.

According to Crowdstrike, the cybersecurity company hired by the DNC to investigate the incident, Cozy Bear was known to have used spear-phishing attacks previously to target a range of public and private organizations.[18] It commonly intruded systems through spear-phishing campaigns that involve sending emails containing links to a malicious software which, if activated by the targeted user, installed one of a range of sophisticated remote access tools that provided the attackers with access to users' systems.[19] According to Crowdstrike, in its operation against the DNC, Cozy Bear mainly used a piece of malicious software called 'SeaDaddy', which then allowed it to 'launch malicious code automatically after a specified period of system uptime or on a specific schedule'[20] and to download additional features – meaning it was capable, in theory, of doing 'virtually anything on the victim system'.[21]

Conversely, Fancy Bear was known to send targeted emails to specific users based on reconnaissance of its targets.[22] This often involved using publicly available information (such as LinkedIn profiles demonstrating that a person was affiliated with a particular organization) as well as information obtained through prior operations.[23] It was also known for registering domain names similar to legitimate names known to be used by an organization and creating websites that closely resemble them.[24] The purpose of these fake websites was to steal the user credentials of those targeted with the spear-phishing attacks.[25] In its operation against the DNC, once it had gained access to DNC systems, Fancy Bear used malicious software that was capable of executing commands remotely, transferring files, and logging keystrokes of users.[26] Fancy Bear is also believed to have been responsible for compromising the email account of the chairman of Hillary Clinton's presidential campaign, John Podesta, which contained approximately 60,000 of his emails.[27]

According to statements given at a US Senate Select Committee on Intelligence in March 2017, at least 109 staff members of the Clinton campaign were targeted by spear-phishing attacks between 10 March and 7 April 2016.[28] The malicious link sent to these people was clicked 36 times, and some of these accounts were breached.[29] Clinton's senior policy adviser, Jake Sullivan, was also targeted by at least fourteen attempts from 19 March 2016.[30] Clinton's personal email was targeted twice in March 2016; however, she was not successfully deceived into providing her credentials.[31] Sixteen emails were also sent to DNC staff between 15 March and 11 April 2016, and three of the accounts targeted were breached on 6 April 2016.[32]

As a result of the cyber attacks by Cozy Bear and Fancy Bear, thousands of emails and files were obtained that were then released to the public during the second half of 2016. For example, on 22 July 2016, WikiLeaks released approximately 44,000 emails and 18,000 attachment files obtained from the DNC networks,[33] and in October 2016, it continued releasing emails and files obtained from Podesta's account.[34] According to US intelligence agencies, Russia had also compromised Republican Party computers and networks; however, no information obtained from these computers and networks was released to the public.[35]

In addition to the spear-phishing attacks against the DNC, electoral systems were also targeted through similar attacks. According to a leaked intelligence report from the NSA in June 2017, the attacks occurred in late

October or early November 2016 and involved spear-phishing emails sent to 122 addresses associated with users in local government organizations that potentially were involved in managing voter registration systems.[36] This report also indicated that Russia had conducted cyber attacks against a US company that supplied voting software; however, it was unknown whether these attacks were successful.[37] According to media reports in September 2017, altogether the electoral systems of 21 US states had been targeted by Russian cyber attacks.[38] In February 2018, it was reported that the voter registration systems or websites had in fact been compromised in seven US states (Alaska, Arizona, California, Florida, Illinois, Texas, and Wisconsin).[39] These figures are largely consistent with a US Senate Select Committee on Intelligence report released in May 2018, which noted that it was possible that at least 21 states had been targeted.[40] According to this report, Russian actors had also gained 'access to restricted elements of the election infrastructure' and had been in a position to at least 'alter or delete voter registration data' in a small number of states.[41] However, the attackers did not appear to have been in the position to manipulate individual votes or the total number of votes.[42] This is consistent with the ICA report released in January 2017, which also noted that, while 'elements of multiple state or local electoral boards' were accessed, the types of systems that had been targeted or compromised were 'not involved in vote tallying'.[43]

According to US intelligence agencies, Russia – under the direction of President Putin – was responsible for conducting these operations with the aim of undermining Clinton's chance of winning the election, as it had developed a 'clear preference' for Donald Trump.[44] The cyber attacks involved targeted emails that sought to mislead human users so that the attackers could obtain unauthorized access to their organizations' systems, install malicious software and exfiltrate data from those systems. These data were then released in a systematic and strategic way with the aim of undermining the Democratic Party's candidate's electability. Accordingly, the cyber attacks did not involve material damage, such as damage to computer hardware, and it is understood that they did not significantly disrupt the operation of computers or manipulate the vote counting process. Nonetheless, the attacks involved more than just the collection of data, as the data were subsequently actively used for a strategic purpose as part of Russia's broader interference operation.

The ontological constraints of the law

This section considers Russian interference in the 2016 US presidential election and international law on the use of force and non-intervention. It first briefly looks at the various ways in which the incident has been characterized under international law. It then demonstrates that, under the orthodox account of the law, the incident is generally regarded as outside the scope of Article 2(4), given the lack of material effects caused by the cyber attacks.

Due to the non-material nature of the effects, most authors consider the incident through the non-intervention principle. It will be shown that the harm caused by the attacks does not subscribe to the conception of violence embodied in Article 2(4) particularly because there was no physical damage or injury to the entities subjected to harm. Instead, the overall impact of the attacks was on the US election *process*. Further, given issues surrounding the establishment of the element of coercion, which is a requisite for an act to amount to a prohibited intervention under international law, the incident highlights problems surrounding the application of the non-intervention principle to the cyber context.

Characterizing the types of cyber attacks used against the DNC and electoral boards, as well as the incident generally, under international law has been approached in various ways. According to Fleur Johns and Annelise Riles, the incident presents a 'fascinating case for public international law (PIL) … [as it] fits awkwardly, if at all, into the rubric of interstate conflict with which PIL has long grappled'.[45] Johns and Riles therefore suggest that private international law offers a 'new legal technology' for thinking about the incident and cyber security more broadly.[46] Jens Ohlin also considers a number of international law rubrics to conceptualize the incident, including privacy, espionage, and non-intervention.[47] Ultimately, he adopts the approach that international law on self-determination provides the most appropriate rubric.[48] Similarly, Sean Watts notes that, 'International law offers a menu of potential characterizations' of the incident, but that 'the most appealing here are that the hacks amount to either a prohibited intervention in the internal affairs of the US' or a violation of its sovereignty.[49]

Russian interference and the use of force threshold

While the incident was characterized as an 'act of war' by some US officials, it is highly questionable whether it would amount to a use of force (let alone an armed attack) under the existing understanding of international law. As demonstrated in Chapter 4, the orthodox view of cyber attacks and Article 2(4) essentially requires material effects – such as damage or destruction, or injury or death – for cyber attacks to qualify as a use of force. Further, for an incident to constitute an 'act of war' under international law, thus allowing the US to respond with self-defensive force, it must be sufficiently serious in terms of its scale and effects to amount to an armed attack.[50] Given that the cyber attacks involved compromising computers and networks, and the release of information to the public, there were no material effects of this kind that would effectively qualify the incident as a use of force under existing law.

This is the position adopted by most authors in relation to the incident. For example, according to Michael Schmitt, the 'hacking and dumping' of emails was 'not a violation of the UN Charter's prohibition on the use of force … [and] not a situation that would allow the US to respond in self-defense militarily'.[51] Similarly, according to Duncan Hollis, the incident was 'obviously not a case violating Article 2(4)', as the distribution of confidential data did not involve any 'force'.[52] Watts likewise notes how 'it is enormously difficult to imagine a persuasive characterization of the DNC hacks as either uses of force or armed attacks'.[53] In the same way, other commentators observe that 'hacking and releasing information' would not fall within the scope of Article 2(4), as 'such activities do not implicate force'.[54] Therefore, under existing law, the incident would not amount to a use of force or an 'act of war'.[55] The incident is mainly considered to have involved unauthorized access to information and its subsequent distribution; the overriding position is therefore that it did not involve the type of harm that can be recognized within the scope of Article 2(4).

Russian interference and the non-intervention principle

As the incident is viewed as falling below the use of force threshold, most authors argue that it amounts to a potential violation of the non-intervention principle. However, in this context there is debate about whether the incident involved the element of coercion required to establish a prohibited intervention. According to Schmitt, 'Russia's apparent attempt to influence the outcome of the election by its release of emails through WikiLeaks *probably* violates the international law barring intervention in a state's internal affairs'.[56] Elsewhere he maintains that, given the facts of the incident, this question depends largely on whether it was coercive. According to him, it is 'unclear whether facilitating the release of actual e-mails – as distinct from, for example, using cyber means to alter election returns – amounts to coercion as a matter of law'.[57] Nonetheless, he maintains that the 'sounder view' about the incident is that it was coercive because 'the cyber operations manipulated the process of elections and therefore caused them to unfold in a way that they otherwise would not have'.[58] Similarly, according to Steven Barela, the incident went further than 'conventional espionage', given the extent of the cyber activities and the wider influence campaign. He argues that, by seeking to disrupt a 'free and fair election' and by 'weakening confidence in the legitimacy of the [democratic] process', the incident amounted to a form of coercion in breach of the non-intervention principle.[59]

In contrast, while Ohlin also considers the non-intervention principle in relation to the incident in detail, he ultimately concludes that it did not satisfy the requirement for coercion, and therefore did not amount to a prohibited intervention.[60] He argues that a line must be drawn between what amounts to coercion and what does not, and that the incident, while 'corrosive to the proper functioning of a democracy … it is unclear whether it should count as coercive'.[61] Hollis also notes the challenges of applying the non-intervention principle in relation to the incident, particularly given 'the absence of coercion'.[62] He argues that as an 'information operation', Russia's actions sought to alter the behavior of the US electorate willingly, and that under such circumstances there was no coercion.[63] Similarly, Ido Kilovaty considers the non-intervention principle applicable in relation to the incident.[64] However, given the problems surrounding the notion of coercion in relation to Russia's activities, he argues that the incident would not fall within the scope of the non-intervention principle in its existing form due to lack of coerciveness.[65] While the *Tallinn Manual* was published before the full extent of Russia's activities were known, a specific example given by the Group of Experts involving cyber attacks and the non-intervention principle is where a state uses cyber means to 'alter electronic ballots and thereby manipulate an election' in another state.[66] Given the approach to the notion of coercion adopted by the Group of Experts, which requires a state to be factually compelled to take a particular course of action, it is unlikely that the incident would be considered a prohibited intervention under the *Tallinn Manual*'s approach.[67]

Accordingly, as these accounts of the incident highlight, there is an overriding sense that the incident was a violation of international law, and generally (though not unproblematically), the non-intervention principle is deemed most appropriate for reaching this conclusion.[68] However, by viewing the incident as something 'obviously' below the use of force threshold and as a potential breach of the non-intervention principle, the harm that was caused to the United States is not adequately accounted for. The incident is effectively equated to a form of non-violence only potentially affecting the personality of the United States. Given the problems surrounding whether the incident was coercive in nature, this also reveals problems surrounding the applicability of the non-intervention principle to cyber attacks. Here the law becomes concerned not just with the harm caused by cyber attacks (that is, whether hardware damage occurred, for example) but instead shifts its focus to whether the attacks were designed to coercively compel the United States into engaging in a particular way. This is particularly problematic given that, provided a cyber attack has material effects and is seen to constitute a use of force, the element of coercion is seen as 'particularly obvious' and the law does not require identification of how a state was factually compelled by another state to take one course of action over the other.[69] Accordingly, where the effects are merely disruptive but not clearly coercive, such attacks effectively escape the legal parameters of both the use of force and non-use of force principles.

Again, this distinction between cyber attacks based on whether they result in material effects – such as injury to human beings or damage to physical objects – derives from the ontologically constrained conception of violence embodied in Article 2(4). Existing law does not sufficiently account for or recognize the degree to which states can be harmed in new ways that do not involve attacks against physical objects or human beings – for example, through attacks against an election process.[70] The cyber attacks used as part of Russia's interference operation during the 2016 US presidential election highlight the inadequacy of the existing legal boundaries for the types of interstate interactions permitted in and through cyberspace. The near-exclusive focus on physical effects in the use of force discourse, as well as the need to establish the element of coerciveness to satisfy the non-intervention principle in relation to non-material cyber attacks, undermines the law's ability to properly contain the new forms of violence to which states can be subject. Russia's cyber attacks mainly sought to undermine the integrity and disrupt the operation of the election process without causing material effects. Thus, despite the incident being considered harmful towards US interests,[71] the harm caused to the election process is not recognized as a form of violence capable of falling within the ambit of Article 2(4).

An informational approach

This section develops an informational approach to offer an alternative way to consider the harm caused by the cyber attacks against the United States. It first locates the US election process within the democratic system of government of the United States as an information entity, and then considers the harm caused by the cyber attacks in terms of entropy. It will demonstrate how the non-material cyber attacks used against the US election process can be seen to constitute a form of informational violence against the United States.

The US entity

Like other state entities, the US entity has a range of information flows moving in and out of it, and can be seen as a developed information society. In 2015, approximately 87 per cent of US households had a computer, and 82 per cent of households had Internet access.[72] The United States also has a high level of access to ICTs, a developed ICT infrastructure and high levels of ICT use in society.[73] The United States is also an autonomous entity, having obtained its independence from Great Britain in the late eighteenth century. While it is a member of various international organizations such as the Organization of American States, NATO, and the United Nations, and it interacts with these and other state entities, it has autonomy because it has the ability to act independently from other entities. Given this autonomy, it has the capacity to determine the internal processes through which its public office holders, for example, are chosen.

The form or pattern of the United States is evident in the information structures through which it is configured. With a federal system of government made of various legislative and executive organs at different levels, and a court system with the Supreme Court at the apex of the hierarchy, there is a persistent form or pattern to this entity. The US Constitution is considered the supreme law of the land, and it provides the key protocol according to which the United States functions. It separates various levels and branches of government, assigns their respective tasks and functions, and provides the proper information communication channels between these components. Given its democratic system of government, a key process by which the individuals who occupy various positions within these components (such as the Congress and the Executive Office of the President) are determined is the election process. These processes are essential to the proper operation of this entity, allowing it to flourish according to its nature and maintain its autonomy from other entities.

The US Constitution vests executive power in the President of the United States of America and determines the process by which the President is chosen. It provides that each US state appoints a number of electors equal to the number of the members of Congress to which they are entitled, and the electors vote to determine the President in what is known as the Electoral College.[74] However, as a democratic system of government, the electors of most US states vote according to the result of the popular vote in those states. Elections provide eligible individuals with a 'formal and institutional channel' for political participation through which public office-holders are chosen.[75] In this context, there are numerous protocols determining the age of those entitled to vote, the secret nature of the vote and the ways in which these votes are calculated and translated into an output determining the identity of the office holder(s). A presidential election occurs every four years once each political party has determined its candidate for the election through the presidential primaries and caucuses. The President is generally determined by calculating which candidate receives at least 270 out of 538 votes in the Electoral College.[76]

In order for eligible voters to input their vote into the election process, it is a requirement in almost all US states that these individuals have previously registered to vote.[77] The Help America Vote Act (HAVA) was passed in 2002 and seeks to optimize this process in order to 'allow faster, more reliable, and centralized registration of voters'.[78] The HAVA does so by requiring US states to create a 'computerized statewide voter registration list' to 'serve as the single system for storing and managing the official list of registered voters'.[79] In order to then verify the identities of individuals at the polling place, most states require registered voters to identify themselves with photographic or other identification documents.[80] Subsequently, eligible voters can input their vote into the voting system. The HAVA defines a 'voting system' as 'the total combination of mechanical, electromechanical, or electronic equipment (including the software, firmware, and documentation required to program, control, and support the equipment)' used to define ballots, cast and count votes, report or display election results, and maintain and produce an audit trail.[81] Similarly, according to the US Electoral Assistance Commission, the voting system is 'more than voting machines' as it consists of a 'collection of unified components, that when functioning properly, covert inputs to outputs'.[82] It constitutes 'the core technology that drives and integrates the election system' – the 'most visible component of the election system', 'the [tangible] part the voter touches', and 'the part that produces results and determines outcomes of elections'.[83] The voting system therefore provides the interface through which eligible voters can input their votes into the election process.

Accordingly, as an information system, the United States can be seen to consist of a range of components and processes. Among those of particular importance in relation to the Russian interference incident are the democratic processes through the outcome of elections are determined; the political parties and organizations made up of numerous individuals that interact to organize politically around their candidates; individual voters as the entities with the capacity to input votes into the election process; and voting systems and the technical and organizational infrastructure that allow voting to occur across the United States. The system created by these components and processes is integral to the functioning of the United States as a democracy.

Like other state entities, the purpose of the United States is to care for and protect its region of the infosphere. This involves a responsibility to protect everything from its natural environment, the virtual environment of cyberspace, and the various information processes through which it operates. Given how its system of government, and the democratic process in particular, functions, the overall flourishing and well-being of the United States depend on its ability to care for and protect these processes and their key components from increases in entropy.

Russian cyber attacks and entropy

With the United States viewed as an information system, the cyber attacks used by Russia against the United States can be analyzed in terms of the entropy they produced. While the degree of entropy produced by the spear-phishing attacks against US political organizations was minor, the systematic and strategic release of information obtained from DNC networks in particular produced more significant increases in entropy by disrupting the proper operation of the US democratic process and undermining the autonomy of the United States as an entity.

Spear-phishing attacks against the DNC

The cyber attacks in mid-2015 and early 2016 involving spear-phishing attacks can be seen to have resulted in minor increases in entropy. These attacks sought to compromise the interactions between human users and their computer systems. They did so by seeking to mislead human users into installing malicious software onto their computer systems, or misleading them into providing their credentials, which then allowed the attackers to obtain unauthorized access to those systems and install malicious software. This then enabled the attackers to extract thousands of files from those computer systems and networks. The successful spear-phishing attacks in particular caused increases in entropy by compromising the DNC's networks.

The first wave of the spear-phishing attacks in mid-2015 by Cozy Bear targeted over 1000 recipients, including many with US government email addresses.[84] They thus targeted individuals occupying positions within key components of the United States. These emails contained a link to domains that appeared to be associated with legitimate US organizations that hosted malware.[85] While not all of these attacks were successful, at least one user activated the link, resulting in the installation of malware that granted Cozy Bear access to the DNC networks.[86] In this context, Cozy Bear used the SeaDaddy malware, for example, which provided it with the ability to take any action it wanted on the affected systems.[87] By misleading human users into unknowingly installing this hostile entity onto their computer systems, the attackers were able to compromise the integrity of those systems. They thus compromised the proper interactions between the human users who activated the malicious link and their computer systems. This allowed Cozy Bear to compromise the integrity of the DNC network.

The second wave of attacks in early 2016 by Fancy Bear also compromised the integrity of the DNC network.[88] Fancy Bear targeted its spear-phishing attacks against particular individuals based on information obtained through reconnaissance of public online profiles of these individuals and past information-collection operations.[89] Unlike the attack by Cozy Bear that compromised the DNC network through malware that the users would unsuspectingly install onto their computers, the Fancy Bear attack misled users into providing their credentials to the attackers, and this allowed it to install malicious files onto DNC systems. The targeted emails used by Fancy Bear 'tricked recipients into changing their passwords through a fake webmail domain hosted on APT28 [Fancy Bear's] operational infrastructure'.[90] Then, using the user credentials that had been obtained, Fancy Bear was able to obtain access to these networks and extract data from senior members of the Democratic Party.[91] It is understood that Podesta's credentials were compromised in this attack.[92] These attacks also compromised the interactions between human users and computer systems by utilizing websites designed to appear legitimate to mislead users into providing their credentials to the attackers, which allowed them to compromise the targeted systems.

Both waves of attacks by Cozy Bear and Fancy Bear caused minor increases in entropy within the DNC as a component of the US entity. While email communications generally constitute natural information flows into and within the United States, the spear-phishing emails can be regarded as hostile entities, as they were embedded with links to fake domains or to those hosting malware. Instead of normal information flows enabling individuals and organizations to communicate via the Internet, these entities were designed specifically to cause increases in entropy by undermining the interactions between human users and computer systems in order to undermine the integrity of the networks of these users' organizations. The targeted nature of the spear-phishing attacks against 109 staff members of the Clinton campaign, including multiple emails targeted at senior staff members and Clinton's personal email account,[93] demonstrated that the attackers sought to undermine these accounts and the DNC network. The successful spear-phishing attacks in particular caused increases in entropy as they compromised the DNC network by exploiting vulnerabilities in human information-processing capabilities and spam filter software, as these entities and protection mechanisms were unable to prevent these entities from causing harm.[94] The security software was unable to recognize these emails as malicious and capable of causing entropy, and similarly the human users were deceived into activating the links to install the malware or into providing their credentials to the attackers. By corrupting these interactions and obtaining unauthorized access to the DNC networks, and thereby undermining its integrity, the spear-phishing attacks caused a small increase in entropy.

The extraction of the information itself – that is, the thousands of private emails and attachments that were obtained from the DNC – can also be viewed as an increase in entropy, given that the properties of these entities were altered when their confidential nature was undermined. By itself, this can only be seen as a minor increase in entropy, as this information was not deleted or modified in any way that would have caused a larger increase in entropy. However, the way in which this information was used for malicious purposes can be seen to have constituted a more serious form of informational violence.

The strategic and systematic release of information

The release of information obtained from DNC networks was deliberately designed to disrupt the proper functioning of the United States as an information system. Compared with the increase in entropy caused by the spear-phishing attacks that compromised DNC networks, the entropy caused by the release of information obtained from those networks was more significant. The information was released with the aim of interfering with the interaction between voters, the voting system, and the election process, and therefore disrupting the proper operation of a process central to the operation of the United States. The release of information therefore caused significant increases in entropy, undermining the autonomy of the United States and disrupting its normal functioning as an entity.

Elections constitute a process that is integral to the functioning of the United States as an information system with a democratic system of government. The election process is complex and involves human beings, voting systems, and numerous protocols that govern the operation of this process. Russia sought to disrupt the proper operation of this process. Unlike, for example, DDoS attacks designed to disrupt the operation of voting systems, the release of information was intended to influence the decision-making process of human voters, to undermine their interaction with voting systems and the election process, and by doing so, to disrupt the proper operation of the election process.

This disruptive effect was achieved through the systematic and strategic release of information through various intermediaries at critical points in time during the election. For example, on 22 July 2016, three days before the Democratic National Convention in Philadelphia, WikiLeaks released 44,053 emails with 17,761 attachments. The contents of these emails demonstrated, for instance, that the DNC favored Clinton over her rival Bernie Sanders for the Democratic Party's nomination.[95] Additionally, from 7 October 2016 onwards, WikiLeaks began releasing more emails that sought to cast Clinton in a negative light. This was the same day that the 'Access Hollywood' video had emerged, which was viewed as damaging to Trump's campaign, and the first time emails obtained from Podesta's account were released.[96] Instead of releasing all the emails in its possession simultaneously, WikiLeaks began releasing emails on this day and continued to do so on a daily basis for the last month of the presidential campaign.[97] While the Republican Party networks had also been compromised, no information was released by WikiLeaks and others that demonstrated an effort to undermine the Republican Party's campaign.[98] The release of information thus was timed strategically, and it occurred systematically over prolonged periods of time during the election campaign. It was specifically targeted at influencing the decision-making process of voters in order to undermine the Democratic Party's candidate's chance of winning the election. Accordingly, the release of information was aimed at disrupting the proper operation of the election process and its outcome.

Therefore, given the type of information obtained from DNC networks and the way in which it was released, the attackers sought to influence the decision-making process of human voters in order to undermine their interaction with the voting system and the election process. While it is unknown whether Russia's actions in fact affected the outcome of the election,[99] the systematic and strategic release of information demonstrated a malicious effort to disrupt the operation of the election process, and therefore undermine the autonomy of the United States. The interactions among entities central to the operation of the election process were undermined, and by seeking to disrupt its operation and influence its outcome in this way, the ability of the United States to determine the outcome of its internal democratic processes independently and consistently with its own protocols was undermined. The release of information infringed the ability of the United States to flourish according to its nature as an information entity constituted by a democratic system of government, and in doing so, caused significant increases in entropy.

Spear-phishing attacks on electoral boards

The attacks against electoral boards in numerous states also resulted in increases in entropy; however, as no voter registration information and no votes were deleted or manipulated, the impact on the functioning of the United States was smaller compared with the release of information obtained from DNC networks. The attacks against electoral boards are believed to have occurred in late October or early November 2016, and they also involved spear-phishing emails sent to 122 addresses associated with local government organizations and those involved in managing voter registration systems.[100] Altogether, the electoral systems of 39 US states had been targeted by these types of attacks,[101] and of these, the voter registration systems or websites of seven US states are reported to have been effectively compromised.[102] The successful spear-phishing attacks in this context caused small increases in entropy, as the integrity of these systems was compromised. For example, in one state the voter database was compromised, and in another the username and password of an election official was compromised.[103] Compared with the spear-phishing attacks that compromised DNC networks, this increase in entropy was more significant, given that the targeted systems were more central components in the operation of the election process itself. On the other hand, it was less significant when compared with the entropy caused by the release of information that sought to disrupt the election process. This is particularly the case given that no voters were removed from voting rolls and no votes were reported to have been changed,[104] and the systems involved in vote tallying were not compromised.[105] These attacks therefore did not undermine the vote calculation process by manipulating or disrupting it. Had this been the case, the attacks would have resulted in more significant increases in entropy, given the extent to which the ability of the United States to function as an autonomous entity would have been undermined. This would likely have been greater than that caused by the release of information obtained from DNC networks, given the deeper and more direct intrusion into the operation of the election process and its outcome.

US responses

Finally, the US responses to the incident showed that as an entity it viewed these as hostile information flows that were potentially harmful and capable of causing increases in entropy. In December 2016, President Barack Obama noted how the 'data theft and disclosure' activities that Russia had undertaken sought to 'interfere with the US election process' and 'harm US interests'.[106] Further, he issued a range of sanctions on Russian entities and individuals, and authorized the release of technical information about Russia's actions in cyberspace to allow others to 'identify, detect, and disrupt Russia's global campaign of malicious cyber activities'.[107] Additionally, in

March 2018, the Trump administration issued a range of sanctions with the aim of 'confronting and countering malign Russian cyber activity', including its attempted efforts to interfere in the US elections.[108] The sanctions targeted, for example, Russia's Internet Research Agency, which had 'tampered with, altered, or caused a misappropriation of information with the purpose or effect of interfering with or undermining election processes and institutions' during the 2016 presidential election.[109] Through these means, the United States demonstrated that as an entity it regarded Russia's activities as hostile and capable of causing entropy. Further, it sought to protect itself by imposing constraints on the human and institutional entities involved in the cyber attacks, and by releasing technical information to undermine Russia's capability of causing further increased in entropy within the infosphere.

Therefore, the cyber attacks used by Russian actors against the DNC and electoral boards, as well as the systematic and strategic release of information obtained from DNC networks, sought to disrupt the proper operation of the US election process. The unauthorized access to the DNC networks and electoral boards itself resulted in a minor increase in entropy (compromising the integrity of those networks or websites). However, the release of the information obtained from DNC networks was designed to influence the decision-making process of human voters, undermine their proper interaction with voting systems and the election process, and disrupt the proper operation of the election process. It thus resulted in a more significant increase in entropy. Accordingly, when considered as a whole, Russia's actions demonstrated a concentrated effort to undermine the ability of the United States to operate according to its usual trajectory as a democratic system of government and undermine its autonomy as an entity.

Conclusion

Existing analyses of the incident in light of the law on the use of force and non-intervention largely adopt the position that the incident falls below the use of force threshold, and highlight problems surrounding the identification of the coercive element in order to consider the incident as amounting to a violation of the non-intervention principle. Essentially, despite the targeted nature of Russia's cyber attacks against individuals, organizations, and systems that formed integral components of the US election process, and the active effort to disrupt the proper operation of the election process, the attacks used in this context did not cause the type of harm that subscribes to the conception of violence embodied in Article 2(4). This is the seemingly 'obvious' conclusion to those who consider the application of Article 2(4) to the incident (even if only to exclude it). Given the non-material nature of the effects against an integral internal process of a state (opposed to damage or injury to physical objects or human beings within a state), most legal analyses therefore focus on the non-intervention principle in relation to the incident. This is problematic on a conceptual level because, under existing law, had the attacks used in the incident resulted in some form of physical damage – such as damage to computer hardware – the incident would more readily have been seen as a potential use of force under Article 2(4). It also rests on an artificial threshold distinction between cyber attacks with material and non-material effects, and this position does not adequately account for the ways in which, in this case, cyber means can be used to attack and undermine the proper operation of democratic systems of government. Additionally, the cyber attacks used as part of Russia's interference operation demonstrate the limitations of the non-intervention principle in the cyber context, especially given difficulties in identifying the element of coerciveness. While the US elections targeted by the cyber attacks were clearly within its internal affairs as a sovereign state, it is difficult to clearly identify how the United States was deprived of its freedom of choice in relation to the outcome of the election and forced to act in a particular way so that the incident would amount to a violation of the non-intervention principle.

An informational approach to the incident enables an analysis that takes into account the harm caused by the attacks against a range of entities and the election process, and how the attacks therefore sought to undermine the proper operation of the United States as an entity. This is despite the incident not being sufficiently coercive to amount to a violation of the non-intervention principle or involving the type of harm to constitute a use of force under existing law.

Given the nature of the spear-phishing attacks that enabled the attackers to install malware onto DNC computers in order to exfiltrate data from its network, the attacks undermined the interactions between human beings and computer systems. Similar attacks were used to compromise the systems of electoral boards in numerous US states. The strategic and systematic release of information that followed was aimed at disrupting the proper operation of the election process by undermining the interactions between voters, the voting system and the election process. While there was no physical injury to human beings or damage to material objects, the attacks nonetheless impacted on various entities and processes – human beings, computer systems and networks, and the election process – and they were designed to disrupt the proper operation of the election process and undermine the autonomy of the United States as an entity. In doing so, the release of information in particular can be seen to have caused significant increases in entropy and resulted in a form of informational violence against the United States.

Notes

1 David Sanger and Nick Corasaniti, 'DNC Says Russian Hackers Penetrated Its Files, Including Dossier on Donald Trump' *New York Times* (14 June 2016) <https://nyti.ms/2k8WBxs> accessed 5 February 2018.

2 Eric Lipton, David Sanger and Scott Shane, 'The Perfect Weapon: How Russian Cyberpower Invaded the US.' *New York Times* (13 December 2016) <https://nyti.ms/2jASgpt> accessed 5 February 2018.
3 Office of the Director of National Intelligence, 'Assessing Russian Activities and Intentions in Recent US Elections' (Intelligence Community Assessment, 6 January 2017) 3 <www.dni.gov/files/documents/ICA_2017_01.pdf> accessed 5 February 2018 ('ICA Report'). In January 2017, the US Office of the Director of National Intelligence released a declassified version of the ICA report. Full technical details and information about how the conclusions were reached was redacted; however, the conclusions of the unclassified version were the same as in the highly classified version. The ICA report did not assess the impact of Russian activities on the outcome of the election, only the motivation and scope of Russia's intentions and its use of cyber and other means to influence public opinion in the United States. ICA Report (n 3) i.
4 ICA Report (n 3) 1.
5 ibid.
6 ibid 5.
7 Theodore Schleifer and Deirdre Walsh, 'McCain: Russian Cyberintrusions an "Act of War"' CNN (31 December 2016) <http://edition.cnn.com/2016/12/30/politics/mccain-cyber-hearing/index.html> accessed 5 February 2018.
8 Andrew Blake, 'Cheney Calls Russian Election Meddling "an Act of War"' *Washington Times* (28 March 2017) <www.washingtontimes.com/news/2017/mar/28/cheney-calls-russian-election-meddling-act-war> accessed 5 February 2018.
9 The release of data obtained from the DNC may not constitute a cyber attack in the traditional sense. See, for example, Lucas Kello, *The Virtual Weapon and International Order* (Yale University Press 2017) 222. However, through an informational approach to the incident, the systematic and strategic release of data can be seen as a hostile information flow targeted at disrupting the operation of the election process, which is central to the functioning of the United States. As such, it can be regarded as a computer-enabled action used to disrupt an information system, namely the United States when it is viewed as an information entity.
10 US Department of Homeland Security and Federal Bureau of Investigation, *Grizzly Steppe – Russian Malicious Cyber Activity* (Joint Analysis Report, 29 December 2016) 2–3 <www.us-cert.gov/sites/default/files/publications/JAR_16-20296A_GRIZZLY%20STEPPE-2016-1229.pdf> accessed 5 February 2018 ('Grizzly Report').
11 Lipton, Sanger and Shane (n 2).
12 ibid.
13 Sam Thielman and Spencer Ackerman, 'US Believes Russian Hackers are Behind Democratic National Committee Leak' *The Guardian* (27 July 2017) <www.theguardian.com/us-news/2016/jul/26/russia-hackers-democratic-national-committee-email-leak> accessed 5 February 2018.
14 Mark Galeotti, 'Size Doesn't Matter for Spies Anymore' *Foreign Policy* (31 January 2018) <http://foreignpolicy.com/2018/01/31/size-doesnt-matter-for-spies-anymore> accessed 5 February 2018.
15 Dmitri Alperovitch, 'Bears in the Midst: Intrusion into the Democratic National Committee' (*Crowdstrike*, 15 June 2016) <www.crowdstrike.com/blog/bears-midst-intrusion-democratic-national-committee> accessed 5 February 2018.
16 'What is Social Engineering?' (*Symantec*) <https://us.norton.com/internetsecurity-emerging-threats-what-is-social-engineering.html> accessed 5 February 2018.
17 Paul Thompson, 'Cognitive Hacking and Digital Government: Digital Identity' (2004) 2(2) *Journal of Systemics, Cybernetics and Informatics* 9, 10.

18 Alperovitch (n 15).
19 ibid.
20 ibid.
21 ibid.
22 Thielman and Ackerman (n 13).
23 ibid. According to cybersecurity experts, the tailored nature of these tools (as well as formal coding practices indicating programmers that are methodological and diligent) meant that the attackers had the time and resources to test them, to ensure they functioned in the particular environment; this indicated that they were carried out by state-based actors opposed to criminals that simply targeted large numbers of people. ibid.
24 Alperovitch (n 15).
25 ibid.
26 ibid.
27 Lipton, Sanger and Shane (n 2).
28 Thomas Rid, 'Disinformation: A Primer in Russian Active Measures and Influence Campaigns' (Hearings before the Select Committee on Intelligence, United States Senate, 30 March 2017) 4 <www.intelligence.senate.gov/sites/default/files/documents/os-trid-033017.pdf> accessed 5 February 2018.
29 ibid.
30 ibid.
31 ibid.
32 ibid.
33 Lipton, Sanger and Shane (n 2).
34 Rosalind Helderman and Tom Hamburger, 'Hacked Emails Appear to Reveal Excerpts of Speech Transcripts Clinton Refused to Release' *Washington Post* (7 October 2016) <http://wapo.st/2e0rYMm> accessed 5 February 2018.
35 ICA Report (n 3) 3; Luke Harding, 'What We Know about Russia's Interference in the US Election' *The Guardian* (17 December 2016) <www.theguardian.com/us-news/2016/dec/16/qa-russian-hackers-vladimir-putin-donald-trump-us-presidential-election> accessed 5 February 2018.
36 Matthew Cole and others, 'Top Secret NSA Report Details Russian Hacking Effort Days Before 2016 Election' *The Intercept* (6 June 2017) <https://interc.pt/2rufxx6> accessed 5 February 2018.
37 ibid.
38 Callum Borchers, 'What We Know About the 21 States Targeted by Russian Hackers' *The Washington Post* (23 September 2017) <http://wapo.st/2xwfQdD> accessed 5 February 2018. According to some reports, a total of 39 states were targeted. See Michael Riley and Jordan Robertson, 'Russian Cyber Hacks on US Electoral System Far Wider Than Previously Known' Bloomberg (13 June 2017) <www.bloomberg.com/news/articles/2017-06-13/russian-breach-of-39-states-threatens-future-u-s-elections> accessed 14 March 2018.
39 'Russians Compromised Election Systems in Seven States: NBC News' Reuters (28 February 2018) <www.reuters.com/article/us-usa-trump-russia-election/russians-compromised-election-systems-in-seven-states-nbc-news-idUSKCN1GC01E> accessed 14 March 2018. For example, in the state of Illinois in mid- to late 2016, the state voter database was compromised, providing the attackers with access to voters' personal information. See Riley and Robertson (n 38).
40 US Senate Select Committee on Intelligence, 'Russian Targeting of Election Infrastructure During the 2016 Election: Summary of Initial Findings and Recommendations' (8 May 2018) 1 <www.burr.senate.gov/imo/media/doc/RussRptInstlmt1-%20ElecSec%20Findings,Recs2.pdf> accessed 10 May 2018.
41 ibid 1–2.
42 ibid 2.

43 ICA Report (n 3) 3.
44 ibid 1.
45 Fleur Johns and Annelise Riles, 'Beyond Bunker and Vaccine: The DNC Hack as a Conflict of Laws Issue' (2016) 110 *AJIL Unbound* 347.
46 ibid 350–1.
47 Jens D Ohlin, 'Did Russian Cyber Interference in the 2016 Election Violate International Law?' (2017) 95(7) *Texas Law Review* 1579.
48 ibid 1594–7.
49 Sean Watts, 'International Law and Proposed US Responses to the D.N.C. Hack' (*Just Security*, 14 October 2016) <www.justsecurity.org/33558/international-law-proposed-u-s-responses-d-n-c-hack> accessed 5 February 2018.
50 Michael N Schmitt (ed), *Tallinn Manual 2.0 on the International Law Applicable to Cyber Operations* (2nd edn, Cambridge University Press 2017) 341.
51 Ellen Nakashima, 'Russia's Apparent Meddling in US Election is Not an Act of War, Cyber Expert Says' *Washington Post* (7 February 2017) <www.washingtonpost.com/news/checkpoint/wp/2017/02/07/russias-apparent-meddling-in-u-s-election-is-not-an-act-of-war-cyber-expert-says> accessed 5 February 2018.
52 Duncan B Hollis, 'Russia and the DNC Hack: What Future for a Duty of Non-Intervention?' (*Opinio Juris*, 25 July 2016) <http://opiniojuris.org/2016/07/25/russia-and-the-dnc-hack-a-violation-of-the-duty-of-non-intervention> accessed 5 February 2018.
53 Watts (n 49).
54 Logan Hamilton, 'Beyond Ballot-Stuffing: Current Gaps in International Law Regarding Foreign State Hacking to Influence a Foreign Election' (2017) 35 *Wisconsin International Law Journal* 179, 193–4.
55 See also Ryan Goodman, 'International Law and the US Response to Russian Election Interference' (*Just Security*, 5 January 2017) <www.justsecurity.org/35999/international-law-response-russian-election-interference> accessed 5 February 2018.
56 Nakashima (n 51) (emphasis added).
57 Michael N Schmitt, 'Grey Zones in the International Law of Cyberspace' (2017) 42(2) *Yale Journal of International Law Online* 1, 2 <https://campuspress.yale.edu/yjil/files/2017/08/Schmitt_Grey-Areas-in-the-International-Law-of-Cyberspace-1cab8kj.pdf> accessed 5 February 2018.
58 ibid 8.
59 Steven Barela, 'Cross-Border Cyber Ops to Erode Legitimacy: An Act of Coercion' (*Just Security*, 12 January 2017) <www.justsecurity.org/36212/cross-border-cyber-ops-erode-legitimacy-act-coercion> accessed 5 February 2018.
60 Ohlin (n 47) 1593
61 ibid. Ohlin then goes on to argue that a better fit comes from the principle of self-determination. Essentially, by distorting the will of the American people – the very essence of democratic forms of government – the incident amounted to a violation of the 'right of all peoples to determine for themselves their political destiny'. ibid 1595–6.
62 Duncan B Hollis, 'The Influence of War: The War for Influence' (3 April 2018) 10 <https://ssrn.com/abstract=3155273> accessed 4 May 2018.
63 Hollis considers various elements of Russia's actions separately, and maintains that the unauthorized access to information in DNC networks constituted a form of espionage and did not involve coercion; similarly, Russian activities through social media were not coercive, as they only sought to impact people's opinions. In contrast, he suggest that the 'timed dumps' of information through WikiLeaks, for example, may have involved coercion; however, according to

Hollis, even here 'it is not clear what the threatened consequences were, let alone who its targets were'. ibid 11

64 Ido Kilovaty, 'Doxfare: Politically Motivated Leaks and the Future of the Norm on Non-Intervention in the Era of Weaponized Information' (2018) 9 *Harvard National Security Journal* 147.

65 Kilovaty argues for an expansion of the scope of the non-intervention principle to cover instances of disruptive cyber attacks where it is difficult to identify the coercive effects. See ibid 174. This argument has merit, as it seeks to recognize the harmful impact such attacks can have and aims to address an important problem with the application of the non-intervention principle to cyber attacks. However, in this book it is proposed that simply viewing such activities through the non-intervention principle is problematic in itself, as it equates cyber attacks of this kind to forms of non-violence in the law's periphery.

66 Schmitt (n 50) 313.

67 The Group of Experts defined coercion as 'an affirmative act designed to deprive another state of its freedom of choice, that is, to force that State to act in an involuntary manner or involuntarily refrain from acting in a particular way'. They distinguished coercion from other forms of pressures, such as 'persuasion, criticism, public diplomacy, propaganda … retribution, mere maliciousness, and the like'. They noted that, 'unlike coercion, such activities merely involve either influencing (as distinct from factually compelling) the voluntary actions of the target State, or seek no action on the part of the target state at all'. According to the Group of Experts, to amount to coercion, the act in question 'must have the potential for compelling the target State to engage in an action that it would otherwise not take (or refrain from taking an action it would otherwise take)'. ibid 317–19.

68 Ohlin, for example, refers to a 'commonsense intuition about the impropriety of the Russian hacking during the election'. Ohlin (n 47) 1580. Schmitt maintains that the incident epitomized Russia's strategy of exploiting grey zones of international law in which the applicable legal principles are inadequately demarcated. See Schmitt (n 57) 1, 2.

69 According to the ICJ, 'The element of coercion … is particularly obvious in the case of an intervention which uses force.' *Case Concerning Military and Paramilitary Activities in and Against Nicaragua (Nicaragua v United States of America)* (Merits) [1986] ICJ Rep 14, 108. In the cyberspace context, according to the *Tallinn Manual*, a cyber attack amounting to a use of force 'is always coercive and therefore constitutes intervention'. Schmitt (n 50) 319.

70 Similarly, Herbert Lin and Jaclyn Kerr note how cyber-enabled information or influence warfare operations pose 'a new kind of threat to democratic nations – a threat that evades established laws and conventions and turns the strengths of democracies, namely their openness and guaranteed freedoms, against them'. In this way, the threat posed by these activities 'is much like the threat from traditional cyber weapons that affect the confidentiality, integrity, and availability of information and information systems'. Herbert Lin and Jaclyn Kerr, 'On Cyber-Enabled Information/Influence Warfare and Manipulation' (8 August 2017) 20–1 <https://ssrn.com/abstract=3015680> accessed 14 March 2018.

71 For example, according to the Obama administration, the incident was harmful towards US interests but only violated 'established international norms of behavior' as opposed to rules of international law. See White House, Office of the Press Secretary, 'Statement by the President on Actions in Response to Russian Malicious Cyber Activity and Harassment' (Media Release, 29 December 2016) <https://obamawhitehouse.archives.gov/the-press-office/2016/12/29/statement-president-actions-response-russian-malicious-cyber-activity> accessed 14 March 2018; David P Fidler, 'The .US

Election Hacks, Cybersecurity, and International Law' (2016) 110 *AJIL Unbound* 337, 341.

72 International Telecommunication Union, *Measuring the Information Society Report* (ITU, 2016) 243 <www.itu.int/en/ITU-D/Statistics/Documents/publications/misr2016/MISR2016-w4.pdf> accessed 5 February 2018.

73 The International Telecommunication Union's ICT Development Index (IDI) combines various indicators to 'monitor and compare developments in ICT between countries and over time'. These include the ICT readiness of the country (its level of networked infrastructure and access to ICTs), the ICT intensity (the level of ICT use in society) and the ICT impact (the outcomes of efficient and effective ICT use, or the ICT skills). ibid 8. The US IDI for 2016 was 8.17, ranked 15th in the world. ibid 12.

74 US Constitution Art 2 § 1.

75 According to Theodore Lowi and others, 'Elections offer a formal and institutional channel' for political participation. See Theodore Lowi and others, *American Government: Power and Purpose* (13th edn, WW Norton 2015) 312–13.

76 'Presidential Election Process' (USA.gov) <www.usa.gov/election> accessed 14 March 2018.

77 'Register to Vote and Confirm or Change Registration' (USA.gov) <www.usa.gov/register-to-vote> accessed 14 March 2018.

78 Kele Williams, 'Key Provisions of the Help America Vote Act' (Fact Sheet, Brennan Center for Justice, New York University School of Law, 20 June 2004) 2 <www.brennancenter.org/analysis/key-provisions-help-america-vote-act> accessed 14 March 2018.

79 Help America Vote Act of 2002, 42 USC 15483 § 303 (2002).

80 Wendy Underhill, 'Voter Identification Requirements/Voter ID Laws' (National Conference of State Legislatures, 5 January 2018) <www.ncsl.org/research/elections-and-campaigns/voter-id.aspx> accessed 14 March 2018.

81 Help America Vote Act of 2002, 42 USC 15481 § 301 (2002).

82 US Election Assistance Commission, 'Ten Things to Know About Selecting a Voting System' (EAC, 14 October 2017) 1 <www.eac.gov/documents/2017/10/14/ten-things-to-know-about-selecting-a-voting-system-cybersecurity-voting-systems-voting-technology> accessed 14 March 2018.

83 ibid.

84 Grizzly Report (n 10) 2.

85 ibid 2–3.

86 ibid.

87 Alperovitch (n 15).

88 Grizzly Report (n 10) 3.

89 Thielman and Ackerman (n 13).

90 Grizzly Report (n 10) 3.

91 ibid.

92 Lipton, Sanger and Shane (n 2).

93 Rid (n 28) 4.

94 Grizzly Report (n 10) 2.

95 Lipton, Sanger and Shane (n 2).

96 Amy Chozick, 'John Podesta Says Russian Spies Hacked His Emails to Sway Election' *New York Times* (11 October 2016) <https://nyti.ms/2dUbXUQ> accessed 14 March 2018.

97 Lipton, Sanger and Shane (n 2).

98 Harding (n 35).

99 US intelligence agencies, for example, maintained that assessing this was outside the scope of their activities. See ICA Report (n 3) i.

100 Cole and others (n 36).

101 Riley and Robertson (n 38).

102 'Russians compromised election systems in seven states: NBC News' (n 39).
103 Borchers (n 38).
104 'Russians compromised election systems in seven states: NBC News' (n 39).
105 ICA Report (n 3) 3.
106 White House, Office of the Press Secretary (n 71).
107 ibid.
108 US Department of the Treasury, 'Treasury Sanctions Russian Cyber Actors for Interference with the 2016 US Elections and Malicious Cyber-Attacks' (Media Release, 15 March 2018) <https://home.treasury.gov/news/press-releases/sm0312> accessed 16 March 2018.
109 ibid. In particular, these sanctions targeted the Internet Research Agency, as it had 'created and managed a vast number of fake online personas that posed as legitimate US persons to include grassroots organizations, interest groups, and a state political party on social media'. As part of this process, it had 'posted thousands of ads that reached millions of people online' and 'organized and coordinated political rallies during the run-up to the 2016 election, all while hiding its Russian identity'. ibid.

Bibliography

Alperovitch D, 'Bears in the Midst: Intrusion into the Democratic National Committee' (*Crowdstrike*, 15 June 2016) <www.crowdstrike.com/blog/bears-midst-intrusion-democratic-national-committee> accessed 5 February 2018

Barela S, 'Cross-Border Cyber Ops to Erode Legitimacy: An Act of Coercion' (*Just Security*, 12 January 2017) <www.justsecurity.org/36212/cross-border-cyber-ops-erode-legitimacy-act-coercion> accessed 5 February 2018

Blake A, 'Cheney Calls Russian Election Meddling "an Act of War"' *Washington Times* (28 March 2017) <www.washingtontimes.com/news/2017/mar/28/cheney-calls-russian-election-meddling-act-war> accessed 5 February 2018

Borchers C, 'What We Know About the 21 States Targeted by Russian Hackers' *Washington Post* (23 September 2017) <http://wapo.st/2xwfQdD> accessed 5 February 2018

Case Concerning Military and Paramilitary Activities in and Against Nicaragua (Nicaragua v United States of America) (Merits) [1986] ICJ Rep 14

Chozick A, 'John Podesta Says Russian Spies Hacked His Emails to Sway Election' *New York Times* (11 October 2016) <https://nyti.ms/2dUbXUQ> accessed 14 March 2018

Cole M and others, 'Top Secret NSA Report Details Russian Hacking Effort Days Before 2016 Election' *The Intercept* (6 June 2017) <https://interc.pt/2rufxx6> accessed 5 February 2018

Fidler DP, 'The US Election Hacks, Cybersecurity, and International Law' (2016) 110 *AJIL Unbound* 337

Galeotti M, 'Size Doesn't Matter for Spies Anymore' *Foreign Policy* (31 January 2018) <http://foreignpolicy.com/2018/01/31/size-doesnt-matter-for-spies-anymore> accessed 5 February 2018

Goodman R, 'International Law and the US Response to Russian Election Interference' (*Just Security*, 5 January 2017) <www.justsecurity.org/35999/international-law-response-russian-election-interference> accessed 5 February 2018

Hamilton L, 'Beyond Ballot-Stuffing: Current Gaps in International Law Regarding Foreign State Hacking to Influence a Foreign Election' (2017) 35 *Wisconsin International Law Journal* 179

Harding L, 'What We Know About Russia's Interference in the US Election' *The Guardian* (17 December 2016) <www.theguardian.com/us-news/2016/dec/16/qa-russian-hackers-vladimir-putin-donald-trump-us-presidential-election> accessed 5 February 2018

Helderman R and Hamburger T, 'Hacked Emails Appear to Reveal Excerpts of Speech Transcripts Clinton Refused to Release' *The Washington Post* (7 October 2016) <http://wapo.st/2e0rYMm> accessed 5 February 2018

Help America Vote Act of 2002, 42 USC 15301 et seq (2002)

Hollis DB, 'Russia and the DNC Hack: What Future for a Duty of Non-Intervention?' (*Opinio Juris*, 25 July 2016) <http://opiniojuris.org/2016/07/25/russia-and-the-dnc-hack-a-violation-of-the-duty-of-non-intervention> accessed 5 February 2018

——— 'The Influence of War: the War for Influence' (3 April 2018) <https://ssrn.com/abstract=3155273> accessed 4 May 2018

International Telecommunication Union, *Measuring the Information Society Report* (ITU, 2016) <www.itu.int/en/ITU-D/Statistics/Documents/publications/misr2016/MISR2016-w4.pdf> accessed 5 February 2018

Johns F and Riles A, 'Beyond Bunker and Vaccine: The DNC Hack as a Conflict of Laws Issue' (2016) 110 *AJIL Unbound* 347

Kello L, *The Virtual Weapon and International Order* (Yale University Press 2017)

Kilovaty I, 'Doxfare: Politically Motivated Leaks and the Future of the Norm on Non-Intervention in the Era of Weaponized Information' (2018) 9 *Harvard National Security Journal* 147

Lin H and Kerr J, 'On Cyber-Enabled Information/Influence Warfare and Manipulation' (8 August 2017) <https://ssrn.com/abstract=3015680> accessed 14 March 2018

Lipton E, Sanger D and Shane S, 'The Perfect Weapon: How Russian Cyberpower Invaded the US' *New York Times* (13 December 2016) <https://nyti.ms/2jASgpt> accessed 5 February 2018

Lowi T and others, *American Government: Power and Purpose* (13th edn, WW Norton 2015)

Nakashima E, 'Russia's Apparent Meddling in US Election is Not an Act of War, Cyber Expert Says' *Washington Post* (7 February 2017) <www.washingtonpost.com/news/checkpoint/wp/2017/02/07/russias-apparent-meddling-in-u-s-election-is-not-an-act-of-war-cyber-expert-says> accessed 5 February 2018

Office of the Director of National Intelligence, 'Assessing Russian Activities and Intentions in Recent US Elections' (Intelligence Community Assessment, 6 January 2017) <www.dni.gov/files/documents/ICA_2017_01.pdf> accessed 5 February 2018

Ohlin JD, 'Did Russian Cyber Interference in the 2016 Election Violate International Law?' (2017) 95(7) *Texas Law Review* 1579

'Presidential Election Process' (USA.gov) <www.usa.gov/election> accessed 14 March 2018

'Register to Vote and Confirm or Change Registration' (USA.gov) <www.usa.gov/register-to-vote> accessed 14 March 2018

Rid T, 'Disinformation A Primer in Russian Active Measures and Influence Campaigns' (Hearings before the Select Committee on Intelligence, United States Senate, 30 March 2017) 4 <www.intelligence.senate.gov/sites/default/files/documents/os-trid-033017.pdf> accessed 5 February 2018

Riley M and Robertson J, 'Russian Cyber Hacks on US Electoral System Far Wider than Previously Known' Bloomberg (13 June 2017) <www.bloomberg.com/news/

articles/2017-06-13/russian-breach-of-39-states-threatens-future-u-s-elections> accessed 14 March 2018

'Russians Compromised Election Systems in Seven States: NBC News' Reuters (28 February 2018) <www.reuters.com/article/us-usa-trump-russia-election/russians-compromised-election-systems-in-seven-states-nbc-news-idUSKCN1GC01E> accessed 14 March 2018

Sanger D and Corasaniti N, 'DNC Says Russian Hackers Penetrated Its Files, Including Dossier on Donald Trump' *New York Times* (14 June 2016) <https://nyti.ms/2k8WBxs> accessed 5 February 2018

Schleifer T and Walsh D, 'McCain: Russian Cyberintrusions an "Act of War"' CNN (31 December 2016) <http://edition.cnn.com/2016/12/30/politics/mccain-cyber-hearing/index.html> accessed 5 February 2018

Schmitt MN, 'Grey Zones in the International Law of Cyberspace' (2017) 42(2) *The Yale Journal of International Law Online* 1 <https://campuspress.yale.edu/yjil/files/2017/08/Schmitt_Grey-Areas-in-the-International-Law-of-Cyberspace-1cab8kj.pdf> accessed 5 February 2018

——— (ed), *Tallinn Manual 2.0 on the International Law Applicable to Cyber Operations* (2nd edn, Cambridge University Press 2017)

Thielman S and Ackerman S, 'US Believes Russian Hackers are Behind Democratic National Committee Leak' *The Guardian* (27 July 2017) <www.theguardian.com/us-news/2016/jul/26/russia-hackers-democratic-national-committee-email-leak> accessed 5 February 2018

Thompson P, 'Cognitive Hacking and Digital Government: Digital Identity' (2004) 2(2) *Journal of Systemics, Cybernetics and Informatics* 9

Underhill W, 'Voter Identification Requirements/Voter ID Laws' (National Conference of State Legislatures, 5 January 2018) <www.ncsl.org/research/elections-and-campaigns/voter-id.aspx> accessed 14 March 2018

United States Constitution (US)

United States Department of Homeland Security and Federal Bureau of Investigation, *Grizzly Steppe – Russian Malicious Cyber Activity* (Joint Analysis Report, 29 December 2016) <www.us-cert.gov/sites/default/files/publications/JAR_16-20296A_GRIZZLY%20STEPPE-2016-1229.pdf> accessed 5 February 2018

United States Department of the Treasury, 'Treasury Sanctions Russian Cyber Actors for Interference with the 2016 US Elections and Malicious Cyber-Attacks' (Media Release, 15 March 2018) <https://home.treasury.gov/news/press-releases/sm0312> accessed 16 March 2018

United States Election Assistance Commission, 'Ten Things to Know About Selecting a Voting System' (EAC, 14 October 2017) <www.eac.gov/documents/2017/10/14/ten-things-to-know-about-selecting-a-voting-system-cybersecurity-voting-systems-voting-technology> accessed 14 March 2018

United States Senate Select Committee on Intelligence, 'Russian Targeting of Election Infrastructure During the 2016 Election: Summary of Initial Findings and Recommendations' (8 May 2018) <www.burr.senate.gov/imo/media/doc/RussRptInstlmt1-%20ElecSec%20Findings,Recs2.pdf> accessed 10 May 2018

Watts S, 'International Law and Proposed US Responses to the D.N.C. Hack' (*Just Security*, 14 October 2016) <www.justsecurity.org/33558/international-law-proposed-u-s-responses-d-n-c-hack> accessed 5 February 2018

'What is Social Engineering?' (*Symantec*) <https://us.norton.com/internetsecurity-emerging-threats-what-is-social-engineering.html> accessed 5 February 2018

White House, Office of the Press Secretary, 'Statement by the President on Actions in Response to Russian Malicious Cyber Activity and Harassment' (Media Release, 29 December 2016) <https://obamawhitehouse.archives.gov/the-press-office/2016/12/29/statement-president-actions-response-russian-malicious-cyber-activity> accessed 14 March 2018

Williams K, 'Key Provisions of the Help America Vote Act' (Fact Sheet, Brennan Center for Justice, New York University School of Law, 20 June 2004) <www.brennancenter.org/analysis/key-provisions-help-america-vote-act> accessed 14 March 2018

8 Information ethics and international law on the use of force

Introduction

As the case studies explored in the three preceding chapters have demonstrated, an informational approach offers an alternative way to view the harm caused by cyber attacks against the state. Essentially, given its basis in an informational ontology, this approach allows recognition of a broader spectrum of violence than existing law on the use of force. It thus provides a way by which the law can better account for the harm caused by cyber attacks against societies that are becoming increasingly reliant on ICTs for their proper functioning.

This chapter provides a summary of the informational approach developed in relation to the case studies explored in this book and examines the doctrinal implications of this approach for international law on the use of force and cyber attacks. It begins by revisiting some of the recent calls in the international community to regulate harmful state activities in and through cyberspace. It then provides a summary and comparison of the informational approach developed for each of the case studies examined in the three preceding chapters. Finally, the chapter examines the doctrinal implications that flow from an informational approach in this context. It considers the consequences of an ontological update to the conception of violence embodied in Article 2(4) in relation to the use of force threshold, the legally permitted responses to cyber attacks, the effects of an informational approach for the non-intervention principle, and how this approach aligns with the purpose of the law on the use of force.

International law and the containment of informational violence

Writing in the late 1960s, Richard Falk maintained that the primary task of international law in international society was 'to prohibit, or at least to contain effectively violence and threats of violence within tolerable limits. Nonviolent and less violent means must be developed as feasible alternatives for the resolution of international conflict.'[1] The end of World War II and the creation of the UN Charter saw the emergence of a new rule of international law in response to the death and destruction experienced during the preceding decades. It was drafted in the shadow of the wars that the world had experienced, and during a time when the technological capability of states to inflict harm – machine guns, artillery, tanks, aerial bombardment, and nuclear weapons bringing about human suffering on a global scale – was still in recent memory.[2] In contrast to the position under classical international law in which war was seen as a sovereign prerogative,[3] the UN Charter's Article 2(4) prohibition on the use of force heralded a new era for international relations between states – one in which violence was sought to be contained through law.

The 2007 Distributed Denial-of-Service (DDoS) attacks against Estonia, depicted by that country's president as 'Web War One', marked the first time a state was subject to cyber attacks that were significant in both scale and duration.[4] In contrast to the issues raised by largely hypothetical cyber attack incidents that had been the focus of much of the literature on cyber attacks and the use of force since the 1990s,[5] and while not amounting to a 'digital Pearl Harbor' in terms of the death and destruction associated with the Japanese entry into World War II, the Estonia incident demonstrated the increasing vulnerability of states reliant on ICTs to a new form of violence in and through cyberspace. The incident also provided significant impetus for international lawyers and policy-makers to consider the application of international law to state activities in this context. It thus highlighted the need to create clarity for the rules of state behavior in cyberspace and paved the way for the *Tallinn Manual* process.[6]

The effort to create agreement on the application of international law in cyberspace continues today, as evidenced by recent calls to establish norms of behavior in states' peacetime cyber activities by the United Nations and the Group of Seven (G7).[7] For example, in the 2015 UN Group of Governmental Experts (GGE), states recognized that the misuse of ICTs could undermine international peace and security, and that international law and the UN Charter in particular applied in the cyber context.[8] In 2016, the G7 also affirmed the applicability of international law and the UN Charter in cyberspace, and went so far as to affirm that 'under some circumstances' cyber attacks can amount to a use of force or an armed attack as understood in existing law.[9] Despite this apparent progress in states beginning to reach agreement on these critical issues, in 2017 the UN GGE failed to reach consensus, with many states divided on the applicability of central rules of international law to cyberspace.[10] While there has been significant progress since the 2007 attacks on Estonia in terms of what norms of behavior should apply in cyberspace,[11] uncertainty and divisions remain about the precise application of international law to state activities in this context.

Despite these efforts in the international community, as well as like-minded calls by the private sector to create a 'Digital Geneva Convention' to protect civilians from cyber attacks by states,[12] the use of various types of cyber attacks by states remains prevalent. In recent years, these have included the Russian interference in the 2016 US presidential election, which the United States described as representing 'a significant escalation in directness, level of activity, and scope of effort' compared with prior efforts to interfere with US elections.[13] In 2016 and 2017, the WannaCry and NotPetya incidents occurred,[14] with the latter being described by the US government as the most destructive and costly cyber attack the world has ever experienced.[15] This was followed by revelations in early 2018 about Russian cyber attacks compromising routers and other network infrastructure devices since 2015 enabling control of traffic through those devices.[16] This current state of affairs has been described by the president of Microsoft in the following terms:

> We suddenly find ourselves living in a world where nothing seems off limits to nation-state attacks. Conflicts between nations are no longer confined to the ground, sea and air, as cyberspace has become a potential new and global battleground. There are increasing risks of governments attempting to exploit or even weaponize software to achieve national security objectives, and governmental investments in cyber offense are continuing to grow.[17]

As such, despite calls that international law and the UN Charter apply to state activities in cyberspace, the use of various cyber attacks – including the use of non-destructive and seemingly 'non-violent' cyber operations by states against other states during peacetime – continues to be prevalent in interstate relations.

Accordingly, there is little question of the threat that cyber attacks pose to international peace and security – especially when used by states (either directly or through intermediaries) against other states in pursuit of their strategic interests. However, as demonstrated in the preceding chapters, as the central doctrinal mechanism through which international law seeks to contain interstate violence, the law on the use of force is limited in its capacity to regulate cyber attacks. It embodies an ontologically constrained conception of violence that undermines its ability to adequately recognize the harm caused by non-material cyber attacks in particular. As a result, due to their seemingly non-violent nature under traditional understandings of what constitutes violence, various cyber operations conducted by states escape the legal and conceptual bounds of key provisions of international law seeking to limit and contain interstate violence.[18] This is increasingly problematic given the degree to which states, together with society more generally, rely on ICTs for their proper functioning, and given the increased potential of non-material cyber attacks to adversely impact on the functioning of these societies.

As the case studies explored in this book show, even cyber attacks with non-material effects are capable of harming states that have integrated ICTs into central aspects of society, from social services to election processes to critical infrastructure. New forms of cyber violence can harm states and threaten international peace and security, and this calls for new ways of thinking about violence and the law regulating interstate violence. By viewing the state informationally and the harm caused by cyber attacks in terms of entropy, an informational approach offers an alternative way to do so. It allows consideration of the harm caused by cyber attacks to a broader range of entities (from human beings and physical objects to data and virtual processes) and offers a less anthropocentric and materialist way of thinking about violence. Accordingly, it allows consideration of even non-material cyber attacks as a form of informational violence against the state.

An informational approach to the cyber attacks against Estonia, Iran, and the United States

As demonstrated in Chapter 5, under existing law, the 2007 cyber attacks against Estonia are generally not considered to have amounted to a use of force. This was particularly because they were mainly disruptive in nature and did not result in injury to human beings or damage to physical objects.[19] However, through an informational approach, the 2007 cyber attacks could be seen to have caused significant increases in entropy by disrupting the operation of Estonia as an information entity. The DDoS attacks in particular caused disruptions to the operation of government and social services, and other services integral to the functioning of civil society, such as banking and Internet access. Given the scale and duration of the attacks, they infringed on Estonia's ability to interact and its autonomy as an entity, and constituted a form of informational violence against it. Viewed in this way, the 2007 cyber attacks against Estonia should be regarded as a prohibited form of interstate violence under Article 2(4).

The Stuxnet incident, in contrast, is more widely seen to have crossed the use of force threshold and amounted to a violation of Article 2(4) under existing law.[20] Unlike the Estonia incident, which is seen as primarily disruptive, in Chapter 6 it was shown how Stuxnet caused material damage to approximately 1000 centrifuges and therefore involved the requisite type of harm to be recognized within the conception of violence embodied in Article 2(4). However, this one-dimensional account of violence does not adequately capture the non-material harm caused by Stuxnet. Stuxnet also undermined the integrity, or disrupted the operation, of thousands of entities associated with the functioning of Iran's uranium enrichment facility at Natanz. In doing so, it disrupted the operation of a process central to the functioning of Iran as an autonomous entity. Unlike the Estonia incident, in which the violence was only informational, the Stuxnet incident involved a combination of both informational and physical violence. Further, as demonstrated in Chapter 6, even if Stuxnet had simply disrupted the operation of the centrifuges without causing material damage to them, it should similarly be viewed as a form of violence prohibited by Article 2(4).

The cyber attacks used as part of the Russian interference operation against the United States during the 2016 presidential election are generally not seen to have involved a form of harm that can be considered to constitute a use of force in violation of Article 2(4). Unlike the Estonia incident, which some argue that the law should be extended to be viewed as a use of force,[21] it is seemingly obvious to most commentators that the Russian interference incident did not involve a form of violence prohibited by Article 2(4).[22] The United States was not subject to DDoS attacks lasting multiple weeks disrupting the operation of its voter registration systems. Similarly, while malware was installed onto systems within DNC networks to exfiltrate data from them, no sophisticated computer viruses with technical capabilities similar to Stuxnet were used – for example, to manipulate the vote tally while making it appear that the votes were being counted normally, or to cause hardware damage to DNC or electoral board systems. Instead, there was unauthorized access to data stored in computer systems, and this was followed by a wide-scale release of these data to the public. Essentially, computer systems and networks were compromised, and the confidentiality of data was also compromised, but there was no significant disruption to the operation of computer systems or networks, or any hardware damage. For these reasons, the incident ultimately did not involve a type of harm that could be considered within the scope of Article 2(4) under existing law. However, through an informational approach, the election process could be seen as central to the proper operation of the United States as an information entity, and the attacks could be seen to cause increases in entropy by disrupting the normal operation of this process. The spear-phishing attacks targeted individuals within US political organizations and, where successful, compromised the interactions between these individuals and their organizations' computer systems and networks. This enabled the attackers to install malware that allowed them to extract information from the computer systems of these organizations. While the spear-phishing attacks themselves only resulted in minor increases in entropy, the subsequent strategic release of this information into the infosphere was carried out with the aim of undermining the proper operation of the United States as an information system. It was this release of information in particular that caused significant increases in entropy by disrupting the proper operation of the US presidential election process. Viewed in this way, the incident can be seen as a serious form of informational violence that should fall within the conceptual scope of Article 2(4), and not simply considered a form of non-violent interference into the internal affairs of the United States.

The current conception of violence embodied in Article 2(4) was shaped by the world wars and the traditional modes of warfare experienced during those conflicts. The various forms of 'cyber warfare' experienced in recent years – from the 2007 cyber attacks against Estonia, the Stuxnet incident, and the Russian interference operation to numerous other instances of cyber attacks by states – need to inform an updated conception of violence for Article 2(4) in the twenty-first century. DDoS attacks can disrupt the operation of virtual online services and processes relied on by states for the proper functioning of government and civil society. Artificial virtual entities like Stuxnet can be designed to operate with degrees of autonomy and with the ability to harm countless entities in real and virtual environments. Election processes can be disrupted through the systematic and strategic release of information obtained through targeted efforts to compromise computer systems. Informational violence is increasingly real, and in order for international law to be able to contain violence on a doctrinal level, the ontology underpinning the law on the use of force needs to be updated to accommodate Article 2(4)'s ability to recognize new forms of violence that should not be regarded as feasible means of solving disputes between states.

Doctrinal implications for international law

This section examines some of the doctrinal implications of an informational approach to cyber attacks and international law on the use of force. It considers the use of force threshold and the legally permitted responses to cyber attacks, namely, self-defense and countermeasures. It then examines the implications of this approach for the non-intervention principle, and looks at how this approach aligns with the purpose of the law on the use of force more generally.

The prohibition on the use of force

Adopting an informational approach offers an alternative way to think about violence and the harm caused by cyber attacks against the state, as well as a way to overcome the law's ontological constraints. By updating the conception of violence embodied in Article 2(4), forms of informational violence can also be viewed through the use of force principle, meaning the harm caused by cyber attacks can be taken more seriously. Michael Schmitt also argues that the law on the use of force is likely to develop in the future to recognize the dependence of modern societies on ICTs and provide them with more legal protection. According to him:

> It will impose obligations on states to act as responsible inhabitants of cyberspace, lower the point at which cyber operations violate the prohibition on the use of force, allow states to respond forcefully to some non-destructive cyber operations, and enhance the protection of cyber infrastructure, data, and activities during armed conflicts.[23]

Essentially, as states become increasingly dependent on ICTs for their proper functioning, the law will need to recognize informational violence as capable of harming states.

By adopting this way of thinking about violence, a broad range cyber operations by states – from information collection operations to destructive cyber attacks – can be seen to result in differing degrees of entropy and harm to various entities. However, it is not suggested that all such activities should fall within the scope of Article 2(4). Instead, adopting this approach is about recognizing the increasing degree to which states are reliant on ICTs, and can therefore also be harmed through non-material cyber attacks. In particular, those activities that seek to actively interrupt or disrupt the proper functioning of states warrant being viewed as a form of violence within the scope of Article 2(4).

It may appear that adopting this approach has the effect of lowering the use of force threshold to cover even minor instances of informational violence – for example, cyber espionage operations in which the confidentiality of information is compromised. However, this is not what is advocated. While each cyber attack incident must be considered on a case-by-case basis (and the *Tallinn Manual* criteria can be practically helpful in this),[24] by considering the degree of entropy caused by cyber attacks, the effects-based analysis is less restricted to solely injury or death, or damage or destruction in the physical world. Instead, the harm caused by cyber attacks can be considered more broadly in terms of the entropy caused to a range of entities – whether virtual or real. This offers a less anthropocentric and materialist way of thinking about violence, as it allows consideration of the harm caused to various parts of the infosphere and entities therein. An informational approach to this analysis is particularly useful, given the degree to which ICTs are embedded into all aspects of life – from the functioning of government to the daily lives of people in society.

Self-defense and countermeasures

Apart from the use of force threshold, this does mean that the armed attack threshold providing states with the legal justification to use kinetic force in self-defense should be triggered more lightly in response to cyber attacks. The purpose of the law on the use of force is to limit the use of violence in interstate relations, and a broader account of what constitutes violence should not open the door to legally justified uses of force in response to any instance of informational violence. Nonetheless, this way of thinking about violence can help provide the conceptual grounding for states to respond to serious forms of informational violence with physical violence where appropriate. For example, a cyber attack against a state's stock exchange or critical infrastructure, causing serious disruptions to society – even without material effects directly caused by the attacks – could qualify as a use of force rising to the level of an armed attack and warrant the use of kinetic force in self-defense.[25] Such an attack would amount to significant increases in entropy, justifying the use of violence against the entity responsible for the attack.

On the other hand, where the harm caused by cyber attacks is less severe, the law on countermeasures provides states with a legal framework permitting the use of proportionate and necessary measures in response to cyber attacks.[26] Again, it must be emphasized that if international law deems a broader range of malicious cyber attacks wrongful, and the implication of this is that states can respond with countermeasures, this should not be regarded as providing the legal justification for the use of any form of cyber attacks in retaliation that could lead to an escalation of conflict. It is important to note that international law in this context provides numerous conditions on the use of countermeasures, including in relation to their aim and duration, and them not involving a use of force.[27] Therefore, in order to minimize the risk of escalation, adopting an informational approach should not be regarded as legitimizing retaliatory cyber attacks against all forms of informational violence because states nonetheless have numerous other options available to them when they are subject to cyber attacks by other states, including sanctions and acts amounting to retorsion under international law.[28]

The non-intervention principle

Updating Article 2(4)'s conception of violence also has implications for the non-intervention principle. Under the position in existing law – as evident, for example, in the *Tallinn Manual*'s approach, cyber attacks that are seen to fall below the use of force threshold are generally regarded as possible violations of the non-intervention principle.[29] By adopting an informational approach to Article 2(4), it is possible that some cyber attacks that currently would fall within the realm of the non-intervention principle would now also be included within the realm of Article 2(4). However, given the issues surrounding the non-intervention principle and its application in the cyber context, this is preferable to casting non-material cyber attacks outside the scope of this key provision of international law. In addition to the often illusive nature of the non-intervention principle as a rule of customary international law, there are problems inherent in the application of this principle to the cyber context, as evidenced by a tendency to use the non-intervention principle as a secondary category into which to push non-material cyber attacks in particular. Further, to establish a prohibited intervention in the cyber context, various issues surround the element of coercion, which is a requisite to establish a violation of this principle.

As a principle of customary law that is often read as implied in the UN Charter, the meaning and scope of the non-intervention principle remains unclear, particularly in the cyber context. For example, even the *Tallinn Manual*'s Group of Experts note how 'the precise contours and application of the prohibition of intervention are unclear in light of ever evolving and increasingly intertwined international relations'.[30] Prior to the UN Charter, the principle was understood to refer only to 'forceful' means, whereas in the modern context it is generally seen to also cover non-forceful means of coercion. In relation to cyber attacks in particular, the principle is mainly referred to when such attacks fall below the use of force threshold, and generally where they lack material effects. For example, some argue that the cyber attacks against Estonia only constituted a violation of the non-intervention principle because they were not destructive in nature and sought to coerce Estonia into changing its policy about the location of the war memorial statue that was at the center of the 2007 incident.[31] While in this context the coercive aim of the attacks was clear, given the nature of cyber attacks and cyberspace more generally, this is not always so obvious. The application of the non-intervention principle can thus be problematic even in relation to non-material cyber attacks, given the need to demonstrate the element of coercion. This is highlighted particularly by the Russian interference in the 2016 US presidential election, as it may not always be clear what, for example, the specific change in policy that the state responsible for cyber attacks is trying to compel the other state to undertake. The incident demonstrated that various forms of cyber attacks could be used to undermine or disrupt the operation of key internal processes of a state without being coercive under international law and therefore amounting to a violation of the non-intervention principle.[32] The need to establish the element of coercion for non-material cyber attacks to amount to prohibited interventions is further problematized by the fact that where cyber attacks result in material effects and qualify as uses of force, the element of coercion is considered a given.[33] Essentially, according to this logic, non-material cyber attacks must be clearly coercive to constitute prohibited interventions, whereas cyber attacks with material effects naturally do so.

Accordingly, given the tendency to equate non-material cyber attacks almost categorically as forms of non-violence in breach of the non-intervention principle alone, a legal and conceptual barrier is created that requires cyber attacks to involve some form of material effects to be taken seriously under international law. Where material effects are lacking, the element of coercion becomes central to establishing a violation of international law on non-intervention. Given the complex nature of various types of cyber attacks and the threat they pose to states increasingly reliant on ICTs and to international peace and security, the non-use of force principle is a more appropriate means of regulating these activities as the UN Charter's central provision seeking to contain interstate violence.

The purpose of the law on the use of force

As a cornerstone provision of modern international law, the purpose of Article 2(4) within the UN Charter framework is to contain violence and, by limiting the circumstances in which states can use force to solve their disputes, to help foster predictability and stability in international relations. Updating Article 2(4)'s conception of violence enables an expanded doctrinal containment of violence and legal recognition of the new types of harmful activities in cyberspace in which states should be prohibited from engaging in. This is necessary given the existing law's inability to adequately recognize non-material cyber attacks in particular within the ambit of Article 2(4), as evident in the tendency to relegate these activities to forms of non-violence within the scope of the non-intervention principle alone. By depicting the majority of non-material cyber attacks as forms of non-violence and casting them into Article 2(4)'s periphery, the existence of this informational violence outside the law threatens to destabilize it.[34] The current extent of the use of various malicious cyber attacks by states – including the use of active cyber defense measures like hack-backs in response to such attacks[35] – can be viewed as a reversion to times in which states could resort to violent forms of engagement to solve their disputes. Some scholars liken the situation to a Hobbesian state of nature in which the rule of law is resisted to the extent that it becomes difficult to distinguish the state of 'cyber war' from peace.[36] The existence of this state of ubiquitous informational violence is destabilizing for international law on the use of force because, while the prohibition on the use of force is an accepted rule of international law, various malicious cyber attacks in peacetime remain prevalent but often occur in a legal grey area of uncertainty that can also increase the risk of escalation of conflict between states.[37] Unless recognized as a form of violence within the law, seemingly non-violent cyber attacks will continue to fall outside Article 2(4)'s conception of violence and thereby threaten international law's containment of violence.

Therefore, in light of the central purpose of Article 2(4) as the modern *jus ad bellum* to limit interstate violence and the outbreak of war, it runs counter to this purpose for the law to lack the adequate ability to recognize the harm that can be caused through cyber attacks. Updating Article 2(4)'s conception of violence is necessary on a conceptual level to strengthen the legal barrier against the current prevalence of such activities and, optimally, to limit the use of malicious cyber attacks by states. Given that Article 2(4)'s central purpose is to contain interstate violence, an informational approach offers a way for it to retain its relevance in doing so.

Conclusion

In the twenty-first century, with states increasingly reliant on ICTs for their proper functioning, the use of cyber attacks – whether destructive or disruptive – is not a feasible 'non-violent' means for states to use to resolve their disputes or in pursuit of their strategic interests. An informational approach offers a means through which to update Article 2(4)'s conception of violence on an ontological level. This enables cyber attacks involving harm to a broader range of entities to be recognized as a form of violence that international law on the use of force should contain on a doctrinal level, and it renders the law more suited to regulating the new forms of violence currently prevalent in cyberspace. This is warranted due to the nature of Article 2(4) as a central provision of international law designed to limit states from using violent means of engagement, and the issues surrounding the application of the non-intervention principle in the cyber context that result in the marginalization of cyber attacks with non-material effects in particular.

Notes

1 Richard Falk, *Legal Order in a Violent World* (Princeton University Press 1968) 41.

2 Antonio Cassese, for example, writes how the drafters of the UN Charter 'had been profoundly shocked by the Second World War and they ardently desired to set up an institution capable of preventing the repetition of such large-scale tragedy'. Antonio Cassese, *Violence and Law in the Modern Age* (Polity Press 1988) 32.

3 Stephen Neff describes how in the nineteenth century war was 'recognized by international lawyers as an accepted and routine means of conducting everyday international business'. Stephen C Neff, *War and the Law of Nations: A General History* (Cambridge University Press 2005) 161.

4 Toomas H Ilves, 'Address by the President of Estonia' (Speech at the 67th Session of the United Nations General Assembly, New York, 26 September 2012) <https://vp2006-2016.president.ee/en/official-duties/speeches/7991-address-by-h-e-toomas-hendrik-ilves-president-of-estonia-to-the-67th-session-of-the-united-nations-general-assembly-un-headquarters-new-york-september-2012> accessed 24 April 2018.

5 See, for example, Walter G Sharp, *CyberSpace and the Use of Force* (Aegis Research Corporation 1999); Michael N Schmitt, 'Computer Network Attack and the Use of Force in International Law: Thoughts on a Normative Framework' (1999) 37 *Columbia Journal of Transnational Law* 885.

6 Michael N Schmitt (ed), *Tallinn Manual on the International Law Applicable to Cyber Warfare* (Cambridge University Press 2013) 1–4.

7 Owen Bowcott, 'Dispute Along Cold War Lines Led to Collapse of UN Cyberwarfare Talks' *The Guardian* (23 August 2017) <www.theguardian.com/world/2017/aug/23/un-cyberwarfare-negotiations-collapsed-in-june-it-emerges> accessed 24 April 2018; Group of Seven, 'G7 Ise-Shima Leaders' Declaration' (G7 Ise-Shima Summit, Japan, 26–27 May 2016) <www.mofa.go.jp/files/000160266.pdf> accessed 24 April 2018.

8 UN Group of Governmental Experts on Developments in the Field of Information and Telecommunications in the Context of International Security, *Report of the Group of Governmental Experts on Developments in the Field of Information and Telecommunications in the Context of International Security* (22 July 2015) UN Doc A/70/174, 6, 12.

9 Group of Seven, 'G7 Principles and Actions on Cyber' (G7 Ise-Shima Leaders' Declaration annex, G7 Ise-Shima Summit, Japan, 26–27 May 2016) 1 <www.mofa.go.jp/files/000160279.pdf> accessed 24 April 2018.

10 Eneken Tikk and Mika Kerttunen, *The Alleged Demise of the UN GGE: An Autopsy and Eulogy* (Cyber Policy Institute, 2017) 16–18 <http://cpi.ee/wp-content/uploads/2017/12/2017-Tikk-Kerttunen-Demise-of-the-UN-GGE-2017-12-17-ET.pdf> accessed 24 April 2018.

11 See also Martha Finnemore and Duncan B Hollis, 'Constructing Norms for Global Cybersecurity' (2016) 110(3) *American Journal of International Law* 425, 436–8.

12 Brad Smith, 'The Need for a Digital Geneva Convention' (*Microsoft on the Issues*, 14 February 2017) <https://blogs.microsoft.com/on-the-issues/2017/02/14/need-digital-geneva-convention> accessed 24 April 2018.
13 Office of the Director of National Intelligence, 'Assessing Russian Activities and Intentions in Recent US Elections' (Intelligence Community Assessment, 6 January 2017) 5 <www.dni.gov/files/documents/ICA_2017_01.pdf> accessed 5 February 2018.
14 Alex Hern, 'WannaCry, Petya, NotPetya: How Ransomware Hit the Big Time in 2017' *The Guardian* (30 December 2017) <www.theguardian.com/technology/2017/dec/30/wannacry-petya-notpetya-ransomware> accessed 24 April 2018.
15 US Department of the Treasury, 'Treasury Sanctions Russian Cyber Actors for Interference with the 2016 US Elections and Malicious Cyber-Attacks' (Media Release, 15 March 2018) <https://home.treasury.gov/news/press-releases/sm0312> accessed 16 March 2018.
16 David D Kirkpatrick and Ron Nixon, 'US–UK Warning on Cyberattacks Includes Private Homes' *New York Times* (16 April 2018) <https://nyti.ms/2J0S8t2> accessed 24 April 2018.
17 In this context, he calls for the creation of a 'Digital Geneva Convention to protect civilians on the internet'. Smith (n 12).
18 For example, even the 2017 *Tallinn Manual*'s Group of Experts could not reach consensus on the issue of the use of force threshold – particularly where there is no physical damage – and instead adopted an approach that focuses on factors that states are likely to consider in determining this issue. Michael N Schmitt (ed) *Tallinn Manual 2.0 on the International Law Applicable to Cyber Operations* (2nd edn, Cambridge University Press 2017) 333. See also Michael N Schmitt, 'Grey Zones in the International Law of Cyberspace' (2017) 42(2) *The Yale Journal of International Law Online* 1, 15 <https://campuspress.yale.edu/yjil/files/2017/08/Schmitt_Grey-Areas-in-the-International-Law-of-Cyberspace-1cab8kj.pdf> accessed 24 April 2018.
19 See, for example, Russell Buchan, 'Cyber Attacks: Unlawful Uses of Force or Prohibited Interventions?' (2012) 17(2) *Journal of Conflict & Security Law* 211, 219.
20 See, for example, Heather Harrison Dinniss, *Cyber Warfare and the Laws of War* (Cambridge University Press 2012) 81; Schmitt, *Tallinn Manual* (n 18) 342.
21 Michael N Schmitt, 'Cyber Operations and the *Jus Ad Bellum* Revisited' (2011) 56(3) *Villanova Law Review* 569, 577; Sheng Li, 'When Does Internet Denial Trigger the Right of Armed Self-Defense?' (2013) 38(1) *Yale Journal of International Law* 179, 199–201.
22 See, for example, Duncan B Hollis, 'Russia and the DNC Hack: What Future for a Duty of Non-Intervention?' (*Opinio Juris*, 25 July 2016) <http://opiniojuris.org/2016/07/25/russia-and-the-dnc-hack-a-violation-of-the-duty-of-non-intervention> accessed 5 February 2018; Sean Watts, 'International Law and Proposed US Responses to the DNC Hack' (*Just Security*, 14 October 2016) <www.justsecurity.org/33558/international-law-proposed-u-s-responses-d-n-c-hack> accessed 5 February 2018.
23 Michael N Schmitt, 'The Law of Cyber Warfare: *Quo Vadis*?' (2014) 25 *Stanford Law and Policy Review* 269, 299.
24 The *Tallinn Manual* criteria are useful in making this assessment. Schmitt, *Tallinn Manual* (n 18) 334–6. Further, these criteria can be improved by, for example, incorporating into the assessment of when a cyber attack constitutes a use of force a need to consider the degrees of increases in entropy caused by a cyber attack when assessing its 'severity'; and the amount of entities harmed, as well as how important they are to the functioning of a state when considering a cyber attack's 'invasiveness' and 'measurability'. See also Ugo Pagallo, 'Cyber Force and the Role of Sovereign States in Informational Warfare' (2015) 28(3) *Philosophy & Technology* 407, 414–15.

25 This is consistent with the view taken by some of the *Tallinn Manual*'s Group of Experts. Schmitt, *Tallinn Manual* (n 18) 342–3.

26 International Law Commission, Responsibility of States for Internationally Wrongful Acts, UNGA Res 56/83 (12 December 2001) UN Doc A/RES/56/83 Art 22; Oona A Hathaway, 'The Drawbacks and Dangers of Active Defense' in Pascal Brangetto, Markus Maybaum and Jan Stinissen (eds), *2014 6th International Conference on Cyber Conflict* (NATO CCD COE Publications 2014) 45–7; Michael N Schmitt, 'Peacetime Cyber Responses and Wartime Cyber Operations' (2017) 8(2) *Harvard National Security Journal* 239, 253–60.

27 International Law Commission, Responsibility of States for Internationally Wrongful Acts (n 26) Arts 49–53. See also. Hathaway (n 26) 45–7.

28 Hathaway (n 26) 47–50; Schmitt (n 26) 258.

29 This is evident in the idea that, while cyber attacks generally require physical effects to constitute a use of force, the *Tallinn Manual*'s Group of Experts expressly notes that, 'The fact that the cyber operations result in no physical consequences does not detract from their characterization as a prohibited intervention.' Schmitt, *Tallinn Manual* (n 18) 318.

30 ibid 314.

31 See Buchan (n 19) 226.

32 Some argue that the scope of the non-intervention principle should be expanded to cover disruptive but non-coercive cyber attacks. See Ido Kilovaty, 'Doxfare: Politically Motivated Leaks and the Future of the Norm on Non-Intervention in the Era of Weaponized Information' (2018) 9 *Harvard National Security Journal* 147, 174. Similarly, a minority of the *Tallinn Manual*'s Group of Experts maintained that the 'context and consequences' of a cyber attack should be considered in determining whether the incident should be considered to rise to the level of being coercive. See Schmitt, *Tallinn Manual* (n 18) 319.

33 See *Case Concerning Military and Paramilitary Activities in and Against Nicaragua (Nicaragua v United States of America)* (Merits) [1986] ICJ Rep 14, 108; Schmitt, *Tallinn Manual* (n 18) 319.

34 As noted in Chapter 3, according to Walter Benjamin, the law has an interest in the monopoly of violence in order to preserve itself, as 'violence, when not in the hands of the law, threatens it not by the ends that it may pursue but by its mere existence outside the law'. Walter Benjamin, 'Critique of Violence' in Marcus Bullock and Michael W Jennings (eds), *Walter Benjamin: Selected Writings* (Belknap Press of Harvard University Press 2002) 239.

35 See Hathaway (n 26).

36 George Lucas, *Ethics and Cyber Warfare: The Quest for Responsible Security in the Age of Digital Warfare* (Oxford University Press 2017) 9.

37 Schmitt, 'Grey Zones' (n 18) 21.

Bibliography

Benjamin W, 'Critique of Violence' in Bullock M and Jennings MW (eds), *Walter Benjamin: Selected Writings* (Belknap Press of Harvard University Press 2002)

Bowcott O, 'Dispute Along Cold War Lines Led to Collapse of UN Cyberwarfare Talks' *The Guardian* (23 August 2017) <www.theguardian.com/world/2017/aug/23/un-cyberwarfare-negotiations-collapsed-in-june-it-emerges> accessed 24 April 2018

Buchan R, 'Cyber Attacks: Unlawful Uses of Force or Prohibited Interventions?' (2012) 17(2) *Journal of Conflict & Security Law* 211

Case Concerning Military and Paramilitary Activities in and Against Nicaragua (Nicaragua v United States of America) (Merits) [1986] ICJ Rep 14

Cassese A, *Violence and Law in the Modern Age* (Polity Press 1988)

Dinniss HH, *Cyber Warfare and the Laws of War* (Cambridge University Press 2012)

Falk R, *Legal Order in a Violent World* (Princeton University Press 1968)

Finnemore M and Hollis DB, 'Constructing Norms for Global Cybersecurity' (2016) 110(3) *American Journal of International Law* 425

Group of Seven, 'G7 Ise-Shima Leaders' Declaration' (G7 Ise-Shima Summit, Japan, 26–27 May 2016) <www.mofa.go.jp/files/000160266.pdf> accessed 24 April 2018

——— 'G7 Principles and Actions on Cyber' (G7 Ise-Shima Leaders' Declaration annex, G7 Ise-Shima Summit, Japan, 26–27 May 2016) 1 <www.mofa.go.jp/files/000160279.pdf> accessed 24 April 2018

Hathaway OA, 'The Drawbacks and Dangers of Active Defense' in Brangetto P, Maybaum M and Stinissen J (eds), *2014 6th International Conference on Cyber Conflict* (NATO CCD COE Publications 2014)

Hern A, 'WannaCry, Petya, NotPetya: How Ransomware Hit the Big Time in 2017' *The Guardian* (30 December 2017) <www.theguardian.com/technology/2017/dec/30/wannacry-petya-notpetya-ransomware> accessed 24 April 2018

Hollis DB, 'Russia and the DNC Hack: What Future for a Duty of Non-Intervention?' (*Opinio Juris*, 25 July 2016) <http://opiniojuris.org/2016/07/25/russia-and-the-dnc-hack-a-violation-of-the-duty-of-non-intervention> accessed 5 February 2018

Ilves TH, 'Address by the President of Estonia' (Speech at the 67th Session of the United Nations General Assembly, New York, 26 September 2012) <https://vp2006-2016.president.ee/en/official-duties/speeches/7991-address-by-h-e-toomas-hendrik-ilves-president-of-estonia-to-the-67th-session-of-the-united-nations-general-assembly-un-headquarters-new-york-september-2012> accessed 24 April 2018

International Law Commission, Responsibility of States for Internationally Wrongful Acts, UNGA Res 56/83 (12 December 2001) UN Doc A/RES/56/83

Kilovaty I, 'Doxfare: Politically Motivated Leaks and the Future of the Norm on Non-Intervention in the Era of Weaponized Information' (2018) 9 *Harvard National Security Journal* 147

Kirkpatrick DD and Nixon R, 'US–UK Warning on Cyberattacks Includes Private Homes' *New York Times* (16 April 2018) <https://nyti.ms/2J0S8t2> accessed 24 April 2018

Li S, 'When Does Internet Denial Trigger the Right of Armed Self-Defense?' (2013) 38(1) *Yale Journal of International Law* 179

Lucas G, *Ethics and Cyber Warfare: The Quest for Responsible Security in the Age of Digital Warfare* (Oxford University Press 2017)

Neff SC, *War and the Law of Nations: A General History* (Cambridge University Press 2005)

Office of the Director of National Intelligence, 'Assessing Russian Activities and Intentions in Recent US Elections' (Intelligence Community Assessment, 6 January 2017) <www.dni.gov/files/documents/ICA_2017_01.pdf> accessed 5 February 2018

Pagallo U, 'Cyber Force and the Role of Sovereign States in Informational Warfare' (2015) 28(3) *Philosophy & Technology* 407

Schmitt MN, 'Computer Network Attack and the Use of Force in International Law: Thoughts on a Normative Framework' (1999) 37 *Columbia Journal of Transnational Law* 885

——— 'Cyber Operations and the Jus Ad Bellum Revisited' (2011) 56(3) *Villanova Law Review* 569

——— 'The Law of Cyber Warfare: *Quo Vadis*?' (2014) 25 *Stanford Law and Policy Review* 269

——— 'Grey Zones in the International Law of Cyberspace' (2017) 42(2) *Yale Journal of International Law Online* 1 <https://campuspress.yale.edu/yjil/files/2017/08/Schmitt_Grey-Areas-in-the-International-Law-of-Cyberspace-1cab8kj.pdf> accessed 24 April 2018

——— 'Peacetime Cyber Responses and Wartime Cyber Operations' (2017) 8(2) *Harvard National Security Journal* 239

——— (ed), *Tallinn Manual on the International Law Applicable to Cyber Warfare* (Cambridge University Press 2013)

——— (ed), *Tallinn Manual 2.0 on the International Law Applicable to Cyber Operations* (2nd edn, Cambridge University Press 2017)

Sharp WG, *CyberSpace and the Use of Force* (Aegis Research Corporation 1999)

Smith B, 'The need for a Digital Geneva Convention' (*Microsoft on the Issues*, 14 February 2017) <https://blogs.microsoft.com/on-the-issues/2017/02/14/need-digital-geneva-convention> accessed 24 April 2018

Tikk E and Kerttunen M, 'The Alleged Demise of the UN GGE: An Autopsy and Eulogy' (Cyber Policy Institute, 2017) <http://cpi.ee/wp-content/uploads/2017/12/2017-Tikk-Kerttunen-Demise-of-the-UN-GGE-2017-12-17-ET.pdf> accessed 24 April 2018

UN Group of Governmental Experts on Developments in the Field of Information and Telecommunications in the Context of International Security, *Report of the Group of Governmental Experts on Developments in the Field of Information and Telecommunications in the Context of International Security* (22 July 2015) UN Doc A/70/174

US Department of the Treasury, 'Treasury Sanctions Russian Cyber Actors for Interference with the 2016 U.S. Elections and Malicious Cyber-Attacks' (Media Release, 15 March 2018) <https://home.treasury.gov/news/press-releases/sm0312> accessed 16 March 2018

Watts S, 'International Law and Proposed US Responses to the D.N.C. Hack' (*Just Security*, 14 October 2016) <www.justsecurity.org/33558/international-law-proposed-u-s-responses-d-n-c-hack> accessed 5 February 2018

9 Conclusion

Introduction

In 1996 Krystyna Gorniak-Kocikowska predicted that, given the global nature of cyberspace and the nature of the 'computer revolution',

> the ethic of the future will have a global character. It will be global in a spatial sense, since it will encompass the entire Globe. It will also be global in the sense that it will address the totality of human actions and relations.[1]

This is in contrast to the ethical theories of Immanuel Kant and Jeremy Bentham that, despite their claims to universalism, she sees as the manifestation and culmination of a particular European Enlightenment.[2] Also in 1996, writing in relation to the impact of ICTs on public international law and warfare, Sean Kanuck argued that

> Just as territorial boundaries and natural resources formed the theoretical foundation for an international legal paradigm in an age of geopolitical borders, so too must a conceptual framework based on information undergird the legal institutions of the twenty-first century.[3]

He maintained that the basis for this new system must be interactions and not physical territory.[4]

This book has answered the call for a 'new international legal paradigm' for the information age that moves beyond 'territorial boundaries and natural resources'. Floridi's information ethics offers a conceptual framework based on information, and it is concerned with the interactions of all information entities. It thus provides an 'ethic of the future' that is designed to 'address the totality of human actions and relations' in the information age.

This chapter examines the wider conceptual implications of an informational approach for international law and thinking about violence and the state. It shows that, beyond cyber attacks and international law on the use of force, information ethics also provides conceptual tools that are useful for thinking about different forms of violence and the role of the state in the infosphere more generally. The chapter begins with an overview of the 'turn to information ethics' undertaken in this book before examining the wider relationship between law and informational violence, and the state as an information entity.

The turn to information ethics

As demonstrated in Chapter 2, Floridi's information ethics is one of a number of efforts to provide a more universal ethics that is concerned with the impact of the interactions of all entities on the infosphere. It is grounded in a philosophy of information, and it adopts an informational view of the world, placing the ability to interact as central to what constitutes being.[5] It offers an environmental ethics concerned with the well-being of all of the entities and environments that make up the global infosphere. It thus extends its ethical concern beyond anthropocentric or even 'biocentric' theories towards an 'ontocentric' one.[6] The universal or global basis stems in part from the idea that the ethical dimensions of information and ICTs concern everyone.[7] Floridi's information ethics seeks to be universal in the sense of being all-inclusive because, given that all entities can be seen as information entities, its ethical framework seeks to address issues affecting all of them.[8] Therefore, information ethics incorporates not only the digital world of cyberspace, the world's natural environment, and humans and other sentient beings as the focus of its ethical concern, but instead all of these entities, environments and the global infosphere that they constitute. Accordingly, information ethics provides an ethic with a truly global character that encompasses the totality of interactions and relations between information entities.

In this book, information ethics was drawn on essentially to consider the harm that cyber attacks can cause to the state. This was driven by a sense that state activities in and through cyberspace appear to fall outside central international legal doctrines regulating interstate violence, particularly because of the novel forms of harm that they involve. It therefore examined the ways in which states are capable of harming other states in and through cyberspace, and how the harm caused by cyber attacks fits in with existing laws regulating intestate violence. The focus was placed on the law on the use of force – the central doctrine through which modern international law seeks to contain the outbreak of interstate conflict and violence. Here information ethics was used to critique the ontologically constrained conception of violence that limits law's capacity to regulate cyber attacks, and to offer an alternative way in which to think about violence and the state as the entity subject to violence. This was also shown to be a means to update the law's conception of violence, enabling new forms of violence to be recognized within the ambit of Article 2(4).

Accordingly, information ethics was used in this book to problematize and rethink some of the fundamental tenets of international law in light of the conceptual challenges brought about by ICTs. However, the book also demonstrated how information ethics can be used to consider a concrete international problem, thus contributing to the development of information ethics as a field. As highlighted in Chapter 2, information ethics has been subject to criticisms – particularly in relation to the ontological equality principle and the notion of entropy as evil. Among these criticisms was the questioning of why all things should have value in themselves, and the practical question of how to assess differences in value between information entities. While Floridi's responses to these criticisms were outlined in Chapter 2, the analysis of the case studies undertaken in this book also supports the practical viability of an informational approach. It was shown that information ethics can be applied in concrete situations to consider the entropy caused to a range of information entities and also assess differences in the degrees of entropy produced. The case studies illustrate how the expansion of ethical concern beyond human beings and material objects to also purely information entities and processes can have practical utility too – for instance, when considering the harm caused by cyber attacks.[9]

In addition to this contribution to information ethics as a field, the informational approach developed in this book can be used to think about law, technology, and violence more generally. Information ethics provides a conceptual basis on which to rethink the law's anthropocentrism and materialism in informational terms that are uniquely universal. Beyond cyber attacks and the law on the use of force, this is useful given the range of issues that new technologies are raising for the law – for instance, in relation to various non-human entities that are capable of operating with increasing levels of autonomy. Recognizing a broader range of entities as having moral value also raises questions about the role and purpose of the state, and whether it has a responsibility to care for and protect not only human entities, but all entities within its region of the infosphere. Further, where states engage in activities that are harmful to these entities, the violence inherent in the degradation or destruction of information entities can be seen in a way that is not limited by the law's existing worldview.

Law and informational violence

Considering informational violence and the law more broadly, there are fundamental differences in terms of how the law conceives this violence and its legality. Often this depends on the actors responsible. For example, where non-state actors engage in activities involving forms of informational violence, such as obtaining unauthorized access to computers and information or launching Distributed Denial-of-Service (DDoS) attacks against websites, these acts are considered through criminal law, and hence through the domestic laws of the state. Where state actors or non-state actors under the control of states do so, depending on the exact targets and the general motivations of those responsible, the violence can be conceptualized very differently. For instance, where the targets are corporate entities and the information that is undermined is commercially sensitive, this can be classed as economic espionage.[10] In contrast, where the targets are government databases and politically sensitive information is compromised, then it tends to be seen merely as a form of political espionage, about which international law traditionally has little to say.[11] However, these distinctions and classifications are not always clear cut, especially given issues around anonymity and the potential involvement of a multitude of actors.[12] Where cyber attacks involve more significant degrees of harm, and provided they can be attributed to state actors, then – and only then – the law on the use of force paradigm potentially becomes applicable. Accordingly, the entities responsible for activities involving informational violence, the nature of the entities subject to harm and the degree of harm in question greatly impact how the law conceptualizes this violence and whether it is deemed illegal, or implicitly permitted or condoned. Therefore, if a non-state actor without state support obtains unauthorized access to a government's databases and the incident is considered through criminal law, it is effectively deemed a form of illegal and illegitimate violence. In contrast, when a government collects information about individuals or corporations in another state, or accesses information stored in another government's databases without authorization, without international law specifically deeming this illegal, violence in this context effectively is deemed legitimate.

In effect, within cyberspace, the law currently enables states to relatively freely engage in activities involving violence whereas the law is used to restrict non-state actors from doing so. This can be seen as an affirmation of the state's monopoly of violence over forms of informational violence. By criminalizing engagement in informational violence by non-state actors through their domestic laws, states can monopolize informational violence through the law. Internationally, however, instead of being brought within the law regulating interstate violence and into a legal monopoly of violence, informational violence is left outside the law's conception of violence. As a form of violence outside the way the law sees violence on an international level, states effectively are enabled to engage freely in activities involving informational violence, resulting in a 'cyberstate of nature'[13] of sorts. Therefore, while the criminalization of informational violence by non-state actors is express, implicit in this is a more subtle establishment of a monopoly of informational violence outside the law.[14]

By expanding the scope of the notion of violence to a broader ontological spectrum, the potential of states to inflict harm through their various activities in and through cyberspace against a range of entities can be appreciated in a new light. Like nuclear weapons technologies that demonstrated the novel technological capacity of states to annihilate entire cities, while the full extent of states' offensive cyber attack capabilities are unknown, incidents such as Stuxnet and NotPetya offer glimpses into these capabilities and the future of interstate violence. While Stuxnet, for example, was designed to limit collateral damage as it only targeted very specific computer configurations and caused damage subtly, it could have been designed differently. It could have been designed to cause less discriminate harm, more immediate physical damage or more widespread and significant informational harm. This could have involved deletion of the data in the computers to which it spread, like the NotPetya malware in 2017, which disguised itself as ransomware but actually functioned as a 'wiper', rendering computer systems unusable.[15] While the law would not traditionally regard the intentional destruction of data as a form of violence, from an informational perspective it could be seen as a large-scale informational cleansing of sorts. By expanding the ontological scope of the notion of violence, the harmful potential of cyber attacks can be properly appreciated within the context of the increasing ICT dependency of modern states as information societies.

To a degree, this 'infocentric' shift in focus can be seen as a dislodgment of the human that is at the very foundation of law. Both human rights law and international humanitarian law are premised on fundamental assumptions about what entities constitute human beings, who, through the provision of rights, should be protected from violence. The aim here is not to trivialize the notion of violence and equate the deletion of data to the killing of human beings in terms of moral reprehensibility. Instead, as a means of rethinking the law's anthropocentrism and materialism, which were shown to limit the law's capacity to regulate interstate violence, an informational approach offers a change of perspective. It is worth noting that in human rights law, and law more generally, while usually seen as formally equal under the law, even human beings are distinguished in terms of their substantive differences. As such, regardless of any formal depiction of humans as information entities (as information organisms or *inforgs* in Floridi's terminology) that enjoy a basic right to exist shared by all other information entities, even when humans are seen informationally, they can still be seen as uniquely complex information structures. It therefore remains possible to make distinctions between these complex information structures – for example, on the basis of their information communication and processing abilities. Even existing law does this in relation to the entities that are given a right to political participation, as distinctions are made based on a human being's age and mental capacity. This 'infocentrism' does not necessarily reduce human beings to mere information entities; instead, it simply offers a perspective from which to consider all entities (including human beings) in similar terms. Accordingly, it not only broadens the scope of the entities capable of being considered subject to harm, but also the scope of the entities capable of performing actions and having legal agency. This is especially useful given the ways in which artificial and increasingly autonomous entities – such as autonomous vehicles and weapons systems, and other non-human entities – are raising novel legal issues in many areas of the law.[16] Therefore, while it may problematize the law's anthropocentrism, it allows for consideration of the various non-human entities that have the information processing and communication abilities to increasingly perform actions previously reserved purely for human beings as legal agents.[17]

The informational integrity of the state entity

In addition to providing a way of thinking about violence differently, this book has also offered an alternative image of the state. As shown in Chapter 3, when viewed in informational terms, the state can be seen as an information system and its essence as an entity arising from its primary purpose: to care for and protect all entities within its region of the infosphere. Therefore, as a responsible and caring inhabitant of the infosphere pursuant to the laws of information ethics, the state also has a responsibility to do so. In the wider context of international law, the notion of 'responsibility to protect' emerged at the beginning of the twenty-first century in human rights law as the idea that states have a responsibility to protect human beings within their territories.[18] On the other hand, in international environmental law, the notion of sustainable development emerged in the late twentieth century as the idea that the natural resources on which present and future generations depend should also be protected.[19] The idea of the responsibility to care for and protect all entities within a state's region of the infosphere is a conscious amalgamation of the basic ideas behind these concepts and their extension to the infosphere. On a premise broader and more inclusive than human or state equality, drawing on the notion of ontological equality, this extends the idea that not only human beings or the natural environment should have rights and be protected to the premise that everything by virtue of its existence has a (basic) right to exist and flourish according to its nature. This means that, as a starting point, states should have a responsibility to care for and protect all entities within their region of the infosphere. It does not mean that the rights of databases or natural resources will always trump those of human beings, but simply that when viewed informationally, the rights of all entities can be taken into consideration. The notion of a responsibility to care for and protect seeks to capture a concern for the well-being of the recipient of actions, and for all the entities involved in their interactions, as the premise of what is considered good within the global infosphere.

Additionally, given that state entities also have a basic right to exist and flourish, this means that they too have a right to be free from harm. This in turn should entail a corresponding duty to do no harm to others. In practical terms, this can be seen to align with, for example, the principle of due diligence in the cyberspace context. This principle is akin to the duty of states to prevent transboundary harm that exists in international environmental law. It essentially requires states to exercise due diligence in not allowing their territory or cyber infrastructure to be used for activities that cause harm in other states.[20] For example, the *Tallinn Manual*'s Group of Experts maintain that the principle should apply in the cyberspace context by analogy to how it applies in international environmental law, requiring the harm to involve 'serious adverse consequences' for the principle to be applicable.[21] In recognition of a wider range of consequences in this context, they explicitly note that the harm in question does not need to involve physical effects and could involve cyber attacks interfering with or disruptive to the operation of society.[22] Therefore, the due diligence principle can be seen as practically compatible with the notion of states being responsible and caring inhabitants of the infosphere.

Finally, it is worth returning to the ideas of Gorniak-Kocikowska and Kanuck, which were outlined at the beginning of this chapter. Specifically, it was predicted that the future ethic will be global in the spatial sense, and it was proposed that international law's next conceptual paradigm needs to shift away from territory towards information and interactions. Against international law's universalism – historically, a particular European universalism[23] – information ethics offers a uniquely universal foundation for the law that is based on information. From an informational perspective, the informational substance that all entities share is universal. With this as the law's conceptual foundation and its universal premise, a readjustment of the law's focus away from the human individual and the territorial state is required. This enables a shift in its conceptual foundation towards information and interactions. In international law, by considering states as information entities that increasingly interact with other entities within the global infosphere, law can be designed with a concern for the 'quality and healthiness' of the interactions between these entities and their contribution to the enrichment of the infosphere.[24] This can also involve recognition and protection of the 'informational integrity' of states as information entities. The focus thus shifts away from the traditional account in which territory is seen as the essence of the state's existence and the law's conceptual basis towards one based on the interactions of information entities. Beyond cyber attacks and the use of force, this means various other activities can be considered within the same conceptual framework in terms of their impact on the infosphere. From trade restrictions to online censorship and environmental pollution, the potential entropy and the degree to which these activities enrich the well-being of the global infosphere can be considered. In addition to state activities and interactions, the actions and interactions of a wider range of entities, such as individuals, corporations, and international organizations that increasingly interact within the international system, can also be brought under the same conceptual umbrella. Therefore, by offering a conceptual framework based on information that is truly global in the spatial sense, information ethics has the ability to offer a new paradigm for law regulating interactions in the information age.

Notes

1 Krystyna Gorniak-Kocikowska, 'The Computer Revolution and the Problem of Global Ethics' (1996) 2(2) *Science and Engineering Ethics* 177, 179.
2 ibid 182–3.
3 Sean P Kanuck, 'Information Warfare: New Challenges for Public International Law' (1996) 37 *Harvard International Law Journal* 272, 274.
4 ibid 292.

5 According to Floridi, 'the criterion for existence – what it means for something to be completely and ultimately real – is also changing. Oversimplifying, ancient and medieval philosophers thought that only that which is immutable, that is, God, could be said to exist fully. Anything that changes, such as an animal, moves from non-existence (there was no animal) to existence (the animal was born) back to non-existence (the animal is dead). Modern philosophers preferred to associate existence to the possibility of being subject to perception. The most empirically minded insisted on something being perceivable through the five senses in order to qualify as existing. Today, immutability and perceivability have been joined by interactability. Our philosophy seems to suggest that "to be is to be interactable", even if that with which we interact is only transient and virtual.' See Luciano Floridi, *The Fourth Revolution* (Oxford University Press 2014) 43.

6 See Luciano Floridi, 'Information Ethics: on the Philosophical Foundation of Computer Ethics' (1999) 1(1) *Ethics and Information Technology* 33, 43.

7 See Charles Ess, 'Universal Information Ethics? Ethical Pluralism and Social Justice' in Emma Rooksby and John Weckert (eds), *Information Technology and Social Justice* (Information Science Publishing 2007) 70.

8 See Luciano Floridi, 'Information Ethics: a Reappraisal' (2008) 10(2–3) *Ethics and Information Technology* 189, 190–1.

9 While this book focused mainly on the harm caused by cyber attacks and did not assess their morality, the latter is also possible from an informational perspective. See, for example, how Floridi's moral laws of information ethics have been applied to cyber warfare by Mariarosaria Taddeo and Ugo Pagallo. Mariarosaria Taddeo, 'Just Information Warfare' (2016) 35(1) *Topoi* 213, 221–2; Ugo Pagallo, 'Cyber Force and the Role of Sovereign States in Informational Warfare' (2015) 28(3) *Philosophy & Technology* 407, 416–19. For a critique of informations ethics' utility in this context over traditional ethical theories, see Matt Sleat, 'Just Cyber War? *Casus Belli*, Information Ethics, and the Human Perspective' (2017) 44(2) *Review of International Studies* 324.

10 See Michael S Schmidt and David E Sanger, '5 in China Army Face US Charges of Cyberattacks' *New York Times* (19 May 2014) <https://nyti.ms/2lcnYZg> accessed 17 April 2018.

11 For example, in 2015 the personal details of 21.5 million current and former US federal employees (including fingerprints of over five million people) were compromised by a 'Chinese espionage operation': see 'US government hack stole fingerprints of 5.6 million federal employees' *The Guardian* (24 September 2015) <www.theguardian.com/technology/2015/sep/23/us-government-hack-stole-fingerprints> accessed 17 April 2018.

12 For example, in 2014 the Sony Corporation's computer systems were compromised and large amounts of data were stolen or deleted. A non-state actor group claimed responsibility for the incident, and it is believed it acted with the support of North Korean state agencies. In response, the US government issued sanctions against North Korean officials. See Michael Cieply and Brooks Barnes, 'Sony Cyberattack, First a Nuisance, Swiftly Grew into a Firestorm' *The New York Times* (30 December 2014) <https://nyti.ms/2k4Hxn4> accessed 17 April 2018; Kim Zetter, 'Sony Got Hacked Hard: What We Know and Don't Know So Far' *Wired* (3 December 2014) <www.wired.com/2014/12/sony-hack-what-we-know> accessed 17 April 2018; David E Sanger and Michael S Schmidt, 'More Sanctions on North Korea After Sony Case' *New York Times* (2 January 2015) <https://nyti.ms/2tGT5lL> accessed 17 April 2018.

13 Seumas Miller, 'Cyberattacks and "Dirty Hands"' in Fritz Allhoff, Adam Henschke, and Bradley Jay Strawser (eds), *Binary Bullets: The Ethics of Cyberwarfare* (Oxford University Press 2016) 241. See also George Lucas, *Ethics and Cyber Warfare: The Quest for Responsible Security in the Age of Digital Warfare* (Oxford University Press 2017) 9.

14 David Fidler, for example, suggests that Stuxnet's development and use by the United States and Israel may see the development of international law into the direction of 'cyber-specific rules that increase the political and legal space in which states can use cybertechnologies against one another' – rules that push established boundaries of the use of force threshold permitting states 'to explore and exploit cybertechnologies as instruments of foreign policy and national security'. David P Fidler, 'Was Stuxnet an Act of War? Decoding a Cyberattack' (2011) 9(4) *IEEE Security & Privacy* 56, 58.
15 Alex Hern, '"NotPetya" Malware Attacks Could Warrant Retaliation, Says NATO-affiliated Researcher' *The Guardian* (3 July 2017) <www.theguardian.com/technology/2017/jul/03/notpetya-malware-attacks-ukraine-warrant-retaliation-nato-researcher-tomas-minarik> accessed 17 April 2018.
16 See, for example, Tim McFarland and Jai Galliott, 'Autonomous Systems in a Military Context (Part 1): A Survey of the Legal Issues' (2016) 4(2) *International Journal of Robotics Applications and Technologies* 34.
17 Floridi and Sanders, for instance, examine the concept of agency in relation to artificial agents. See Luciano Floridi and Jeff W Sanders, 'On the Morality of Artificial Agents' (2004) 14(3) *Minds and Machines* 349. As to legal agents, Bert-Jaap Koops, Mireille Hildebrandt and David O Jaquet-Chiffelle consider whether, for example, software agents and robots should be given some form of limited legal personhood. Bert-Jaap Koops, Mireille Hildebrandt and David Olivier Jaquet-Chiffelle, 'Bridging the Accountability Gap: Rights for New Entities in the Information Society?' (2010) 11(2) *Minnesota Journal of Law, Science & Technology* 497. For a critique of Floridi's notion of moral agents, see David Grant and Lyria Bennett Moses, *Technology and the Trajectory Myth* (Edward Elgar 2017) 204–8.
18 Where the state fails to do so, then the responsibility shifts to the international community. Anne Orford, *International Authority and the Responsibility to Protect* (Cambridge University Press 2011) 1–2.
19 See Nico J Schrijver, *The Evolution of Sustainable Development in International Law: Inception, Meaning and Status* (Martinus Nijhoff 2008) 23–4.
20 Michael N Schmitt (ed), *Tallinn Manual 2.0 on the International Law Applicable to Cyber Operations* (2nd edn, Cambridge University Press 2017) 30.
21 ibid 36–7.
22 ibid 37–8.
23 See, for example, Emmanuelle Jouannet, 'Universalism and Imperialism: The True–False Paradox of International Law?' (2007) 18(3) *European Journal of International Law* 379, 380–2.
24 The Onlife Initiative, 'The Onlife Manifesto' in Luciano Floridi (ed), *The Onlife Manifesto: Being Human in a Hyperconnected Era* (Springer 2015) 46.

Bibliography

Cieply M and Barnes B, 'Sony Cyberattack, First a Nuisance, Swiftly Grew Into a Firestorm' *New York Times* (30 December 2014) <https://nyti.ms/2k4Hxn4> accessed 17 April 2018

Ess C, 'Universal Information Ethics? Ethical Pluralism and Social Justice' in Rooksby E and Weckert J (eds), *Information Technology and Social Justice* (Information Science Publishing 2007)

Fidler DP, 'Was Stuxnet an Act of War? Decoding a Cyberattack' (2011) 9(4) *IEEE Security & Privacy* 56

Floridi L, 'Information Ethics: On the Philosophical Foundation of Computer Ethics' (1999) 1(1) *Ethics and Information Technology* 33

——— 'Information Ethics: a Reappraisal' (2008) 10(2–3) *Ethics and Information Technology* 189

——— *The Fourth Revolution* (Oxford University Press 2014)

Floridi L and Sanders JW, 'On the Morality of Artificial Agents' (2004) 14(3) *Minds and Machines* 349

Gorniak-Kocikowska K, 'The Computer Revolution and the Problem of Global Ethics' (1996) 2(2) *Science and Engineering Ethics* 177

Grant D and Bennett Moses L, *Technology and the Trajectory Myth* (Edward Elgar 2017)

Hern A, '"NotPetya" Malware Attacks Could Warrant Retaliation, Says NATO-affiliated Researcher' *The Guardian* (3 July 2017) <www.theguardian.com/technology/2017/jul/03/notpetya-malware-attacks-ukraine-warrant-retaliation-nato-researcher-tomas-minarik> accessed 17 April 2018

Jouannet E, 'Universalism and Imperialism: The True–False Paradox of International Law?' (2007) 18(3) *European Journal of International Law* 379

Kanuck SP, 'Information Warfare: New Challenges for Public International Law' (1996) 37 *Harvard International Law Journal* 272

Koops BJ, Hildebrandt M and Jaquet-Chiffelle DO, 'Bridging the Accountability Gap: Rights for New Entities in the Information Society?' (2010) 11(2) *Minnesota Journal of Law, Science & Technology* 497

Lucas G, Ethics and Cyber Warfare: The Quest for Responsible Security in the Age of Digital Warfare (Oxford University Press 2017)

McFarland T and Galliott J, 'Autonomous Systems in a Military Context (Part 1): A Survey of the Legal Issues' (2016) 4(2) *International Journal of Robotics Applications and Technologies* 34

Miller S, 'Cyberattacks and "Dirty Hands"' in Allhoff F, Henschke A, and Strawser BJ, *Binary Bullets: The Ethics of Cyberwarfare* (Oxford University Press 2016)

Onlife Initiative, 'The Onlife Manifesto' in Floridi L (ed), *The Onlife Manifesto: Being Human in a Hyperconnected Era* (Springer Open 2015)

Orford A, International Authority and the Responsibility to Protect (Cambridge University Press 2011)

Pagallo U, 'Cyber Force and the Role of Sovereign States in Informational Warfare' (2015) 28(3) *Philosophy & Technology* 407

Sanger DE and Schmidt MS, 'More Sanctions on North Korea After Sony Case' *New York Times* (2 January 2015) <https://nyti.ms/2tGT5lL> accessed 17 April 2018

Schmidt MS and Sanger DE, '5 in China Army Face US Charges of Cyberattacks' *New York Times* (19 May 2014) <https://nyti.ms/2lcnYZg> accessed 17 April 2018

Schmitt MN (ed), Tallinn Manual 2.0 on the International Law Applicable to Cyber Operations (2nd edn, Cambridge University Press 2017)

Schrijver NJ, The Evolution of Sustainable Development in International Law: Inception, Meaning and Status (Martinus Nijhoff 2008)

Sleat M, 'Just Cyber War? *Casus Belli*, Information Ethics, and the Human Perspective' (2017) 44(2) *Review of International Studies* 324

Taddeo M, 'Just Information Warfare' (2016) 35(1) *Topoi* 213

'US Government Hack Stole Fingerprints of 5.6 Million Federal Employees' *The Guardian* (24 September 2015) <www.theguardian.com/technology/2015/sep/23/us-government-hack-stole-fingerprints> accessed 17 April 2018

Zetter K, 'Sony Got Hacked Hard: What We Know and Don't Know So Far' *Wired* (3 December 2014) <www.wired.com/2014/12/sony-hack-what-we-know> accessed 17 April 2018

Index

For Product Safety Concerns and Information please contact our EU
representative GPSR@taylorandfrancis.com
Taylor & Francis Verlag GmbH, Kaufingerstraße 24, 80331 München, Germany

www.ingramcontent.com/pod-product-compliance
Ingram Content Group UK Ltd.
Pitfield, Milton Keynes, MK11 3LW, UK
UKHW022131190926
475702UK00013B/1738

* 9 7 8 0 3 6 7 7 3 2 2 1 9 *